· *Discovering Our Past* ·

· *Discovering Our Past* ·

A BRIEF INTRODUCTION TO ARCHAEOLOGY

WENDY ASHMORE

Rutgers, The State University of New Jersey

ROBERT J. SHARER

University of Pennsylvania

Mayfield Publishing Company
Mountain View, California

Library of Congress Cataloging-in-Publication Data

Ashmore, Wendy.
  Discovering our past.
  Bibliography: p. 223
  Includes index.
  1. Archaeology.   I. Sharer, Robert J.   II. Title.
CC75.A74   1988   930.1   87-24796

International Standard Book Number: 0-87484-748-6

Manufactured in the United States of America

10   9   8   7   6   5

Mayfield Publishing Company
1240 Villa St.
Mountain View, California 94041

Figure 8.1 on page 171: From *An Introduction to the Study of Southwestern Archaeology*, by A. V. Kidder. Copyright © 1924 by Yale University Press. Revised edition Copyright © 1962 by Yale University. All rights reserved.

Quotation on page 206 is reproduced by permission of the Society for American Archaeology from *American Antiquity*, volume 27, number 1, 1961.

Sponsoring editor, Janet M. Beatty; *production editor*, Wendy Calmenson, The Book Company; *manuscript editor*, Loralee Windsor; *text and cover designer*, Wendy Calmenson, The Book Company; *cover photographer*, Pete Turner, The Image Bank. The text was set in 10/12 Janson by G&S Typesetters and printed on 50 lb. 4 Finch Opaque by Malloy Lithographing.

· *Preface* ·

As CHILDREN, PEOPLE OFTEN learn to associate archaeologists with adventurous exploits and quests for long-lost civilizations in exotic places. Few people ever truly learn what archaeologists do. This book is designed to debunk the myths and explain what archaeologists really do, and how they do it.

The book begins with a brief review of what archaeology is today and how it grew over the past few centuries. The rest of the text is organized to follow the steps of actual archaeological research. Beginning at the abstract level of defining a research question, it proceeds to the concrete levels of finding and making sense of the evidence from the past, and then to presentation of the research results to other archaeologists and the public. The book closes with a discussion of the challenges all archaeologists face today—how to reconcile the sometimes conflicting demands of preserving, protecting, and understanding the past.

We have written this book specifically for lower-division college introductory courses, especially surveys of human prehistory that include an overview of archaeological method and theory. It derives from our more comprehensive text, *Archaeology: Discovering Our Past* (Mayfield, 1987). Not only do both texts follow the same basic organization, but their underlying philosophy is the same—viewing archaeology as integral to the broader field of anthropology, as part of a comprehensive study of what it means to be human. Because the bulk of our past predates the invention of writing, the book emphasizes prehistoric archaeology while still recognizing the importance of the field's other component, historical archaeology. In both cases our presentation stresses that the material remains from the past are nonrenewable resources. These resources are fragile and especially precious, because they are often our only clues to what happened in the past. However, there is often more than one way to study these clues, and this book introduces the reader to the kinds of methodological options available. There is no single recipe for doing archaeology, and the best archaeology is that which is based on the best methods available in each research situation.

The book includes a glossary that defines all the major terms used in the text. A brief and select bibliography is designed to amplify the major topics covered. (The reader may wish to consult the bibliography in *Archaeology: Discovering Our Past* for a more diverse selection of readings on these and related topics.)

In preparing this book we have been helped by many people. We especially wish to thank those colleagues who commented specifically on this manuscript. Kenneth L. Feder (Central Connecticut State University), James F. O'Connell (Univerity of Utah), Stuart D. Scott (State University of New York, Buffalo), and Katherine A. Spielmann (Arizona State University). Since this book is a direct descendant of the more comprehensive text, *Archaeology: Discovering Our Past*, we also wish to acknowledge, collectively, the numerous people who assisted us in the evolution of that work. The staff of Mayfield Publishing Company once again provided us with vital and friendly expertise. Janet M. Beatty has been responsible from the very beginning for the development of the book; her friendship is as much appreciated as her professionalism. Mary Forkner handled the early stages of production, assisted by Cathy Willkie. Wendy Calmenson of The Book Company oversaw final production and design, and Loralee Windsor copyedited the manuscript. We are grateful to them all for their considerable time and cheerful efforts.

Wendy Ashmore
Robert J. Sharer

• *Contents* •

· I ·

Introduction

THE TOMB OF Qin Shi Huang, or Emperor *Ch'in*, after whom we take the name *China*, lies beneath a huge artificial mound near Mt. Lishan in central China. Qin Shi Huang (259–210 B.C.) was the unifier and first emperor of China and, according to historical accounts, had a most spectacular tomb built for himself. Over 700,000 laborers toiled for 36 years to construct a huge underground complex that included a palace with walls of bronze and a ceiling set with pearls to represent the stars. Its floor was said to be covered with gold and silver, cast to simulate the mountains and trees of the earth's surface, while flowing mercury represented the rivers and seas. The entire complex was protected by armies with automatic crossbows set to fire on anyone foolish enough to intrude.

The historical descriptions of the tomb and its treasures were not treated seriously until 1974. In that year farmers from the village of Xiyang dug a new well some 1500 meters east of the great mound. Instead of water they found the remains of a great underground army designed to protect the tomb of China's first emperor. Archaeologists were summoned, and after several years of excavation, they revealed the full extent of the discovery (Fig. 1.1). The excavation exposed a huge subterranean chamber—5 meters deep, 230 meters long (east to west), and 62 meters wide (north to south)—containing some 6000 life-sized ceramic soldiers and horses. The clay army is in full battle array and faces east to defend the imperial tomb. Further excavations have revealed two more chambers, one similar in size to the first, the other smaller and apparently representing a command headquarters for the protecting army. In 1980 two half-life-sized bronze chariots, each pulled by four bronze horses, were found west of the bur-

1

FIGURE I.I

Chinese archaeologists clear one of the hundreds of clay soldiers, part of the effigy army created to protect the tomb of Qin Shi Huang, the first Emperor of China, excavated from a collapsed underground vault near the village of Xiyang, Shaanxi Province, China. (Courtesy of Beijing Photo Studio.)

ial mound. Since all these spectacular discoveries have been made on the edge of the tomb complex, there is no telling what wonders may be found when the Chinese archaeologists finally begin to excavate the underground palace of Qin Shi Huang itself.

Discoveries like this dramatize questions about our origins, the relationship between past and present, and, ultimately, who we are and why we behave as we do. What we are today, the way we act in various situations, our customs, our beliefs, our entire civilization, are all the result of an incredibly long and complex tradition of human accomplishment that stretches thousands, even millions, of years into the past. If we are to understand ourselves we must try to understand our past.

The desire for knowledge about ourselves motivates many people to careers in fields such as psychology, sociology, economics, and other social sciences. These fields address different aspects of humanity, but they are all limited to studying our behavior and society today, in the present. To understand ourselves fully we need to know where we came from, our heritage from the past. The study of history does this, but its scope is limited to the last few thousand years—the era of written documents. Only one field, *archaeology*, is designed to explore and reveal the full extent of our past, from our most remote and obscure glimmerings to our greatest glories. In pursuing the past archaeology addresses such questions as: Where and when did human life begin on earth? How and why did some human societies develop increasingly complex cultures, while others did not? How and why do civilizations rise and fall?

ARCHAEOLOGY

This book is about archaeology and how archaeologists conduct their work to better understand the past. Archaeology holds a fascination for many people. The reasons for this are quite varied. Archaeology appeals to some because it seeks answers to questions about ourselves. To others the life of the archaeologist conjures up pictures of adventurous travel to exotic places and dramatic discoveries of "lost" civilizations. This romantic image of the archaeologist is perhaps best represented by the recent movies about the adventures of Indiana Jones. Fiction aside, certainly the general public's image of archaeology is shaped by real reports of spectacular finds in newspapers or on television, such as the discovery of Emperor Qin's ceramic army. Even a discovery made over 50 years ago—Howard Carter's opening of the lost tomb of Tut-ankh-amun in Egypt (Fig. 1.2)—continues to excite the imagination.

But spectacular finds such as these are obviously very rare in archaeology, and few archaeologists are lucky enough to find anything that even approaches the dramatic discovery made by Howard Carter. As we shall see, archaeologists are not motivated by the prospect of adventure or danger, and they certainly do not recover evidence from the past for its monetary or aesthetic value. Instead they are motivated by a desire for information that will help further our understanding of the past.

Archaeology and Pseudoarchaeology

Archaeologists are not the only ones providing information about our past. A multitude of other accounts are readily available in books, magazines, movies, and television programs. These descriptions of the past are often appealing, for they emphasize dramatic mysteries and baffling paradoxes supposedly found in the archaeological record. But these accounts are not based on archaeology. They are part of what is called *pseudoarchaeology*. Pseudoarchaeology refers to descriptions of the past that claim to be based on fact but in actuality are fictional accounts that distort our understanding of the past.

Pseudoarchaeology has been around for a number of years. Included in this tradition are many of the accounts dealing with the "lost civilizations" of Atlantis and Mu, described as ancient continents supporting societies that had developed far in advance of their times but supposedly disappeared beneath the Atlantic and Pacific oceans.

More recently a series of books by Erich von Däniken has tried to explain a host of archaeological "mysteries" as the work of alien astronauts who sup-

FIGURE I.2

Howard Carter opening the inner doors of the tomb of Tut-ankh-amun. (Griffith Institute, Ashmolean Museum, Oxford.)

posedly visited earth in ancient times to "teach" humans the benefits of civilization. As one of his "proofs" for this thesis, von Däniken describes the sculptured scene of the sarcophagus lid from the famous Maya tomb at Palenque, Mexico, as representing an ancient astronaut at the controls of his rocket ship (Fig. 1.3). In making this interpretation, however, von Däniken ignores a vast amount of evidence about Maya art and symbolism—with which the costume and position of the carved figure are quite consistent—and the hieroglyphic inscription that identifies this figure as the ruler buried in the sarcophagus. In this and other cases the pseudoarchaeologist takes evidence out of its original context, and never mentions the contradictory information. A mere superficial similarity between an astronaut's "launch position" and the carved portrait of a dead Maya ruler is treated as if it were positive evidence for the ancient space visitor theory.

The basic question underlying most pseudoarchaeological theories is this: How could ancient humans possibly have developed civilization and built such monuments as the huge pyramids of Egypt? How could they have possessed the skills and energy to erect these and other awesome constructions before the advent of modern technology, without the aid of extraterrestrial power and intelligence? These questions demand answers, but the pseudoarchaeologist phrases them to suggest that ancient peoples could not have accomplished these feats, despite plentiful evidence to the contrary. In fact, as legitimate archaeology has demonstrated time and again, these accomplishments did not require superhuman skills or knowledge, but were produced by our very human ancestors.

FIGURE 1.3

Rubbing made from the sculptured sarcophagus lid found in the tomb beneath the Temple of the Inscriptions at Palenque, Mexico, representing the dead ruler surrounded by Maya supernatural symbols. (Rubbing, permission of Merle Greene.)

Prehistoric peoples were demonstrably capable of far more artistic, engineering, and intellectual endeavors than pseudoarchaeologists are willing to allow them. Tales of extraterrestrial visits make exciting science fiction, but we should keep these imaginative accounts in the realm of fantasy where they belong, as good entertainment. As a science seeking to understand the human past, archaeology has a responsibility to prevent pseudoarchaeologists from robbing humanity of the real achievements of past cultures.

Archaeology Defined

During the past few hundred years archaeology has grown from an amateur's pastime to a scientifically based profession. In that time archaeology has emerged as the field that studies the past through its material remains, using this evidence to order and describe ancient events and to explain the meaning of those events. In the broadest sense, a definition of archaeology includes the subject matter—the study of the past—and the techniques used to describe and explain the past. To study the past, archaeologists have developed a series of methods by which they discover, recover, preserve, describe, and analyze the remains from ancient times (Fig. 1.4), remains commonly referred to as the *archaeological record*. In assessing the meaning of this evidence archaeologists are guided by a body of theory. Ultimately this theory provides the means to interpret archaeological evidence and allows both description and explanation of the past. This book will

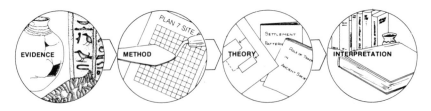

FIGURE 1.4

Archaeological reasoning relates evidence and interpretation by means of method and theory.

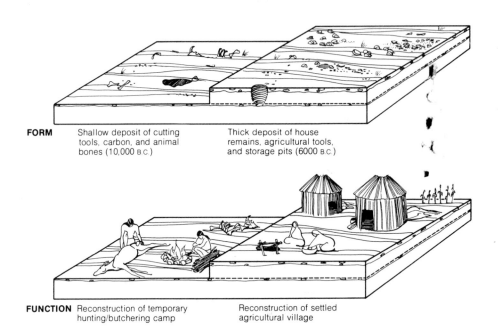

FORM Shallow deposit of cutting tools, carbon, and animal bones (10,000 B.C.)   Thick deposit of house remains, agricultural tools, and storage pits (6000 B.C.)

FUNCTION Reconstruction of temporary hunting/butchering camp   Reconstruction of settled agricultural village

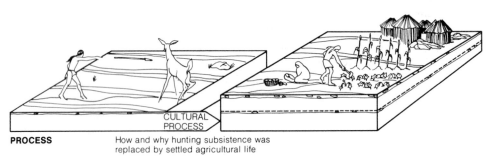

PROCESS How and why hunting subsistence was replaced by settled agricultural life

CULTURAL PROCESS

FIGURE 1.5

Archaeology is concerned with three primary goals: description of form, analysis of function, and explanation of process.

explore both the methods (Chapters 4-6) and the theory (Chapters 3, 7, and 8) used by archaeologists to understand the past.

Archaeology has three principal goals in studying the past (Fig. 1.5). The first of these is to reveal the *form* of the past, the description and classification of the physical evidence that is recovered. Analysis of form allows the archaeologist to outline the distribution of remains of ancient societies in both time and space. The second goal is to discover *function*. By analyzing the form and interrelationships of recovered evidence, the archaeologist attempts to determine their purpose. The determination of function ultimately leads to the reconstruction of ancient behavior. Finally the archaeologist attempts to understand cultural *processes* by using the remains of ancient cultures to explain how and why these cultures changed through time.

ARCHAEOLOGY AND SCIENCE

Science is concerned with gaining knowledge about the natural world and therefore seeks to understand all phenomena that can be observed. Science is not concerned with things that cannot be observed and tested; the latter remain the subjects of theology, philosophy, the occult, and pseudoscience. Science proceeds by a disciplined search for knowledge, pursuing the description, ordering, and meaning of phenomena in a systematic manner. Its method of acquiring knowledge is continuously self-correcting, with perpetual testing and refinement of conclusions from research. The generally accepted set of procedures that have been found to be trustworthy for gaining and testing our knowledge of the real world is called the *scientific method*.

Science advances by reasoning both *inductively* and *deductively*. Inductive reasoning starts from specific observations and proceeds to a generalization based on a series of such observations. Deductive reasoning goes in the opposite direction, deriving specific propositions from a generalization. For instance, if you purchased prerecorded cassette tapes and those of a particular company frequently went bad after only a few playings, you might generalize *inductively* that the company's products were unreliable. If the same company started issuing videotapes, you might reason *deductively* that the quality of these products might also be suspect. You could then *test* your deduction about the company's general manufacturing quality standards by buying and playing some of the new products.

To see how these reasoning processes work within archaeology, let us look at an example. Julian Steward, an anthropologist about whom we will have more to say in a later chapter, conducted extensive fieldwork in the Great Basin of the western United States in the 1920s and 1930s, studying Native American peoples living in this region. From this work, he developed a generalization—reasoning inductively—to describe the distribution of prehistoric Shoshone Indian activities and campsites, relating their locations to the seasonal cycle of food procurement. That is, Steward presented his data as a *model*, a description to summarize the patterns and regularities that reflected the behavior of the ancient Shoshone people.

In the 1960s David Hurst Thomas took Steward's model of Great Basin settlement patterns and—reasoning deductively—derived from it a series of propositions or *hypotheses* (statements of relationships based on a set of assumptions). As Thomas phrased it, "if the late prehistoric Shoshoneans behaved in the fashion suggested by Steward, how would the artifacts have fallen on the ground?" If Steward's model of shifting settlement and seasonal exploitation of food resources in different locations were true, Thomas could expect to find the tools associated with specific activities in predictable locations. Hunting tools and butchering knives, for example, should be found more abundantly in the sagebrush zones, where hunting was argued to have been more important.

Thomas's research supported more than 75% of the hypotheses derived from Steward's model. As a result the model was refined and new hypotheses were generated, which in turn allowed further improvement of the model. This sequence of scientific hypothesis generation and testing could be continued indefinitely.

The contrast between this approach to understanding the past and pseudoarchaeology could not be stronger. Instead of systematically collecting and evaluating all available evidence and using it without bias to develop and test hypotheses to produce the most reasonable reconstruction of the past, pseudoarchaeologists dismiss much of what has been learned about the past, selecting only those bits of information that can be made to fit their preconceived "theories."

Like any science, archaeology deals with a specified class of phenomena: the remains of past human activity. Also, like any science, archaeology attempts objectively to isolate, classify, and explain the relationships among the bits of evidence—in this case, the variables of form, function, time, and space or location. Archaeology can observe the formal and spatial variables directly, but the functional and temporal variables must be inferred. Once these interrelationships are established, the archaeologist infers past human behavior and reconstructs past human society from this evidence.

Although archaeology has become more scientific in its outlook and procedures, its strength stems from the diversity of its interests and practitioners. The value of the traditional historical and other humanistic perspectives within archaeology—such as literary and art historical concerns—should never be discounted.

ARCHAEOLOGY AND HISTORY

Archaeology is obviously related to the field of history in that both disciplines seek knowledge of the human past. The major difference between the two disciplines is the distinction in sources of information; this leads to differences in methodology, the techniques by which the past is studied. History deals primarily with textual sources—written accounts from the past—whereas archaeology deals primarily with the physical remains of the past.

Another contrast between history and archaeology is that history tends to focus not only on literate societies (that is, those that write) but also on their richest and most powerful members, their kings, queens, and high priests. Archaeology is less partial to rich or learned folk. Everyone eats, makes things, discards trash, and dies, so everyone contributes to the archaeological record. Individual archaeologists may concentrate on one or another part or kind of society, but archaeology as a whole treats the whole range of humanity.

History and archaeology are closely allied in several established fields in which the methods of both disciplines are brought to bear on the study of a particular era of the human past. For instance, the long-established field of classical archaeology combines the methods of archaeology with use of historical sources to document the classical civilizations of Greece and Rome. Classical archaeology is also allied to the field of art history, which provides another route—the analysis of art styles and themes—to the understanding of the past.

Most archaeologists, however, are concerned with aspects of the past that cannot be directly supplemented by historical studies. History is limited to the relatively recent era of human development encompassed by the invention and use of writing systems. This "historical era" extends at most only some 5000 years into the past, in the area with the earliest examples of writing, the Near East. When compared with the total length of human cultural development, the era of history represents much less than 1 percent of the overall span of more than two million years (Fig. 1.6). Historical studies are even more limited outside the Near East, and they are not possible in areas where writing systems never developed.

Indeed it is often useful to distinguish archaeological studies on the basis of whether or not the subject society possessed a writing system. *Historical archaeology* refers to archaeological investigations carried out in conjunction with analyses of written records. *Prehistoric archaeology* studies societies and time periods that lack historical traditions. The latter area of archaeology seeks to understand the full sweep of human development on earth, from its earliest traces to its most remote variations. It is prehistoric archaeology, therefore, that is concerned with the bulk of our past and is the primary focus of this book. Although the methods and theoretical approaches discussed here may be applied to any archaeological research, including research directly combined with documentary sources, they do not *depend* on historical supplements.

Of course the distinction between prehistory and history is not always clear. Both historical and archaeological data are fragmentary; they can never provide a complete reconstruction of the past. Thus even when historical records are available, archaeological information can add to our understanding of that past era. A good example in which history was illuminated by archaeology is the excavation of Martin's Hundred, one of the earliest British colonial settlements of tidewater Virginia. Archaeologist Ivor Noël Hume and his associates had

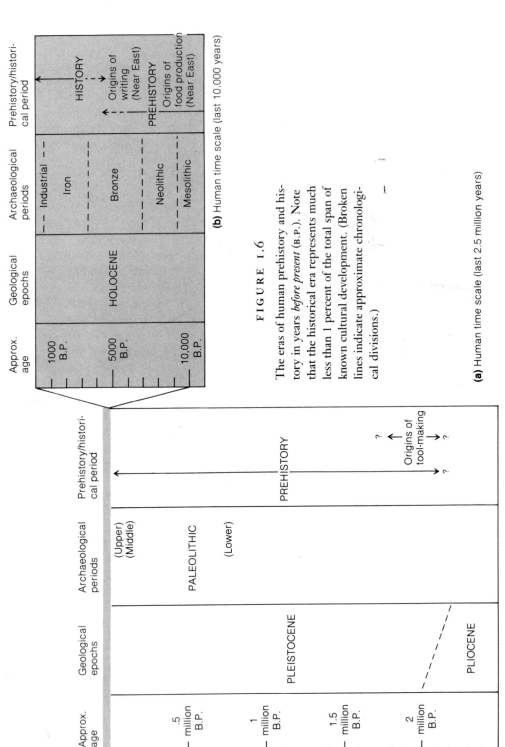

(b) Human time scale (last 10,000 years)

FIGURE 1.6

The eras of human prehistory and history in years *before present* (B.P.). Note that the historical era represents much less than 1 percent of the total span of known cultural development. (Broken lines indicate approximate chronological divisions.)

(a) Human time scale (last 2.5 million years)

originally been seeking traces of the 18th-century Carter's Grove plantation. They happened instead on remains from the early 1600s, remains that turned out to be virtually all that was left of Wolstenholme Towne in a tract known as Martin's Hundred. The tract was established in 1619 by fewer than 200 English settlers, who faced disease and hunger as well as the unknowns of living in the New World. In 1622 the little community was attacked and burned, and nearly 60 of its residents were killed by the Indian attackers. Although Martin's Hundred was reoccupied, Wolstenholme Towne was subsequently lost to history.

Noël Hume's excavations in the 1970s rediscovered the settlement and documented the drama of the massacre. Ash and other traces of the fires were abundant, and several human skeletons attested to a quick, violent end (one bore evidence of scalping) and hasty burial. As dramatic as these findings are, however, the deeper impact of the Martin's Hundred excavations lies in its documentation of daily life in early colonial Virginia. The products and discards of a resident potter speak of local provisioning, while the discovery of helmets and other pieces of armor constitute the earliest such pieces known for colonial America, and traces of the wooden fort furnish a complete ground plan, the oldest example of this architectural form yet recovered. The original settlement was small, but its sometimes poignant traces have yielded important glimpses of life and death in what Noël Hume calls "the teething years of American colonial history."

Knowledge about Martin's Hundred, then, has both archaeology and history as sources. For most of the human past, however, archaeology lacks any sort of historical record to supplement its studies. In such cases prehistoric archaeology has drawn on the resources of several fields, including cultural anthropology and geography. Prehistoric archaeology has traditionally allied itself most closely to anthropology. Through the concept of culture, anthropology provides a framework on which prehistoric archaeology can build both to describe and to explain the past.

ARCHAEOLOGY AND ANTHROPOLOGY

In its broadest sense anthropology is the comprehensive science of humankind—the study of human beings both as biological organisms and as culture-bearing creatures. It also studies human society from two perspectives: a *diachronic* view that stresses development through time, and a *synchronic* view that emphasizes the contemporary state of human societies with little or no time depth.

The field of anthropology is normally divided into a series of subdisciplines (Fig. 1.7). The subdiscipline that studies the human species as a biological organism is usually called physical anthropology. The diachronic aspect of physical anthropology investigates our biological evolution, while the synchronic perspective studies humanity's contemporary biological form and variation. The study of the human species as a cultural organism is usually referred to as cul-

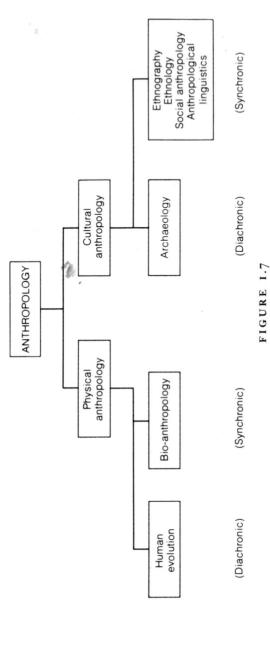

FIGURE 1.7

The field of anthropology can be divided into several subfields. In this view, archaeology represents the part of cultural anthropology that studies the social and cultural past.

tural anthropology. The synchronic aspect of cultural anthropology includes two general approaches to the study of living cultures: ethnography and ethnology. Ethnography refers to particular studies of individual cultures—studies of a single society or of a segment of a complex society, such as a particular community. Ethnology assumes a comparative and generalizing perspective, based on ethnographic data, that attempts to understand the way culture works. By comparing data from many societies, ethnology studies how and why contemporary cultures operate and change. Some anthropologists also specialize in the study of human social institutions (social anthropology) or languages (anthropological linguistics). Archaeology is the diachronic aspect of cultural anthropology, the study of our cultural and social past.

The foregoing description of anthropology is a simplified view of a very complex field. This situation should not be surprising, however, for the pursuits of anthropological research must be as diverse as the varieties of human behavior.

Despite its internal diversity, anthropology is unified by one common factor, the concept of culture. The term *culture* has both a general and a specific connotation. In its general sense *culture* refers to the uniquely human addition to the biological and social dimensions we share with other life forms. It is culture in this general sense that will concern us, and it is this concept that we will attempt to define. But we must also realize that *culture* may be used in a specific sense to refer to the particular and unique cultural systems of individual human societies, as when we speak of the "culture of the Samoan Islanders."

The concept of culture in the general sense is much too complex to define comprehensively in a few paragraphs, encompassing as it does some two million years of human evolution, as well as hundreds of unique and varied contemporary societies throughout the world. Yet one of the most often cited definitions, written more than 100 years ago by Edward Tylor (1871), remains useful today.

That complex whole which includes knowledge, belief, art, morals, law, custom, and any other capabilities and habits acquired by man as a member of society.

Today many archaeologists prefer to define culture as the primary means by which human societies adjust or adapt to their environment, in contrast to the genetic (biological) adaptations of our own and other life forms. According to this view culture comprises the cumulative resources of human societies, perpetuated by language, that provide the primary means for nongenetic adaptation to the environment by regulating behavior on three levels: the technological (relationships with the environment), the social (organizational systems), and the ideational (belief systems).

We will return to this concept later in this book, when we discuss the various views of culture that have developed along with the field of anthropology.

Like anthropology archaeology has benefited from the contributions of many other fields. In pursuing their goals archaeologists often make use of the training and expertise of specialists in other subfields of anthropology, as well as those in disciplines like art history, geography, history, biology, astronomy, physics, geology, and computer science, among others. It is precisely this mix of scientific and humanistic perspectives that so greatly enriches modern archaeology. Together these fields contribute not only to the refinement of archaeological methods but also to the development of a body of archaeological theory by which the evidence of the past is interpreted.

ARCHAEOLOGY AS A PROFESSION

Because archaeology is both fascinating and important—it is the only bridge to our entire past heritage—many people are interested in the prospects for a career in archaeology. It is such a diverse field that there are many different career opportunities for all kinds of interests.

Formal academic training is not a requirement for participation in archaeological research. Many people begin their experience in discovering the past by joining an archaeological dig, or volunteering their time to help a museum preserve or study archaeological collections. Some individuals who are employed full-time in other jobs continue to follow their interest in archaeology as volunteers, working on weekends or during their vacations. But if one is interested in pursuing archaeology as a profession, some sort of formal academic training is necessary.

The teaching and training of archaeology usually begins in the classroom, where methods and theory can be introduced by lectures and discussions. But archaeology cannot be learned solely in a traditional academic setting. Archaeological training must include time spent in the field, so that what is learned in college or university courses can be put into practice. In most cases archaeological field schools first expose students to the practical application of research methods. After such training, students may return to an academic setting and take more advanced courses (in data analysis, theory, etc.) leading to a college degree. Note, however, that most archaeological training in the United States is offered within anthropology programs, and the resulting undergraduate degrees and most graduate degrees are in anthropology, not archaeology.

Archaeological training and practice are generally uniform insofar as most archaeologists subscribe to the definition and goals outlined earlier in this chapter. Yet when it comes to the actual application of method and theory to meet these goals, a considerable diversity becomes apparent. There is more variation than there should be in the standards by which archaeological sites are excavated and the results recorded. In some extreme cases, unfortunately, the lack of proper standards leads to an irreparable loss of information about the past, rather than a gain in knowledge. For example, Kent Flannery describes the following scene at a site in Mexico:

Four stalks of river cane, stuck loosely in the ground, defined a quadrilateral (though not necessarily rectangular) area in which two peones *[laborers] picked and shoveled to varying depths, heaving the dirt to one side. On the backdirt pile stood the archaeologist himself, armed with his most delicate tool—a three-pronged garden cultivator of the type used by elderly British ladies to weed rhododendron. Combing through every shovelful of dirt, he carefully picked out each figurine head and placed it in a brown paper shopping bag nearby—the only other bit of equipment in evidence. This individual was armed with an excavation permit that had been granted because, in the honest words of one official, "he appeared to be no better or worse than any other archaeologist who had worked in the area." When questioned, our colleague descended from the backdirt pile and revealed that his underlying research goal was to define the nature of the "Olmec presence" in that particular drainage basin; his initial results, he said, predicted total success.*

As [we] rattled back along the highway in our jeep, each of us in his own way sat marveling at the elegance of a research strategy in which one could define the nature of a foreign presence in a distant drainage basin from just seven fragmentary figurine heads in the bottom of a supermarket sack. . . .

(FLANNERY 1976:1–2)

This case strikes us as humorous until we realize that it is based on an actual incident, and that, unfortunately, similar situations continue in the name of "archaeology" throughout the world. In part due to this problem, the Society of Professional Archeologists (SOPA) has attempted to define as specifically as possible the professional qualifications and standards for archaeologists. These include the following criteria of training and experience:

1. Education and Training
    a. A professional archaeologist must have received a graduate degree in archaeology, anthropology, history, classics, or another pertinent discipline with a specialization in archaeology;
    b. A professional archaeologist must have supervised experience in basic archaeological field research consisting of at least 12 weeks of field training and 4 weeks of laboratory analysis or curating;
    c. A professional archaeologist must have designed and executed archaeological research, as evidenced by a Master of Arts or Master of Science thesis or an equivalent research report.

2. Experience

    A professional archaeologist must have at least one year of experience in one or more of the following:

    a. Field and laboratory situations under supervision of a professional archaeologist, with a minimum of six months as a supervisor
    b. Analytic study of archaeological collections
    c. Theoretical, library, or archival research
    d. Administration of archaeological research
    e. Management of cultural resources
    f. Museum work
    g. Teaching
    h. Marine survey archaeology

Traditionally most archaeologists have taken academic appointments in universities or museums where they may teach archaeology as well as conduct fieldwork. Today, however, growing numbers of archaeologists are employed by private or governmental agencies, such as the National Park Service, where they engage in full-time field research. This research is usually called *cultural resource management* (or *CRM*), for it emphasizes identification and evaluation of archaeological sites threatened with destruction from road building, housing development, and the like. Because of increasing concern about the damage such construction causes to natural and cultural landscapes—including archaeological sites—protective legislation (discussed further in Chapter 9) has put archaeologists in a position to help manage the changes that take place. Thus CRM is the fastest growing segment of the profession and now accounts for more than half of all the professional archaeologists employed in the United States.

The diversity within the field is also reflected in the existence of no fewer than six professional archaeological societies in the United States alone. These are the Archaeological Institute of America (AIA), the Society for American Archaeology (SAA), the Association for Field Archaeology (AFFA), the American Society of Conservation Archaeologists (ASCA), the Society for Historical Archaeology (SHA), and the Society of Professional Archeologists (SOPA).

SUMMARY

Archaeology is both a popular and a fascinating subject, and it often captures considerable public attention, especially when dramatic discoveries are made. Such discoveries, along with the appeal of exotic adventures, are certainly part of the reason for the popular fascination with archaeology. But a deeper attraction is generated by the substance of archaeology itself—the study of the past—and by the realization that the reconstruction of the past mirrors our present lives.

Archaeology is the one field that studies the full range of our human past. It does so from the recovery and analysis of surviving material remains. Its general goals are to describe the *form* of archaeological evidence and its distribution in time and space; to determine the *function* of these remains and thereby reconstruct ancient behavior; and to define the *processes* of culture to determine how and why cultures change through time.

The purpose and goals of archaeology stand opposed to those of pseudoarchaeology—fictitious reconstructions of the past that ignore facts but cater to human desires for fantasy and mystery. In contrast, archaeology belongs to the general realm of science, for, like any scientific discipline, it involves a search for knowledge based on hard evidence, using a logical and consistent method, and guided by a body of theory. Yet many archaeologists maintain a humanistic perspective as well.

Archaeology is thus allied to a variety of other disciplines. These include *history*, the study of the past from the written record, and *anthropology*, the study of human society, past and present, from both cultural and biological perspectives. The span of history divides the realm of archaeology into *historical* and *prehistoric archaeology*. Anthropology, history, and related fields provide the theories that guide prehistoric archaeology in reconstructing the past from material remains.

The training of professional archaeologists usually combines classroom, laboratory, and field experiences at both undergraduate and graduate levels. Professional standards for archaeological research have been defined, but there is still considerable variation in their application.

· 2 ·

Archaeology's Past

THE DEVELOPMENT OF SCIENCE is one of the hallmarks of Western civilization. Although the origins of science and the scientific method can be traced several thousand years into the past, they have taken their modern form in the 500 years since the European Renaissance. In this growth process, archaeology is a relative newcomer, since it has emerged as a distinct field only during the past 100 years. But archaeology has followed a developmental course similar to other scientific disciplines, and by briefly describing its history we can better understand its present characteristics.

Many scientific fields, including archaeology, originated with the work of amateur collectors. These individuals, often part-time hobbyists, pursue their interests because they value the objects they collect, often as things of beauty or curiosity. For example, the modern field of biology began with European collectors of local plant and animal life, including many 17th- and 18th-century English country parsons and other gentlemen of leisure.

Amassing a collection leads naturally to attempts to bring order to the assembled material. These often produce efforts at *classification*, dividing a collection into groups that share one or more traits. The earliest classifications were usually based on the most obvious characteristics, such as appearance or form.

Attempts to classify collections often led in turn to questions about the meaning of the phenomena being collected. The desire to know more about a collection leads to questions about its origins, its purpose, or the relationship of categories to one another. Such questions were often answered initially with pure speculation, but at times conclusions were developed from systematic observation. More often than not, however, the first answers have long since been replaced by more firmly grounded explanations.

In time, amateur collectors gave way to individuals committed to discovering the meaning behind the assembled facts. First these individuals might define and classify the full range of forms. Then they might attempt to infer purpose from physical appearance and discover the underlying organizing principles inherent in the classification. In other words, a concern with function and meaning replaces concern with simple form. This step often identifies the first professionals within a given discipline. The amateur never disappears completely, and of course nonprofessionals in many fields have continued to make important discoveries right up to the present day. But in every scientific discipline, the emergence of true professionalism corresponds to the rise of full-time specialists interested in understanding rather than mere collecting.

As attention shifts more to questions of function and explanation, it becomes obvious that descriptive classifications based solely on isolated traits cannot provide sophisticated answers about the origins and significance of a set of observable phenomena. The final step toward understanding any phenomenon is the attempt to comprehend the processes of its development—to explain the causes of change.

THE ORIGINS OF ARCHAEOLOGY

These trends of scientific development are visible in the emergence of archaeology as a professional discipline. Archaeology did not spring forth fully developed but emerged gradually from diverse origins. As with other fields of inquiry its roots lie in the work of amateur collectors and speculators; such individuals interested in the human past are often called *antiquarians*. But archaeology did not begin to develop as a separate discipline until its practitioners went beyond the mere collection of ancient remains and developed the means to use these materials as evidence for a reasonable reconstruction of the past.

Countless individuals have encountered remains of the past, whether accidentally, or as in the case of looters, as a result of treasure seeking. As the number of discoveries accumulated, some individuals began to realize that remains being found in the earth had an importance beyond curiosity or monetary value—they were, in fact, direct clues to the understanding of entire societies that had long since disappeared.

Examples of interest in the past can be found among the earliest known historical accounts. In the first millennium B.C. the Babylonian king Nabonidus sponsored excavations in the ruined cities of his Sumerian predecessors. Wealthy Romans systematically looted many sites of the Mediterranean area for sculpture and other works of art to decorate their palaces and gardens, but they seemed to have little concern for using these finds to understand the past.

FIGURE 2.1

A street in the Roman city of Pompeii, Italy, after excavation and partial reconstruction. (Courtesy of Elizabeth K. Ralph.)

It wasn't until the Renaissance of the 14th to 17th centuries—an era of re-
awakened interest in the arts, literature, science, and learning in general—that
an awareness of the past began to flourish. Excavation and direct recovery of
antiquities became increasingly popular in Italy as Roman ruins were probed
in search of artifacts and art. In 1594 the construction of a water channel near
Naples led accidentally to the most famous discovery of the period, that of the
lost Roman city of Pompeii (Fig. 2.1). Archaeological excavation continues at
this site even now. Discoveries such as these stimulated a general frenzy of digging, often resembling looting more than archaeological inquiry, throughout the
Mediterranean world and beyond. Although much important evidence was destroyed, some knowledge was gained, some monuments and works of art were
saved, and specific excavation techniques began to improve.

Even as looting and destruction of antiquities became more common, some
individuals stood out not only as notable collectors but also as people interested
in learning about the past through classification and study of material remains.
One of the earliest of these was William Camden. In 1587 he produced *Britan-
nia*, the first compilation of all archaeological sites and artifacts then known in
England, a work that marks the beginning of serious interest in British pre-

FIGURE 2.2

The ancient function of Stonehenge, located on the Salisbury Plain of England, remains a subject of popular speculation—regardless of the archaeological evidence.

history. Two other British antiquarians of the 17th and 18th centuries, John Aubrey and William Stukeley, are notable for their pioneering but speculative attempts to interpret the purposes of the great stone enclosures of Avebury and Stonehenge (Fig. 2.2).

Elsewhere in Europe others were beginning to probe their local prehistoric past. In 16th- and 17th-century Scandinavia, for example, royally commissioned antiquarians such as Ole Worm of Denmark and John Bure of Sweden were recording ancient runic inscriptions (Fig. 2.3), excavating early burial sites, and compiling inventories of national antiquities. It is interesting to note that centuries earlier their Viking ancestors seem to have conducted the first archaeological work in North America, excavating a prehistoric site near their settlement on Greenland.

Speculative interpretation of European prehistory gradually gave way to firmer reconstructions as the archaeological evidence accumulated. The first problem to be solved was the recognition of the earliest products of human activity, usually tools made of stone. William Dugdale, a 17th-century British prehistorian, identified ancient stone hand-axes as "weapons used by the Britons before the art of making arms of brass or iron was known." This essentially correct interpretation was a revolutionary advance over the prevailing view that these artifacts were the work of elves or other mythical beings. Another two centuries would pass, however, before the implications of these discoveries for human prehistory would be generally accepted. They were initially ignored or rejected since they conflicted with the dominant view, based on the Old Testament version of creation, that human existence was confined to the 6000 years since the earth's creation.

FIGURE 2.3

Runic inscriptions were used as early as the 16th and 17th centuries to aid archaeological investigation in Scandinavia. (By permission of the British Library.)

Once these earliest artifacts were recognized as products of human manufacture, determination of their true age became a pressing concern. The best indication of the antiquity of human presence in Europe came from a growing inventory of human bones and tools found associated with the bones of extinct animals. For example, in 1797 John Frere described the discovery of chipped flint artifacts in association with bones of extinct animals at the English site of Hoxne: The artifacts lay 12 feet below the earth's surface beneath three higher and therefore later deposits. Frere concluded that these remains belonged "to a very remote period indeed; even beyond that of the present world." In the mid-19th century, a French customs inspector named Boucher de Perthes found a group of crude hand-axes and extinct animal bones among the gravels of the Somme River. By this time the fossilized remains of the earliest inhabitants of Europe had begun to appear. One of the first of these discoveries was made in 1856 in the Neander Valley in Germany. This find is now well known as an example of an ancient Neanderthal man, but at the time the "primitive" and possibly ancient anatomical attributes of these bones were explained away as being caused by disease in a modern individual.

After bitter and heated debate the tide of scientific opinion finally turned in the mid-19th century. By this time geologists such as Charles Lyell had demonstrated the considerable antiquity of the earth and had proposed that the processes responsible for its current form were the same as those of the past—a position known as *uniformitarianism*. They had also shown that many of the human tools discovered with extinct animal bones were indeed so ancient that the literal interpretation of the Book of Genesis was clearly contradicted. In 1859 the publication of Charles Darwin's *On the Origin of Species* provided a systematic scientific theory of evolution that was in harmony with the geological evidence pointing to the earth's great antiquity. Thus by the mid-19th century the combination of archaeological, geological, and biological evidence was able to challenge successfully the theological position on prehistoric human development in the Old World.

Still unresolved, however, was the central issue of New World prehistory: Who had built the now-abandoned cities of the Americas? The ruined mounds, temples, sculptures, and tombs found in North, Central, and South America offered a new mystery whose solution was first sought in wild speculation. European bias saw Old World immigrants as the most likely sources for the ruins of sophisticated societies being discovered in the Americas, variously crediting ancient Egyptians, Hebrews, Phoenicians, Hindus, Chinese, and even the mythical inhabitants of Atlantis and Mu with these accomplishments. The living American Indians were usually dismissed as incapable of such achievements. Even such a sober scientist as Benjamin Franklin attributed the construction of the monumental mounds of the Mississippi Valley to the early Spanish explorer Hernando de Soto!

Accumulating archaeological data, however, eventually established rightful credit for the ancient New World sites. In 1841 and 1843 John Lloyd Stephens and Frederick Catherwood published their accounts of the discovery of spectacular ruins of the lost Maya civilization in the jungles of Mexico and Central America. Stephens's and Catherwood's books revealed the wonders of ancient Maya culture to the populace of England and the United States (Fig. 2.4). Publicity of this kind helped spur the often romantic and destructive search for other "lost" civilizations, not only in the New World but also in Africa and Asia. But Stephens's appraisal of the source of Maya civilization stands in marked contrast to the pseudoarchaeological speculations popular at the time.

We are not warranted in going back to any ancient nation of the Old World for the builders of these cities. . . . There are strong reasons to believe them the creations of the same races who inhabited the country at the time of the Spanish Conquest.

In 1848 E. G. Squier and E. H. Davis published the results of their research into the mounds of the Mississippi and Ohio Valleys, providing one of the first classifications to distinguish burial mounds, temple platforms, and effigy mounds, inferring that these different types of mounds served different functions. But in trying to identify the ancient occupants of these sites they lapsed into pure speculation, refusing to believe that the American Indians or their ancestors could be the builders. In contrast Samuel F. Haven's sober appraisal of American Indian prehistory—*Archaeology of the United States*, published in 1856—used available archaeological evidence to dismiss many fantastic theories about the origins of the Native Americans and concluded that the prehistoric monuments in the United States were built by the ancestors of living

FIGURE 2.4

Publication of drawings by Frederick Catherwood sparked public interest in ancient New World civilizations in the mid-19th century. (From an original print, courtesy of the Museum Library, University Museum, University of Pennsylvania.)

tribal groups. Further research reinforced this conclusion, and by the end of the 19th century the weight of archaeological evidence required recognition of a complex past for Native American societies without the need to resort to pseudoarchaeological tales of Old World visits or other influences.

Also by this time, archaeology was gaining recognition as a separate field of endeavor and a legitimate scholarly pursuit in both the Old and New Worlds. Unfortunately, other forces led to an increase in looting and the destruction of archaeological sites. In particular, as European and American colonists moved more deeply into Asia, Africa, and Latin America, proprietary claims were staked over newly "discovered" areas, including archaeological sites, which were often mined like mineral deposits. For instance, from 1802 to 1821 Claudius Rich, a British consular agent in Baghdad, collected and removed thousands of antiquities and sent them to England. Giovanni Belzoni, working for the British government, systematically looted Egyptian tombs, even using battering rams to enter the ancient burial chambers. And Thomas Bruce, the seventh Earl of

Elgin, removed a series of sculptures, now called the Elgin marbles, from the Parthenon in Athens to their present location in the British Museum, sparking a dispute that continues today.

As destructive as such activities were, they did produce many important discoveries. Foremost among these was the unearthing of the Rosetta Stone in Egypt, which allowed Jean Jacques Champollion to decipher Egyptian hieroglyphs in 1822. Similar discoveries of inscribed clay tablets in Mesopotamia led to the decipherment of cuneiform writing soon thereafter. As a result of these two breakthroughs, historical records from two of the world's earliest civilizations were suddenly available to scholars and public alike.

THE EMERGENCE OF MODERN ARCHAEOLOGY

As the discoveries continued, archaeology became recognized as a distinct professional discipline. Professional archaeology emerged in this period as many of its practitioners became full-time specialists (rather than part-time hobbyists) and as interpretations of the past relied more on evidence than on speculation. By this time the accumulating evidence of humanity's past was impressive. And the increase in finds was accompanied by a gradual refinement of recovery and classification methods that made the record even stronger. But what did all this new information mean? How could it be interpreted?

The problem was immense. Depending on the particular circumstance, archaeologists usually have only scattered remnants of past cultures to work with. One way to visualize the problem is to imagine what could survive from our own civilization for archaeologists to ponder some five or ten thousand years from now. What could they reconstruct of our way of life on the basis of scattered soft drink bottles, porcelain toilets, plastic containers, spark plugs, reinforced concrete structures, and other durable (nonbiodegradable) products of our civilization? In approaching the problem of interpreting the past, the archaeologist needs a framework to help put the puzzle together. Imagine an incredibly complex three-dimensional jigsaw puzzle. If we know nothing about its size, form, or subject matter, the puzzle would be impossible to reconstruct. But if we proposed a scheme that accounted for the puzzle's size, form, and subject, we could use this scheme to attempt to put it together. If one scheme failed to work, we could propose another until we succeeded.

Today the interpretive frameworks used by professional archaeologists and other scientists are generally called *models*. A model is essentially a form of hypothesis that describes the research subject in a simplified way; it is constructed and tested according to the scientific method (see Chapter 1).

The earliest archaeological interpretations were based on historical models. The first historical scheme widely used by archaeologists was the well-known *three-age technological sequence*, which held that prehistoric society developed pro-

FIGURE 2.5

A contemporary view of Heinrich Schliemann's excavations at Troy. (From Schliemann 1881.)

gressively through ages of stone, bronze, and iron technology. The idea behind this model can be traced to writings from several ancient civilizations, including those of Greece, Rome, and China.

Credit for promulgating the three-age sequence for European prehistory is generally given to two early 19th-century Danish scholars. Christian Thomsen organized the collections in the Danish National Museum of Antiquities according to this scheme, not only as a convenience but also because it seemed to reflect chronological stages of human progress. His colleague, Jens Worsaae, conducted excavations in burial mounds, thereby verifying that stone tools underlay (and were thus earlier than) those of bronze, which underlay the still later tools of iron.

The sequence grew more detailed with further research. In 1865 Sir John Lubbock distinguished an earlier chipped stone technology (Paleolithic or "Old Stone Age") from a later ground stone technology (Neolithic or "New Stone Age"). In 1871 Heinrich Schliemann used a quasi-historical source—Homer's *Iliad*—to discover the site of Bronze Age Troy, thereby linking the study of prehistoric societies with the later classical civilizations known to history (Fig. 2.5). Also in the 19th century, archaeological method was refined to nearly modern precision by the work of the Englishman, General A. L. Pitt-Rivers.

Thus by the end of the 19th century, European archaeology was based on a well-developed chronological framework that followed a historical model. To this day, many European archaeologists regard their discipline as allied more closely to history than to any other field.

By the early 20th century in America, archaeologists were borrowing the excavation methods of the Old World, but they were taking a rather different approach in their attempts to interpret the past. The difference was due largely to contrasting circumstances. For one thing cultural development in the Americas did not seem to have the time depth found in the Old World; the earliest migration in the New World appeared to be relatively recent, taking place during the last glacial epoch. In addition, the New World, unlike many areas of the Old World, appeared to lack a native historical tradition. This meant that the historical (or historically based) schemes used in the Old World could not be meaningfully applied in the New.

Since the connection with history was not so immediately apparent in the New World, archaeologists turned to anthropology to interpret the remains that were being discovered. This was done by comparing contemporary Native American artifacts with those recovered archaeologically, using those artifacts of known use to infer uses in the past. As a result anthropology, with its unifying concept of culture, ultimately became the main source of interpretive models for New World archaeologists—in essence it replaced history. Indeed many anthropologists of this period, such as F. H. Cushing in the Pueblo area of the American Southwest, did archaeological as well as ethnographic and linguistic fieldwork.

In both Europe and America several related interpretive currents fused into a broad interpretive model referred to as cultural evolution. The three-age system was one contribution to the idea of cultural evolution. Another was the general belief that all cultural change, in technology and other customs, was progressive, from simple to complex and from "primitive" to "civilized." Development of evolutionary theory in biology followed a parallel trend, and the two kinds of evolutionary beliefs reinforced one another. These notions were coupled with the recognition of tremendous diversity among living societies, documented in the course of European colonial expansion, and the need to "explain" (and thereby justify) the political and economic dominance of 19th-century Europeans over many other societies. The result was a model of *unilinear* cultural evolution.

The unilinear theory of cultural evolution developed by Herbert Spencer, Lewis Henry Morgan, Edward B. Tylor, and others was based on comparisons among societies. Data from any source were accepted in assessing a society's "evolutionary status." Above all, cultures were compared to determine their relative positions on a single scale of development or success. The assumption that all human cultures develop along a single or unilinear path is perhaps best expressed by Morgan's evolutionary stages of "savagery," "barbarism," and "civilization." The inflexibility of this scheme stands out as both the principal hallmark and the greatest weakness of 19th-century cultural evolutionary theory.

More than 100 years of hindsight make the errors of the unilinear evolutionists readily apparent to us. Above all these 19th-century theorists were *ethnocentric*. Their assessment of the developmental stages of other societies was heavily biased by their assumption that contemporary Western culture represented the current pinnacle of evolutionary achievement.

Of course the idea that human behavior changes and that societies and cultures evolve remains an important aspect of modern anthropological theory. But by the turn of the 20th century it was evident that the weaknesses in unilinear cultural evolutionary theory outweighed its strong points. As a consequence attempts to write a universal history of human culture were either cast aside or altered to remove the inherent problems of unilinear schemes.

The development of modern anthropology and archaeology took a somewhat different turn in America, through the influence of Franz Boas and his students. They rejected attempts to apply a universal developmental scheme via uncritical cultural comparisons. Instead they saw a need for accumulation of great amounts of well-controlled and documented archaeological, ethnographic, and linguistic data for a single society. These data would then be used to reconstruct the unique culture history of each society.

The emphasis on rigorous collection of data with a localized geographic focus that originated with Boasian anthropology dominated American archaeology until the middle of the 20th century. As a result archaeological research was directed to the establishment of specific culture histories, usually concentrating on tracing form, style, and technological changes in particular artifacts, such as pottery. For the most part, however, culture historians in America shied away from attempting broader comparative statements concerning developmental parallels and contrasts in the prehistoric record.

In the mid-20th century, however, comparative approaches began to regain popularity in American archaeology as part of a growing interest in understanding the processes of prehistoric culture change and stability. The study of artifact styles and reconstruction of localized cultural historical sequences have remained useful, especially in previously unstudied regions. At the same time, more sophisticated questions are now being asked of archaeological data, such as how a given culture was organized internally—how it functioned—at particular points in time. And cultural evolution has again become an acceptable interpretive model, but with the recognition that cultures do not develop according to some predetermined plan. Each society's development is conditioned by the natural ecological setting in which it occurs and by the neighboring societies with which it interacts, as well as its own traditions. Therefore, the specific courses of evolutionary change must be expected to be *multilinear*, rather than following a single universal path, as we shall see in Chapter 8.

SUMMARY

Like many other branches of science, archaeology has its roots in the work of amateur collectors of long ago. As the numbers of antiquities grew, attempts were made to bring order to collections by classification. The search for the meaning of antiquities led to the first attempts at understanding the prehistoric past, but such explanations were largely speculative. In the Old World prehistoric archaeology emerged from attempts to understand human origins and evolution, while in America, the central issue was the antiquity of human populations in the New World.

The emergence of archaeology as a professional, scientific discipline was marked by the rise of full-time specialists committed to understanding the meaning behind the physical remains from the past. This commitment to meaning required models or interpretive frameworks that could be tested against the evidence. Models developed in the Old World, such as the three-age system, were initially derived mainly from history. In the New World, where most native cultures lacked a historical tradition, archaeology became closely allied with the new field of anthropology. For both areas the dominant framework at the end of the 19th century was unilinear cultural evolution, defining the same broad stages for all societies. In the 20th century the weaknesses in this scheme led to more rigorous descriptive approaches. More recently multilinear evolutionary models have emerged, focusing research on the process of culture change, and the individual evolutionary career of each society.

· 3 ·

How Archaeology Works

IN THIS CHAPTER WE examine the information archaeologists work with and the ways it is acquired. You may have read about archaeologists "piecing together the past" by studying ancient pottery, "arrowheads," or other artifacts found by excavation. However, these artifacts represent only one of several categories of evidence with which archaeologists work, and excavation is only one of several means of collecting information about the past.

ARCHAEOLOGICAL DATA

The material remains of past human activity, from the microscopic debris produced by chipping stone tools to the most massive architectural construction, become *data* when the archaeologist recognizes their significance as evidence and collects and records them. The collection and recording of these material remains constitutes the acquisition of archaeological data. Here we are concerned with the three basic classes of data—artifacts, features, and ecofacts—and how they cluster into larger units. These categories are not inflexible. There is some overlap among them, but they illustrate the variety and range of information available.

Artifacts

Artifacts are portable objects whose form is modified or wholly created by human activity (Fig. 3.1). Stone hammers or fired clay vessels are artifacts because they are either natural objects modified for or by human use, such as a hammer-

FIGURE 3.1

Artifacts are portable objects whose form is modified or wholly created by human activity, while ecofacts are nonartifactual remains that nonetheless have cultural relevance. Here a projectile point (an artifact) lies embedded among the bones (ecofacts) of an extinct form of bison at Folsom, New Mexico. (All rights reserved. Photo Archives, Denver Museum of Natural History.)

stone, or new objects formed completely by human action, such as a pottery vessel. The shape and other traits of artifacts are not altered by removal from their place of discovery; both the hammerstone and the vessel retain their form and appearance after the archaeologist takes them from the ground.

Features

Features are nonportable artifacts that cannot be removed from their place of discovery without altering or destroying their original form (Fig. 3.2). Some common examples of features are hearths, burials, storage pits, and roads. It is useful to distinguish between these simple features and composite features such as buildings and other multiple component remains. It is also useful to differentiate features that have been deliberately constructed from others, such as trash heaps, that have grown by simple accumulation. Features usually define an area where one or more activities once took place.

FIGURE 3.2

Features are artifacts that cannot be recovered intact, in this case a partially excavated cremation burial pit.

Ecofacts

Ecofacts are nonartifactual natural remains that nonetheless have cultural relevance (Fig. 3.1). Although they are neither directly created nor significantly modified by human activity, ecofacts provide information about past human behavior. Examples include remnants of both wild and domesticated animal and plant species (bones, seeds, pollen, and so forth). These and other ecofacts such as soils contribute to our understanding of the past because they reflect ancient environmental conditions, diet, and resource exploitation.

Sometimes the line between ecofacts and artifacts is blurred. For example, bones with cut marks from butchering might be considered artifacts (reflecting human technology) as well as ecofacts (yielding clues to the ancient environment).

Sites

Sites are spatial clusters of artifacts, features, and/or ecofacts (Fig. 3.3). A site may consist of only one form of archaeological data—a surface scatter of artifacts, for example—or of any combination of the three different forms. Site boundaries are sometimes well defined, especially if features such as walls or moats are present. Usually, however, a decline in density or frequency of the material remains is all that marks the limits of a site. However boundaries are defined, the archaeological site is usually a basic working unit of archaeological investigation.

Sites can be described and categorized in a variety of ways, depending on the characteristics one wants to note. For instance, location—sites in open valley positions, cave sites, coastal sites, mountaintop sites, and so forth—may reflect

FIGURE 3.3

Sites are spatial clusterings of archaeological remains. Stonehenge is an example of a site with well-defined boundaries. (Copyright Historic Buildings and Monuments Commission for England.)

past environmental conditions, concern for defense, or relative values placed on natural resources located in different areas. Sites may be distinguished by one or more functions they served in the past. For example, one can speak of habitation sites, trading centers, hunting (or kill) sites, ceremonial centers, burial areas, and so on. Sites may also be described in terms of their age and/or cultural affiliation. For example, a Near Eastern site may be described as belonging to the Bronze Age, or a Mexican site may be described as Aztec.

The nature and depth of cultural deposits at a site can reveal the time span of activities: whether occupation was brief or extended. At some sites occupation (and deposition of artifacts) may have been continuous. Other sites may have had multiple occupations with periods of abandonment marked by naturally deposited (nonartifactual or "sterile") layers. Depth of accumulation is not an automatic indicator of length of occupation; at one spot a great deal of material can be deposited very rapidly, while elsewhere a relatively thin deposit of trash might represent layers laid down intermittently over hundreds of thousands of years. Whether thick or thin, the remains of sites may be visible on the ground surface or completely buried and invisible to the naked eye.

FIGURE 3.4

Underwater excavation of the Roman shipwreck at Yassi Ada, off the coast of Turkey. (© National Geographic Society.)

Some "buried" sites lie not underground but underwater, the most common being sunken ships (Fig. 3.4). However, sites that were once on dry land may also become submerged because of changes in water level (sometimes resulting from human activity such as dam building) or land subsidence. A famous example of the latter is Port Royal, Jamaica, a coastal city that sank beneath the sea after an earthquake in 1692.

Regions

Regions are the largest and most flexible spatial clusters of archaeological data. The region is basically a geographic concept: a definable area bounded by topographic features such as mountains and bodies of water (Fig. 3.5). But the definition of an archaeological region may also consider ecological and cultural factors. For instance, a region may be defined as the area used by a prehistoric population to provide its food and water. By considering whole regions the archaeologist can reconstruct aspects of prehistoric society that may not be well represented by a single site.

Obviously, the nature and scope of an archaeological region vary according to the complexity of the prehistoric society and its means of subsistence. Part of the archaeologist's task is to identify the factors that define a particular region under study, as well as to show how these factors changed through time. In

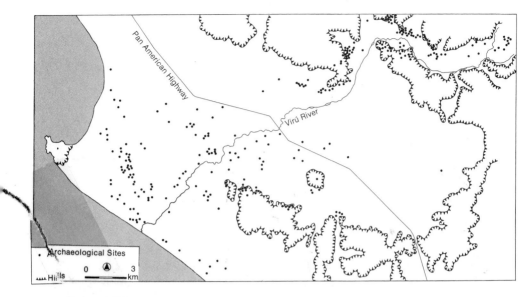

FIGURE 3.5

An archaeological region is often defined by topographic features: In this case, hilly areas and seacoast define the limits of the Virú Valley, Peru. (After Willey 1953.)

other words, the archaeologist usually works within a convenient natural region defined by geographical boundaries and seeks to determine that region's ancient ecological and cultural boundaries as well.

DEPOSITION AND TRANSFORMATION

Archaeological data are the result of two factors: behavioral processes and transformational processes. We will describe them in the order of their involvement with archaeological data.

All archaeological sites represent the products of human activity. While some human behavior, such as storytelling, leaves no tangible trace, many activities produce material remains. The activities responsible for these remains are *behavioral processes* comprising four consecutive stages: acquisition, manufacture, use, and disposal or deposition (Fig. 3.6). Artifacts such as tools are made from acquired raw materials, used for one or more specific purposes, and then discarded when broken or worn. Features such as houses are built from gathered materials, occupied, and then abandoned and destroyed or left to ruin. Ecofacts such as meat animals are hunted, butchered, cooked, eaten, and passed as waste products. The complex aggregate of these activities delineates the same stages in the life span of the site as a whole.

ACQUISITION   MANUFACTURE   USE   DEPOSITION

FIGURE 3.6

Archaeological data represent at least one behavioral cycle of acquisition, manufacture, use, and deposition.

Thus the archaeologist can use all forms of archaeological data to reconstruct the acquisition, manufacture, use, and disposal stages of ancient behavior.
Clues to all four kinds of ancient behavior may be found in characteristics of the
data themselves and in the circumstances of their deposition (Fig. 3.7).

These behavioral processes represent the first stage in the formation of archaeological data. The second step consists of *transformational processes*. These
processes include all conditions and events that affect material remains from the
time ancient use stops (at any point in the behavioral process) to the time the
archaeologist recognizes and acquires them as data. When the specific materials
under study are plants or animals, the archaeologist draws on the field of *taphonomy*: the study of what happens to remains of plants and animals after they die.
One important book on taphonomy is appropriately titled *Fossils in the Making*.

The tangible products of ancient human behavior are never completely in-
destructible, but some survive better than others. As a result the data recovered
by the archaeologist always present a picture of the past that is biased by the
effects of transformational processes (see Fig. 3.7). To gauge bias it is crucial to
determine the processes that have been at work in each archaeological situation.
Both natural and human events act either to accelerate or to retard destruction.
Natural agents of transformation include climatic factors, which are usually the
most basic influences acting on the preservation of archaeological evidence.
Temperature and humidity are generally the most critical: Extremely dry, wet,
or cold conditions preserve fragile organic materials such as textiles and wooden
tools, as well as bulkier perishable items such as human corpses (Fig. 3.8). Organic remains have been preserved under these circumstances along the dry coast
of Peru, in the wet bogs of Scandinavia, and in the frozen steppes of Siberia.

Natural destructive processes such as oxidation and decay and catastrophic
events such as earthquakes and volcanic eruptions also have profound effects on
the remains of the past. Underwater remains may be broken up and scattered by
tidal action, currents, or waves. Catastrophes such as volcanic eruptions may

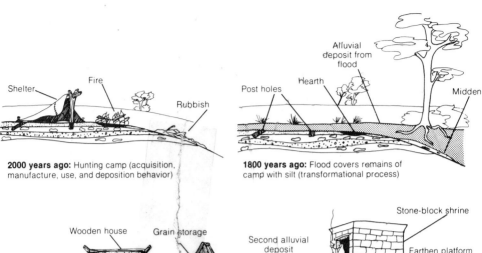

2000 years ago: Hunting camp (acquisition, manufacture, use, and deposition behavior)

1800 years ago: Flood covers remains of camp with silt (transformational process)

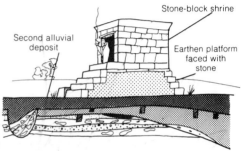

1500 years ago: Farming village built on silt (new cycle of acquisition, manufacture, use, and deposition behavior)

1000 years ago: New flood destroys farming village (transformational process); stone shrine built on new ground surface (new cycles of acquisition, manufacture, use, and deposition behavior)

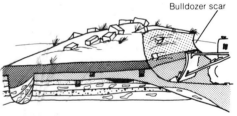

500 years ago: Shrine is abandoned and begins to disintegrate, forming mound (depositional and natural transformational processes)

Today: Mound is mined for fill to be used in highway construction (cultural transformational process)

FIGURE 3.7

The characteristics of archaeological data and their deposition reflect both behavioral and transformational processes.

FIGURE 3.8

Tollund man, a corpse preserved for
some 2000 years in a Danish bog. (Reprinted by permission of Faber &
Faber Ltd. from *The Bog People: Iron-
Age Man Preserved*, by P. V. Glob.)

either preserve or destroy archaeological sites; often the same event may have a
multitude of effects. For example, around 1500 B.C. both an earthquake and a
volcanic eruption struck the island of Thera in the Aegean Sea near Greece (Fig.
3.9). Part of the island blew up; another part collapsed inward and was filled by
the inrushing sea; and still other areas were immediately buried under a blanket
of ash. The population abandoned the island, but the remains of its settlements
were sealed beneath the ash. Recent excavations have disclosed well-preserved
buildings, some intact to the third story—a rarity in more-exposed sites—as
well as beautiful wall paintings and traces of fragile baskets.

One of the most decisive factors in the transformation process is subsequent
human activity. Reoccupation of an archaeological site may destroy all traces of
previous occupation. Earlier buildings are often leveled to make way for new
construction or to provide construction materials. In other cases, however, later
activity may preserve older sites by building over and thus sealing the earlier
remains (see Fig. 3.7). Of course, large-scale human events such as war usually
have destructive consequences for archaeological preservation, as does a flour-
ishing market in antiquities, which encourages the looting and consequent destruction of archaeological sites.

FIGURE 3.10

In this photograph, a human burial has been excavated from most of its matrix, but the relationship of the remains to the matrix is readily apparent. (Courtesy of the Ban Chiang Project, Thai Fine Arts Department/University Museum.)

In summary, archaeologists must determine what conditions and events have transformed the site before they can consider reconstructing past human behavior. Obviously, the behavioral and transformational processes are specific to each site, so each must be evaluated individually. Archaeologists begin to reconstruct these processes from the circumstances under which the data are recovered, including their matrix, provenience, and association.

Matrix refers to the physical medium that surrounds, holds, and supports other archaeological data (Fig. 3.10). Most frequently it consists of combinations of soil, sand, gravel, or rock. The nature of a matrix is usually an important clue to understanding the artifacts, features, or ecofacts it contains. For instance, artifacts recovered from an alluvial matrix (deposited by running water) may have been deposited by the natural action of a river. A matrix may also be produced by human activity, such as the deposition of immense amounts of soil in order to construct an earthen platform. In this case, the soil is not only a matrix for any artifacts or ecofacts contained in it and for other features constructed on it, but also a constructed feature.

Provenience simply refers to a three-dimensional location of any kind of archaeological data on or within the matrix. Horizontal provenience is usually recorded relative to a geographical grid system using known reference points.

FIGURE 3.11

A group of pottery vessels found in association as a result of intentional ritual deposition (primary context). This indicates they were used together as part of an ancient ceremony (ca. first century A.D., El Porton, Guatemala).

Vertical provenience is usually recorded as elevation above or below sea level. Provenience information allows the archaeologist to record (and later to reconstruct) association and context.

Association refers to two or more artifacts (or any other kind of data) occurring together in the same matrix (Fig. 3.11). The associations of various kinds of data are often crucial to the interpretation of past events. For instance, the artifacts found in association with a human burial, such as hunting weapons, may be clues to the individual's sex and livelihood.

Context is a summary evaluation of the significance of the provenience, association, and matrix for a given artifact or other bit of evidence, in light of effects of both behavioral and transformational processes. In other words, context is an assessment of where the evidence is, how it got there, and what has happened to it in the meantime.

There are two basic kinds of archaeological contexts: primary and secondary. Each of these may be divided into two further categories.

Primary context refers to conditions in which both provenience and matrix have been undisturbed since original deposition. Intact archaeological features are always in primary context, although later disturbance can remove portions of such features from primary context. There are two kinds of primary contexts:

1. *Use-related primary context* results from deposition in the place where the artifact was acquired, made, or used. The occurrence of two or more associated artifacts in use-related primary context ideally means that they were used and deposited at the same time. Such an occurrence allows the archaeologist to reconstruct the activity of which the artifacts were a part. Truly undisturbed archaeological contexts, however, are rare, the best examples being burials and tombs. Most contexts have been altered to some degree by transformational processes.

2. *Transposed primary context* is a more specific category since it results from behavior concerned with disposal of refuse (formation of trash heaps or *middens*). In other words, it is the product of the final stage in the behavioral cycle. The association of two or more artifacts in transposed primary context does not allow direct inferences about any ancient behavior other than waste disposal. However, association in transposed primary context does support the conclusion that the artifacts were made and used during the same general period. It can be seen, therefore, that use-related primary context represents a wider range of ancient activities, but archaeological data in primary contexts are more commonly found in transposed situations.

Secondary context refers to a condition in which provenience, association, and matrix have been wholly or partially altered by processes of transformation. There are two kinds of secondary contexts:

1. *Use-related secondary context* results from disturbances by subsequent human activity, ancient or modern.

2. *Natural secondary context* results from disturbance by a variety of nonhuman agents, such as burrowing animals, tree roots, erosion, decay, volcanic eruptions, or earthquakes.

The differences among the types of archaeological context and the significance of accurately determining context, can be illustrated by several examples. In the first place, any artifact may be modified to be reused for different purposes over its use span. Thus a pottery vessel may be manufactured for the transport of water but later modified to use as a container for food or other substances and then (when inverted) as a mold for the shaping of new pottery vessels. If this vessel were abandoned during, or immediately after, any of these activities—say its use as a pottery mold—and remained in an undisturbed matrix with its associated artifacts, ecofacts, and features, its archaeological context upon discovery would be primary (undisturbed) and use-related (as part of pottery making activity). Knowing the provenience, associations, and context (in this case reflected in the finding of an inverted vessel surrounded by other vessels in various stages of manufacture, along with clay-working tools and so forth), the archaeologist would be able to reconstruct both the type of activity and many specific techniques used in this instance of pottery making. Any prior uses, however, would not be directly detected.

As already noted, the survival of use-related primary contexts is relatively rare and depends on both the circumstances of the original behavior and transformation processes that tended to preserve rather than destroy. Discoveries of chipped stone projectile points in clear association with bones of animals have been important keys to the reconstruction of early human activities in the New World. In the mid-1920s, discoveries at Folsom, New Mexico, revealed such points in undisturbed use-related contexts associated with bones of a species of bison that has been extinct for at least 10,000 years (Fig. 3.1). The dates have been supplied by paleontological study, but archaeological association and context were critical in establishing the cultural meaning of these finds.

Many kinds of activity can disturb or erase earlier use-related primary contexts. In some cases, however, subsequent human activity can preserve them—as in the building of a new structure over the recently abandoned pottery workshop described above. In other cases the manner of original deposition may tend to secure use-related primary contexts from disturbance. One of the best examples of such deposition is provided by the preparation of burials and tombs. In many areas of the world ancient people developed elaborate funerary customs. When found undisturbed the resultant tombs provide opportunities to reconstruct ancient ritual activity and belief systems.

A good illustration of this reconstruction can be seen in the Royal Tombs of Ur, an ancient Mesopotamian site in Iraq, excavated by Sir Leonard Woolley in the late 1920s (Fig. 3.12). Careful recording of provenience and associations enabled Woolley to reconstruct a nearly complete funerary scene, including elaborate grave goods and sacrificed victims. From the reconstructions Woolley was able to infer a great deal about royal customs of the time, as well as specific details such as court costume. Only the chamber of the king himself, which had been looted, could not be reconstructed; the rest had been protected and preserved by interment.

Other examples of use-related primary context have been preserved by natural events. The deposition of soil by wind and water has buried countless sites under deep layers of earth; a famous example of a buried site is the ancient Roman city of Pompeii, which was covered by volcanic ash from the eruption of Mount Vesuvius in A.D. 79 (see Fig. 2.1).

Not all primary contexts are use related, however. People in most societies discard items after they are damaged, broken, or no longer useful. Middens are specialized areas for rubbish disposal; they contain artifacts that are usually undisturbed from the moment of their deposition. Furthermore, if used over long periods of time, middens may become stratified or layered, with each layer corresponding to a period of rubbish deposition. Middens are thus in primary context, but because of the nature of their deposition, the only past behavior directly reflected by this context is the general practice of rubbish accumulation and disposal. For this reason, material recovered from middens is in *transposed primary context*. If a midden is used over a long period of time, relative position within the deposit (or within a particular layer of the midden) can be used to assess relative chronological position (Fig. 3.13).

FIGURE 3.12

This plan shows positions of bodies in the "Great Death-Pit" adjacent to the royal tombs at Ur. (From Woolley 1934; by permission of the University Museum, University of Pennsylvania.)

The identification of use-related secondary context can often help the archaeologist understand how artifacts came to be associated. Of course, if the disturbed context is not recognized as such, the interpretation can be badly in error. For example, the contents of a heavily disturbed tomb might include not only some portion of the original furnishings, but also materials such as tools and containers that were brought in and left behind by the looters. During the excavation of the tomb of the Egyptian Pharaoh Tut-ankh-amun, ancient looting was recognized by evidence of two openings and reclosings of the entry; the final sealings of the disturbed areas were marked by different motifs from those on the undisturbed portions. If the disturbance had not been recognized, the associations and arrangements of recovered artifacts might be wrongly interpreted as representing burial ritual behavior.

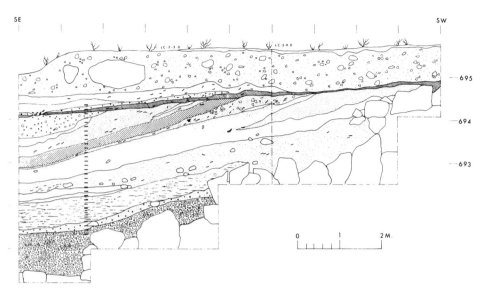

FIGURE 3.13

Cross-section drawing of a stratified midden representing nearly 2000 years of accumulation at Chalchuapa, El Salvador. One of the characteristics of transposed primary context, such as this midden, is that the artifacts from a given layer are contemporaneous but cannot be assumed to represent the same set of ancient activities.

Natural secondary context, which might occur, for example, when burrowing animals have placed later artifacts in apparent association with earlier features, can also make interpretation difficult. At Ban Chiang, a site in northern Thailand, ancient burials are juxtaposed in a very complex fashion, with later pits intruding into or overlapping earlier ones. The job of segregating distinct units was made even more difficult by the numerous animal burrows, including those of worms, crisscrossing the units, so that tracing pit lines and other surfaces was exacting and intricate work.

The archaeologist uses the foregoing kinds of information along with the products of past behavior—archaeological data—to reconstruct both the behaviors and the cultural systems by which they were produced. As the first step in linking the data to a past cultural system, the archaeologist must assess the effects on the data of the processes we have discussed: the kinds of ancient behavior that produced the evidence (behavioral processes), and the natural or human events that have affected the evidence from the time of deposition to the moment of archaeological recovery (transformational processes).

A point to be emphasized is that any kind of excavation—by archaeologists or anyone else—*destroys* matrix, association, and context. The only way to preserve the information these factors convey is in drawings, photographs, and written records. Without them, even the most painstakingly controlled excavation is no more justifiable or useful than a looter's pit.

ACQUIRING DATA

Archaeologists are concerned with gathering evidence of past human behavior as a first step toward understanding that ancient behavior and toward meeting both the specific objectives of their research and the general goals of archaeology (see Chapter 1). Realizing these objectives requires discovery of as much as possible about the characteristics of the data. Ideally archaeologists seek to recover the full range of variation in the archaeological data relevant to their research questions. What was the range of activities carried on at a site? What was the range of places chosen for location and settlement? What was the range of forms and styles of artifacts? To the extent that such variation existed but is not known, the picture of ancient life is unnecessarily incomplete and any inferences drawn may be wrong. In a sense archaeological data are always unrepresentative; not all behavior produces tangible evidence, and not all the evidence will survive. The ideal goal is seldom realized, but understanding the processes that affected the production and preservation of the evidence can compensate to some extent for the unevenness in the availability of data. At this point we need to consider how the archaeologist chooses data acquisition strategies to maximize the usefulness of the evidence that *is* available.

The first step in data acquisition is to define the limits of the region under investigation. This will impose a practical limit on the amount of evidence to be collected. A bounded research area may be referred to as a *data universe*. An archaeological data universe is bounded both in time and geographical space. An investigator may define a data universe as a single site or a portion of site. In a regional situation the research area corresponds to a much larger universe, such as an entire valley or a coastal area containing many sites. The archaeologist may also draw temporal boundaries to seek data corresponding to a relatively short era, such as the Pueblo II period of the American Southwest (ca. A.D. 900–1100), or a much longer span, such as a period of several thousand years corresponding to an entire interglacial period of the Pleistocene (Ice Age).

Once defined, the data universe is subdivided into *sample units*. A sample unit is the unit of investigation; it may be defined by either arbitrary or nonarbitrary criteria. *Nonarbitrary sample units* correspond either to natural areas, such as microenvironments, or to cultural entities, such as rooms, houses, or sites (Fig 3.14). *Arbitrary sample units* are spatial divisions with no inherent natural or cultural relevance (Fig. 3.15). Examples of the latter include sample units defined by a grid system (equal-sized squares). *Sample units should not be confused with data.* If an archaeologist is looking for sites, the sample units will be geographical areas where sites might be located. If sites are the sample units, the data to be gathered will be artifacts, ecofacts, and features within the site.

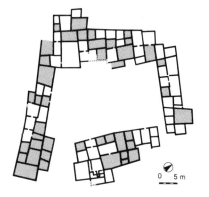

FIGURE 3.14

A universe with nonarbitrary units: In this case, rooms in a prehistoric Southwestern pueblo. The shaded rooms were the ones excavated. (By permission from *Broken K Pueblo, Prehistoric Social Organization in the American Southwest*, by James N. Hill, University of Arizona Anthropological Paper #18, Tucson: University of Arizona Press, copyright 1970.)

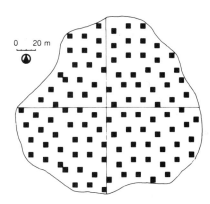

FIGURE 3.15

A universe with arbitrary units at Girik-i-Haciyan, Turkey; the black areas were the units investigated. (After Redman and Watson, reproduced by permission of The Society for American Archaeology, adapted from *American Antiquity* 35:281–282, 1970.)

The choice between arbitrary and nonarbitrary sample units is made by the investigator; it reflects the specific objectives of the study and the nature of the data (see below). But in any case all sample units are (or are assumed to be) comparable. That is, nonarbitrarily defined units are assumed to yield similar or complementary information about ancient behavior. For example, if sites are the sample units, one "cemetery" site will give information similar to that from another cemetery site and complementary to information from "habitation" sites and other sample units within the data population. Arbitrarily defined units, on the other hand, are comparable because they are always regular in size and/ or shape.

The aggregate of all sample units is the *population*. Note that when the universe is a region and the sample units correspond to all the known sites, the population will not include unknown sites or locations in the region without sites, even though these areas are part of the universe. Nevertheless, conclusions drawn about the population are often inferred to be "true" of the research universe as well.

Total data acquisition involves investigation of all the units in the population. Of course the archaeologist never succeeds in gathering every shred of evidence from a given data universe; we are constantly developing new techniques of recovery and analysis that broaden the very definition of archaeological data. A change in the research problem also alters the definition of what materials and relationships are considered appropriate data. It is nonetheless important to distinguish between investigations that attempt to collect all available evidence (by investigation of all sample units) and those that set out to collect only a portion of the available data. Something approaching total data acquisition is often attempted in salvage situations, as when a site or region is threatened with immediate destruction by construction of a new highway or dam.

Sample data acquisition refers to situations in which only a portion or sample of the data can be collected from a given archaeological data pool. The limits of the sample recovered are often influenced by economic constraints: The archaeologist seldom has the funds to study all potential units. Nor is research time unlimited; seasonal weather conditions, scheduling commitments, and other factors often determine the time available to gather evidence. Access to archaeological data may be restricted by natural barriers, lack of roads or lack of permission from property owners. Even when there are no restrictions to access, however, it is still desirable to collect only part of the available archaeological data. Except in situations of threatened site destruction, most archaeologists recommend that a portion of every site be left untouched to allow future scientists a chance to work with intact sources of archaeological evidence using techniques more sophisticated than today's. In this way future research can check and refine the results obtained with present methods.

RESEARCH DESIGN

Whether total or sample coverage is used, research must be planned to ensure that its goals will be addressed and met. Traditionally, archaeological research has been "site-oriented." The major goal was to excavate a particular site and, in many cases, collect spectacular remains. With the emergence of archaeology as a scientific discipline, more systematic approaches have become the rule. Today, regional and problem-oriented investigations are increasingly the norm. This kind of research aims at solving specific problems or testing one or more hypotheses by using controlled and representative samples of data.

Archaeological research design refers to a sequence of stages that guides the conduct of investigation (Fig. 3.16) to ensure the validity of results and make efficient use of time, money, and effort. Each stage has one or more specific purposes. Although the stages may be ideally portrayed as a series of steps, the process is flexible in practice. Aspects of two or more stages may be carried out simultaneously, or the stages may be accomplished in a different order, depending on circumstances. Furthermore, since each research situation is unique, this gener-

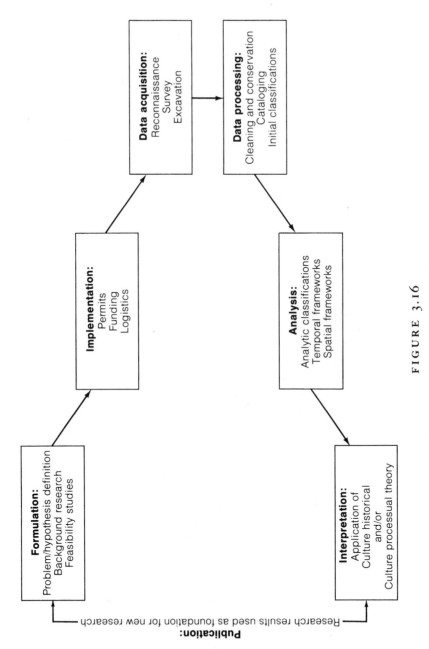

FIGURE 3.16

Diagram of stages of archaeological research.

alized research design must be capable of adapting to a wide variety of specific applications.

Formulation involves definition of the research problem, background investigations, and feasibility studies. Decisions regarding the problem to be investigated and the geographical area of study both limit and guide further work. Once these choices are made, the archaeologist conducts background research to locate and study any previous work that may be relevant to the investigation. Useful information at this point may include geographical, geological, climatological, ecological, and anthropological studies, when available. Such data may be found in publications, archives, laboratories, and so on and through consultations with individual experts. Because archaeological research usually requires fieldwork, the archaeologist must usually do a feasibility study involving a trip to the region or sites to be investigated to evaluate the archaeological situation and local conditions such as accessibility, availability of supplies, and so forth.

Thorough background investigations facilitate the actual research by refining the problem under investigation and defining specific research goals. The goals of most archaeological research include testing one or more specific hypotheses. Some of these may come from previously proposed models, while others may arise during the formulation of the basic research problem. As the research progresses, of course, new hypotheses may be generated and tested. It is important to remember, however, that the initial formulation of research problem(s) leads the archaeologist to look for particular kinds of data and thus sets the course for the entire study.

Implementation involves completing all the arrangements necessary for the success of the planned fieldwork. These arrangements may be complex, especially if the research is to be done in a foreign country. The first step in implementing a study may be to secure the necessary permits for conducting research, usually from government agencies responsible for overseeing archaeological work. The owners of the land on which the work will take place must also grant permission before investigations can proceed. The laws governing archaeological work vary from country to country and from state to state within the United States, so the archaeologist must be aware of the relevant regulations and customs within the area being investigated.

At some point the archaeologist must find funds to finance the research. In some cases this involves submitting a research proposal to private or governmental agencies that fund archaeological investigations. In many CRM situations (see Chapter 1), the agency issuing the contract provides the funding for the research.

When funding and permit have been secured, the archaeologist can turn to making logistic arrangements. Research equipment and supplies must be acquired. In most cases field facilities must be rented or built for safekeeping of the equipment and for laboratory processing and storage of artifacts and field records. Many projects require a staff that must be recruited, transported, housed, and fed, and these arrangements must be completed before the work can begin.

Acquisition involves three basic procedures for the collection of data: reconnaissance, survey, and excavation. At this point we will treat these only briefly, since they will be considered at length in Chapter 4. Reconnaissance is the means for identifying and locating archaeological sites, accomplished by on-the-scene visual search and by remote sensors. Survey is undertaken to record as much as possible about archaeological sites without excavation, through photography, mapping, remote sensors, and collection of surface artifacts. Excavation is undertaken to expose the buried characteristics of archaeological sites, using a variety of techniques to retrieve and record the data revealed.

Data processing refers to the manipulation of raw data (artifacts and ecofacts) and the creation and manipulation of records. Portable remains are usually processed in a field laboratory to insure that they are recorded, preserved, and stored to be available for further analysis. Records referring to these data (descriptions, photographs, and scaled drawings) are also completed and filed to be accessible for later use.

Analysis provides a variety of information useful for archaeological interpretations. For artifacts these studies include classification, determination of age, and various technical analyses designed to identify sources of raw materials, methods of manufacture, and uses. Some of these procedures can be done in the field laboratory, but the more technical or complex analyses are usually undertaken at specially equipped permanent scientific facilities.

Interpretation involves the synthesis of all the results of data collection, processing, and analysis as a means of answering the original goals of the investigation. The use of the scientific method in these procedures is an important characteristic of modern professional archaeology. A variety of models are used in the interpretive process, including both specific and general historical and anthropological frameworks.

Publication completes the research cycle and makes the findings fully accessible so that the results can be used and retested by fellow archaeologists and any other interested individuals. This ensures that any research contributes to the broadest objectives of archaeology and of science in general.

ARCHAEOLOGICAL RESEARCH PROJECTS

Scientific archaeology demands a broad range of expertise. Today's archaeologist must be a theoretical scientist, a methodologist, a technician, an administrator, and more. In reality, of course, it is nearly impossible for one individual to do everything necessary for a particular project; usually the archaeologist must bring together specialists from a wide variety of disciplines. Doing so requires an interdisciplinary approach and coordination of the efforts of many scientists, each of whom focuses on a particular aspect of the research. Scientific teams—usually led by an archaeologist but including botanists, ecologists, geologists, and other specialists—are often created to conduct thorough fieldwork on a re-

FIGURE 3.17

The modern large-scale archaeological excavation at Quiriguá, Guatemala, involved over 100 people and continued over a six-year period. (Quiriguá Project, University Museum, University of Pennsylvania.)

search question. Only by depending on others can the archaeologist ensure that the data collected are used to the maximum degree possible. In some cases the archaeologist may find most of the required support specialists housed under one roof, as in the larger museums and research institutions in many parts of the world. In the United States, the Smithsonian Institution provides one of the most complete support facilities for archaeology.

The size and duration of archaeological research projects depend on the scale of the problems being investigated. A few months' work by a single individual may be all that is required to plan and conduct the data-gathering stages of the research. But even the single individual will need some form of assistance from outside specialists in processing and analyzing the results. Archaeological research concerned with complex civilizations, such as the work being done at large urban sites in the Near East and Mexico, usually calls for a large archaeological staff and a huge labor force (Fig. 3.17). Projects in these and similar areas have employed teams of on-site specialists in research extending over many years.

Like most activities, archaeological research is limited by the availability of time and money. A far greater problem, however, is one that threatens the very existence of archaeological research: the increasing destruction wrought by our rapidly expanding world. The destruction of archaeological remains has reached such proportions that we may well ask, "Does the past have a future?" We will consider the problem of the destruction of archaeological sites in the final chapter of this book.

SUMMARY

The material remains from the past become archaeological data once they are recognized, collected, and recorded. The direct products of past human activity are either artifacts (portable) or features (nonportable). Indirect products of past human activity are called ecofacts. Archaeologists usually examine distributions of data within sites (clusters of data), or, as is increasingly common today, within regions (clusters of sites). Further information is gleaned from recording the specific location (provenience), associations, and matrix (surroundings) of data. The context of data—their behavioral significance—is revealed by evaluation of all these factors. The understanding of context, with care to discriminate among the various kinds of context, is the crucial link that allows the archaeologist to reconstruct the kinds of ancient behavior the recovered data represent.

The material record ideally reflects four major categories of human activity—acquisition, manufacture, use, and deposition—which together constitute behavioral processes. But archaeologists can never recover data representing all kinds of past behavior. Some activity leaves no tangible trace, and the evidence of other kinds of ancient behavior may be altered over time by human and natural transformational processes. These processes act selectively either to preserve or to destroy archaeological evidence. Thus the data available to the archaeologist constitute a sample determined first by ancient human activity (behavioral processes) and then by human or natural forces acting after the remains are deposited (transformational processes).

The resulting data form the base that the archaeologist attempts to recover, either totally (by collection of all available evidence) or by sampling methods. Whatever collection method is used, the archaeologist seeks data that represent, as much as possible, the full range of ancient human activity. With very few exceptions (such as when a site is about to be destroyed), it is generally practical and desirable to collect only a sample of the data.

Archaeological research is usually aimed at solving specific problems or testing specific hypotheses. To guide such investigations, most archaeologists follow a similar research design that begins with formulation of the problem, based on background and feasibility studies, followed by implementation, which includes fund-raising, securing permits, and making logistical arrangements. The next stage is data acquisition, which often includes reconnaissance (locating unknown sites), survey (mapping and collecting surface data), and excavation (removal of matrix to reveal buried data). This is followed by data processing and analysis, leading to interpretation (reconstruction of the past to address the specific research goals) and publication of the research.

To be a successful researcher, today's archaeologist must command a broad range of expertise. He or she must have knowledge of field methods, theory, administration, and a range of technical skills. Seldom can one individual perform all the tasks demanded by the complexity of archaeological investigation, so in almost all cases the archaeologist calls on a variety of specialists for assistance.

The scale of archaeological research ranges from the study conducted by a single person in a few weeks to the work of large research teams over several years or decades. The practical limits to such research are usually determined by time and money, but the severest threat to our understanding of the past is posed by our expanding world's destruction of archaeological data.

· 4 ·

Fieldwork

WITH A WELL-DESIGNED research program in hand, the next consideration is the collection of archaeological data. Archaeologists use three means of collecting evidence about the past: archaeological reconnaissance, surface survey, and excavation. Although excavation dominates the popular image of what archaeologists do, reconnaissance and surface survey are crucial to archaeological research, as are subsequent data processing and classification.

RECONNAISSANCE

Time transforms the sites of past human activity in a variety of ways. Sites such as Stonehenge remain obvious to any observer. Others are nearly destroyed or completely buried; in such cases the task of identification may be extremely difficult. The systematic attempt to identify archaeological sites is called *archaeological reconnaissance*. Identification is both the discovery and the location (determination of geographical position) of sites. Reconnaissance data can be used to formulate or refine hypotheses to be tested in later research stages. This is especially true when the work is taking place in geographical areas with no prior archaeological information or as part of a feasibility study for a larger project.

Archaeological reconnaissance yields data about the range in form (size and internal arrangement) of sites as well as their total number and spatial distribution within a region. The distributional data may reveal patterns in the placement of sites, relative both to each other and to the natural environment, such as

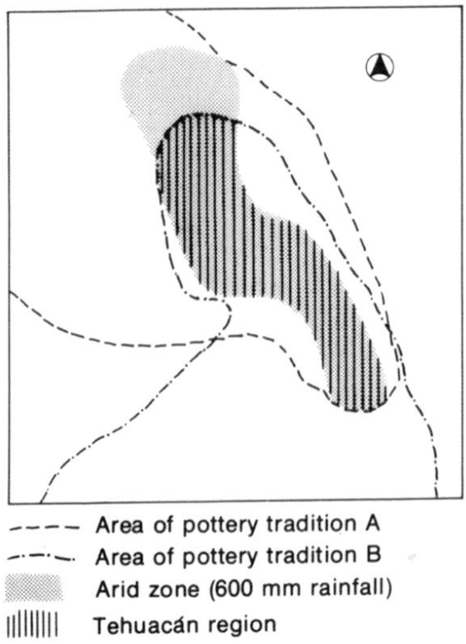

FIGURE 4.1

Definition of the Tehuacán region was based on both cultural and ecological criteria. (After MacNeish et al. 1972.)

- - - - Area of pottery tradition A
- ‒ - ‒ Area of pottery tradition B
▓▓▓ Arid zone (600 mm rainfall)
‖‖‖‖ Tehuacán region

topography; plant, animal, and mineral resources; and water. Sometimes these findings may be used to define the region for later, more intensive study. For the Tehuacán Project in Mexico, one phase of reconnaissance helped to define the study region by indicating the correlation between the limits of the arid Tehuacán Valley (Fig. 4.1) and the distribution limits of two pottery styles.

Uses such as these for archaeological reconnaissance also emphasize the need for studies of the region's environmental resources, either prior to actual archaeological reconnaissance (as part of background research) or in conjunction with the site identification process. Defining ecological zones within a study area can guide the archaeologist in searching for sites if site location can be correlated with distribution of different environmental variables. The archaeologist may thereby gain an initial understanding of possible ecological relationships between past peoples and their environment.

Discovering Archaeological Sites

Not all sites are found through general reconnaissance. To begin with, some archaeological remains are never lost to history: In areas with long literate traditions, such as the Mediterranean basin, the locations and identities of many ancient cities are well documented. Obviously the locations of Athens, imperial Rome, and many other famous places of antiquity have never been forgotten. Most sites, however—even many documented by history—have not fared so well. Many once-recorded sites have been lost, razed by conquerors or ravaged by natural processes of collapse and decay. Ancient Carthage, for example, was systematically destroyed by its Roman conquerors in 146 B.C. Only recently has it been rediscovered near Tunis.

Sometimes histories and even legends provide the clues that lead to the discovery of "lost" cities. The most famous quest of this sort was Heinrich Schliemann's successful search for the legendary city of Troy. As a child, Schliemann was fascinated with the story of Troy and decided that someday he would find that lost city. By age 30 he had become a successful international merchant and had amassed the fortune he needed to pursue his archaeological goals. He had, at the same time, learned more than half a dozen languages and quickened his interest in Troy by reading Homer's tales of the Trojan War in the original Greek. Textual descriptions of the location of the ancient city convinced him that it was to be found at Hissarlik in western Turkey. Accordingly, in 1870 he began excavations that ultimately demonstrated the physical existence of Priam's legendary city. Later it was found that the buried remains Schliemann had called Troy were really an earlier settlement and that he had cut right through the Trojan layers in his determined digging (see Fig. 2.5). Nonetheless Schliemann is credited with the discovery of Troy, and his successful persistence there and later in Greece at Mycenae and Tiryns gave great impetus to the search for the origins of Greek civilization.

Perhaps more archaeological sites come to light by accident than by any other means. The forces of nature—wind and water erosion, natural catastrophes, and so forth—have uncovered many long-buried traces of past human activity. The deposits of Tanzania's Olduvai Gorge, from which Louis and Mary Leakey recovered remains of early human ancestors, were exposed by thousands of years of riverine bed-cutting action. And the famous Neolithic lake dwellings of Switzerland were discovered when extremely low water levels during the dry winter of 1853–1854 exposed the preserved remains of wooden pilings that had once supported houses.

Chance discoveries of ancient sites occur all the time. For example, it was French schoolboys who in 1940 first happened on the Paleolithic paintings of Lascaux cave: The boys' dog fell through an opening into the cave, and when they went after their pet, they discovered the cavern walls covered with ancient paintings. As the world's population increases and the pace of new construction accelerates, more and more ancient remains are uncovered. More often than not new sites are first found by farmers, outdoor enthusiasts, explorers, and construction workers rather than archaeologists. Unfortunately, and often despite the best intentions, many of these sites are destroyed before an archaeologist has a chance to observe and record them.

Archaeological reconnaissance may be conducted in many ways, but the actual techniques and procedures used often depend on the kinds of sites being sought. The methods used to locate surface sites differ greatly from those intended to discover deeply buried sites. In most cases limitations of time and money prevent the archaeologist from covering every square meter of the research area in attempting to identify sites. Carefully selected sampling procedures must therefore be used to maximize the chance that the number and location of sites in the areas actually searched are representative of the universe under study.

(a)   (b)

FIGURE 4.2

Present environmental conditions have a great influence on reconnaissance:
(a) Tropical rain forest greatly reduces visibility, while (b) arid landscapes are
often conducive to detection of surface sites. (Courtesy of the Tikal and Gordion
Projects, University Museum, University of Pennsylvania.)

It is worth noting that some environments are simply more conducive to
reconnaissance than others. Dry climates and sparse vegetation offer nearly
ideal conditions for both visual detection of sites and ease of movement across
reconnoitered terrain (Fig. 4.2). Such environments have greatly aided archaeologists in discovering sites in the Near East, coastal Peru, highland Mexico, the
southwestern United States, and similar areas.

Good quality maps are essential for reconnaissance. They may be supplemented in some cases by aerial photos. Maps are used first to plot the grid
squares or other boundaries for sample units and then to plot the locations of
new archaeological sites discovered. Plotting of sample unit boundaries enables
the archaeologist to indicate which areas have been covered. Sampling adequacy
can then be assessed and possible distributions in unreconnoitered areas can be
posited. Plotting of new sites is necessary for distributional studies within the
sampled area and, of course, for later return to the sites.

Two basic methods are used for archaeological reconnaissance: ground reconnaissance (aerial reconnaissance and subsurface detection) and remote sensing. Each requires specialized techniques, and each is effective in identifying
sites under different conditions.

Ground reconnaissance is the oldest, most common method of searching the
study area. It has been used since the days of antiquarian interest when exploration by such men as William Camden in England or Stephens and Catherwood
in Central America led to the discovery of countless sites. This approach is illus-

FIGURE 4.3

Traces of a building visible on the surface of Shahr-i-Sokhta. (Courtesy of Centro Studie Scavi Archeologici in Asia of IsMEO, Rome.)

trated in recent years by numerous large-scale surveys in the United States and elsewhere. An example is David Hurst Thomas's work in the Great Basin, discussed in Chapter 1.

Most ground reconnaissance is still conducted by walking—the slowest method but the most thorough. Often the efficiency of reconnaissance on foot may be increased by using teams of archaeologists (or an archaeologist and several trained assistants). Attention to changing ground conditions is also useful; for example, in freshly plowed fields, farmers will have brought shallowly buried items to the surface again. Many archaeologists increase the speed of large-scale ground reconnaissance by use of horses, mules, or even motorized transport (four-wheel drive vehicles are frequently necessary).

How does the archaeologist recognize archaeological sites on the ground? Some sites, of course, are identified by their prominence. Many ancient settlements in the Near East are called *tell* or *tepe*—both meaning "hill"—because they stand out as large mounds against a relatively flat plain. In other cases a slight rise or fall in the landscape that appears unnatural may indicate a buried ancient wall or other feature. Many sites are identified by concentrations of surface artifacts such as pottery sherds and stone tools. Shahr-i Sokhta in eastern Iran was recognized as a site because of its densely littered surface. Moreover, at certain times of day differential absorption of salt made the tops of the buried mud-brick walls at Shahr-i Sokhta stand out as white against the rest of the surface of the mound (Fig. 4.3). Many sites, however, lack standing architecture and other obvious surface traces and require more than simple walking and looking for their discovery.

Remote sensing approaches to site discovery involve a number of techniques in which the observer is not in direct contact with the archaeological remains.

FIGURE 4.4

Aerial photograph, shot by remote control, from a balloon moored over the site of Sarepta, Lebanon. (Photo by Julian Whittlesey.)

These techniques may be divided into two major categories: reconnaissance from the air and subsurface reconnaissance from ground level.

Aerial reconnaissance includes a variety of established and developing techniques, the most common being aerial photography. Although the most common approach to aerial photography is to use a small airplane, balloons and helicopters have also been used, as have kites equipped with remote-controlled cameras (Fig. 4.4).

Aerial photography is useful to the archaeologist in a number of ways. It provides data for preliminary analysis of the local environment and its resources, and it yields information on site location. Although aerial photography can reveal sites from their surface characteristics or prominence, one of its most useful applications is in detecting buried sites. Low-growing vegetation, such as grass, grain, and other ground covers, is often sensitive to subsurface conditions. Many plants grow higher and more luxuriantly where ancient human activity, such as the construction of canals, deposition of middens, or interment of burials, has improved soil moisture and fertility. In contrast, solid construction features such as walls or roads immediately below the surface will often impede vegetation growth (Fig. 4.5). The best circumstance for such detection is a uniform, low-growing plant cover, such as may be found in grassy plains, savannahs, or croplands. Areas of luxuriant growth are usually darker than contrasting poor-growth areas.

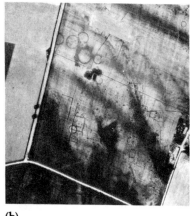

(a)   **(b)**

FIGURE 4.5

A pair of aerial photographs of the same area at different times. Detection of buried archaeological features has been greatly enhanced with the maturation of the barley growing in the field: (a) taken June 4, 1970; (b) taken June 19, 1970. (Courtesy of the Museum Applied Science Center for Archaeology, University Museum, University of Pennsylvania.)

As with data from all remote sensing techniques, aerial reconnaissance data require knowledge of the corresponding *ground truth* for reliable interpretation. That is, one must determine, by checking at ground level, what the various contrasting patterns and features on a photograph represent. Features such as rivers and towns may be self-evident. But even familiar things such as modern golf courses can sometimes go unrecognized by an individual who is not acquainted with the area or experienced in reading aerial photographs. Aerial radar images have also been used for archaeological purposes. Radar is effective in penetrating cloud cover, and it will "see through" dense vegetation to a certain extent.

Exploration of the potential archaeological utility of satellite sensing is just beginning. Some satellites have multispectral scanners that record the intensity of reflected light and infrared radiation. The satellite data are converted electronically to photographic images, which can be built up, in a mosaic, to form a very accurate map. Although the resolution of the images is low and individual features (even those as massive as the great pyramids of Egypt) are barely visible (Fig. 4.6), extensive features such as ancient road networks are often detectable. This suggests to archaeologists that studies involving regional or interregional distributions are the ones most likely to make use of satellite data.

Subsurface detection includes a variety of methods used to identify buried remains. These range from the rather simple and commonplace to those requiring exotic and expensive equipment. Since most of these techniques provide limited

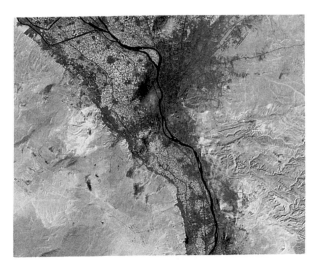

FIGURE 4.6

Satellite image of a portion of the Nile Valley in Egypt,
with the Great Pyramids visible on the desert margin at
lower left. (Landsat imagery courtesy of EOSAT.)

coverage and are time-consuming and costly, they are sometimes used only for
subsurface identification of specific features within archaeological sites. Often,
however, they are the only means available for locating buried sites.

The most direct and simple methods are *augering*, *coring*, and *shovel testing*.
An auger is a large drill run by human or machine power. It is used to find out
the depth of deposits such as topsoil or middens. Corers are hollow tubes that
are driven into the ground. When removed, they yield a narrow column or core
of matrix, providing a quick and relatively inexpensive cross-section of subsurface layers or construction. Simple shallow probes with shovels or posthole diggers are the most common kind of reconnaissance technique in eastern North
America and similar regions, where sites lie invisible, just below ground level.

The *magnetometer* is an instrument that discerns minor variations in the
magnetism present in many materials. Unlike the compass, which measures the
direction of the earth's magnetic field, magnetometers measure the intensity of
the magnetic field. These instruments have been applied successfully to archaeological reconnaissance because some remains create anomalies in the magnetic field. For example, iron tools and ceramic kilns are especially easy to find.
Such buried features as walls made of volcanic stone, ditches filled with humus,
and even burned surfaces may all be detected by the magnetometer (Fig. 4.7).
Its primary use is to locate features within a site.

The first application of the cesium magnetometer, however, was in site reconnaissance during the search for the Greek colonial city of Sybaris. Sybaris had a
history and reputation but no tangible existence. It was founded in 710 B.C. and

(a)   (b)

FIGURE 4.7

Magnetometers are important aids in subsurface detection: (a) The person in the foreground carries the detector, while the two in the background (b) read and record the magnetic values. (© Nicholas Hartmann, MASCA, University Museum, University of Pennsylvania.)

became notorious for the self-indulgence of its inhabitants; in 520 B.C. it was destroyed by its neighbors from the city of Croton. It was known to be located somewhere in or on the plain of the River Crati in the instep of Italy's boot; beyond this, all attempts at locating the ancient city had been unsuccessful. In the 1960s, however, a multiseason, joint Italian-American expedition succeeded in locating Sybaris (Fig. 4.8). The investigators used a variety of approaches, including coring and resistivity techniques, but the center of attention was the magnetometer, which proved to be the instrument that located this elusive site.

Another instrument, the *resistivity detector* (Fig. 4.9), measures differences in the ability of subsurface features to conduct electrical current. Moisture content gives most soils a low resistance to electrical current; solid features such as walls or floors can raise resistance considerably.

The development of newer and better remote-sensing instruments continues. One recent technique uses *radar* to locate buried features. Ground-penetrating radar sends electromagnetic waves into the earth, to be reflected back as "echoes" by subsurface discontinuities such as soil strata and constructed features. But the utility of such simple techniques as walking and looking, and shovel testing, will always remain high.

Locating Archaeological Sites

Discovery is only half the task of reconnaissance. The other half is determining and recording the location of the sites as they are discovered. The central pur-

FIGURE 4.8

Excavations at Sybaris, following reconnaissance by magnetometer, expose
Roman construction superimposed
on the remains of the earlier Greek
colony. (Courtesy of the Museum Applied Science Center for Archaeology,
University Museum, University of
Pennsylvania.)

FIGURE 4.9

Subsurface detection by resistivity at a historical site in Pennsylvania. (Courtesy
of the Museum Applied Science Center for Archaeology, University Museum,
University of Pennsylvania.)

pose of recording is to relate the newly found sites to their spatial setting, to place the previously unknown into the realm of the known. Usually this involves plotting the site location on a map or aerial photograph. Sometimes base maps have to be specially drawn to record the results of reconnaissance. In other cases archaeological sites may already be indicated in some way on a map or be visible on an aerial photo. Although this may help the archaeologist conducting the reconnaissance, it does not remove the need for checking ground truth to ensure that a site actually exists at the indicated location.

When plotting location archaeologists give each new site a designation for identification. Numbers are often the easiest labels; they may run in a single series within a region or be subdivided, as when each grid square on a map has an independent series of numbered sites. The system commonly used in the United States combines a number designation for the state, a letter code for the county, and a number for each site. Thus site 28MO35 refers to the 35th site designated in Monmouth County, New Jersey. Names are also used to designate sites. They can be easier to remember, although they are more cumbersome for reference purposes. The crucial point is that each site must have some designation so that all relevant information about that site—descriptions, surface collections, maps, photographs, and so on—can be linked to it. Although this information may be gathered as part of the identification and location process, its collection actually falls under the headings of survey and excavation, which are discussed next.

SURFACE SURVEY

Surface survey refers to methods used by archaeologists to acquire data from sites without excavation. The overall objective of surface survey is to determine as much as possible about a given site or region, based on both observable surface remains and remote detection of subsurface features.

The choice of surface survey methods depends on the nature of the site or region being studied and the kinds of data being sought. To begin with, in conducting surveys archaeologists attempt to detect and record all surface features. Traces of many substantial ancient remains, such as ruined buildings, walls, roads, and canals, exist on the surface, where they can still be seen and recorded by mapping. On the other hand, buried features may not be directly detectable from the surface. In some cases these buried remains can be located and mapped by one or more of the remote sensing methods described previously. The site of Sybaris was recorded in this manner.

Surface surveys also include detection and recording of artifacts and ecofacts. When these are found on the surface, their provenience is recorded, and then, because they are portable, they may be collected and taken to the field laboratory for further study. Like features, artifacts and ecofacts may be buried, of course, but their detection by remote sensors is usually far more difficult. In some cases augers, corers, and shovels are used to determine the presence or absence of artifacts below ground, but recovery of buried artifacts and ecofacts in large numbers must usually await excavation.

The objectives of reconnaissance and survey can sometimes be met most efficiently by combining them into a single operation. This is especially true if the same sample units can be used both for site identification and for gathering surface data. In some situations, however, these operations are best pursued separately. For instance, an investigation may undertake total coverage of its data universe to identify and locate sites but have the resources to record and collect surface remains for only a sample of the universe.

Whether or not it is combined with reconnaissance, surface survey is usually an essential complement to later excavation. It is even possible to conduct archaeological research with data gathered solely by surface survey. This may be the best and most obvious solution in cases of well-preserved surface sites with little or no depth. If lack of time, money, or necessary permits precludes excavation, surface survey becomes the only means for acquiring data.

Survey Methods

As already mentioned, surface survey involves two basic methods: ground survey and remote sensing. Each of these will be considered in a little more detail before we turn to the results of surface survey.

Ground survey means walking over the site or sites under investigation in order to gather or record whatever surface artifacts, ecofacts, or features may be present. Techniques used to record surface features may differ from those used for surface artifacts and ecofacts. Surface features are recorded by mapping techniques. Archaeologists use several types of maps for this purpose, but most are based on either topographic or planimetric representations. The former depicts elevation differences by means such as contour lines, while the latter presents symbolic representations of features (Fig. 4.10). Surface artifacts and ecofacts may be mapped as well, especially if their spatial distribution may reflect ancient activity areas or patterns. But in many cases the remains may be too numerous for this technique to be practical. In such situations, after keying provenience to mapped sample areas, surface artifacts and ecofacts are simply collected for field laboratory analysis.

Remote sensing is often used to detect and record buried features and sometimes used to detect artifacts as well. The techniques used are the same as described in our discussion of reconnaissance: aerial sensors such as cameras and radar, ground-based sensors including magnetometers and pulse radar, and mechanical devices such as corers and shovels. Although the techniques are the same, their applications in surface survey involve different objectives. Instead of being used to discover unrecorded archaeological sites, they are used to detect and record internal components of sites as part of data acquisition. For example, aerial photography can reveal the form and extent of features such as building

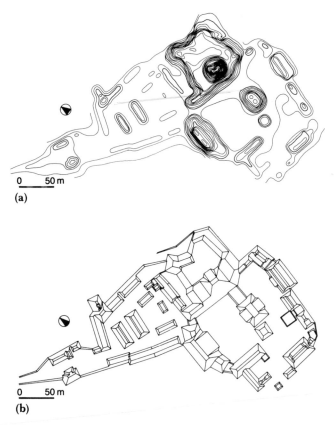

FIGURE 4.10

Comparison of information conveyed by (a) topographic
and (b) planimetric archaeological maps of the same site,
Nohmul, Belize. (Courtesy of Norman Hammond.)

foundations and road networks whether they are present on the surface or detectable underground as crop marks. This information may be significant in itself, or it may be used to guide subsequent excavation.

Preliminary Site Definition

A well-executed surface survey using one or more of the methods described
above provides the archaeologist with a preliminary definition of the study universe, whether it consists of a single site or a region containing many sites. The
preliminary definition should also include data on the *form, density,* and *structure*
of archaeological remains within the study universe. The range in the forms of

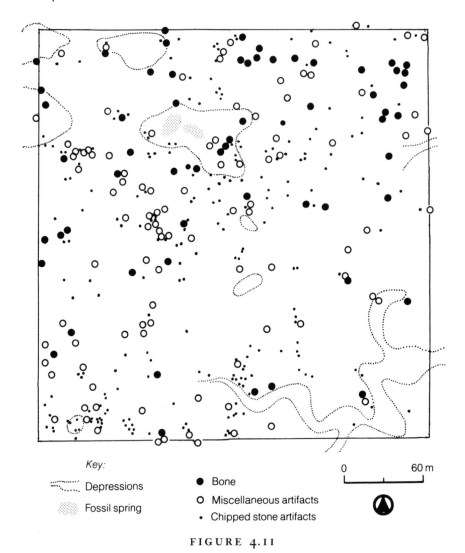

Key:

····· Depressions   ● Bone

░░ Fossil spring   ○ Miscellaneous artifacts

· Chipped stone artifacts

0   60 m

FIGURE 4.11

Detailed plot of surface finds at China Lake, California. (After Davis 1975, reproduced by permission of The Society for American Archaeology, adapted from *American Antiquity* 40:51, 1975.)

features may be assessed by both ground survey (mapping) and remote sensing, while the ranges in the forms of artifacts and ecofacts are assessed from surface collections. Surface survey information may then be used to determine the relative density of each form and their interrelationships (structure). By plotting the spatial distribution of one artifact class, say grinding stones, the investigator may find areas in which these artifacts cluster. It may be possible to relate these

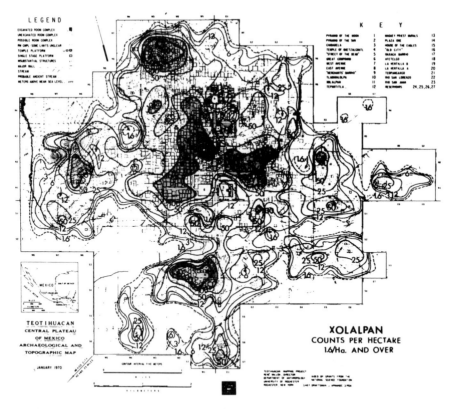

FIGURE 4.12

Surface densities of recovered pottery at Teotihuacán, Mexico, ca. A.D. 450–650. (After Cowgill 1974.)

relative densities to the distribution of other classes of artifacts, ecofacts, and features. Surface survey data of this kind are often presented as maps to show the distribution and density of artifacts, ecofacts, and features within a site. From these maps the archaeologist may be able to formulate working hypotheses to account for the distributional patterns. For example, in the China Lake Valley of California, artifact/ecofact distributions were used to infer that two different stone tool types represented different parts of one tool kit rather than occupation by distinct human groups (Fig. 4.11). At Teotihuacán in central Mexico, George Cowgill has plotted surface potsherd density for different time periods to study the growth and decline of their makers' population (Fig. 4.12). In surface-oriented research, these insights are an "end product" of the investigation. In most cases, however, such survey results are preliminary findings; they guide the archaeologist in choosing where to excavate to explore promising areas and test specific hypotheses.

EXCAVATION

The principal means by which the archaeologist gathers data about the past is *excavation*, which is used both to discover and to retrieve data from beneath the ground surface. As we have seen, surface survey is often an essential prelude to excavation. Collections of artifacts and ecofacts from the surface often provide clues about what lies beneath the ground and help the archaeologist plan excavations. Remote sensors such as magnetometers or pulse radar equipment may also detect the existence of buried archaeological features. But the only way to verify the presence and nature of subsurface data is through excavation.

Data retrieved through excavation are especially important for the archaeologist since subsurface remains are usually the best preserved and least disturbed. Surface artifacts and ecofacts are seldom in primary context and are usually poorly preserved. Surface features such as ancient walls or roads, though generally still in primary context, are often less well preserved than similar features buried, and therefore protected, below the surface. Excavation increases the archaeologist's chances of finding well-preserved data of all kinds. Most importantly, excavation often reveals *associations* of artifacts, ecofacts, and features in primary contexts. As we have seen, this kind of data is the most useful to the archaeologist for inferring ancient function and behavior.

The two basic goals of excavation are (1) to reveal the three-dimensional patterning or structure in the deposition of artifacts, ecofacts, and features, and (2) to assess the functional and temporal significance of this patterning. Where were stone tools, pottery vessels, and animal bones found, relative to each other and to house remains or other areas in which they were used? Determination of this three-dimensional patterning depends on establishing provenience and associations of the individual artifacts, ecofacts, and features, with respect both to each other and to their surrounding matrix. At the same time, evaluation of provenience and association allows the archaeologist to assess context. As pointed out in Chapter 3, it is attention to these relationships—the links among the elements of archaeological data, as established by records of provenience, association, and context—that clearly differentiates the archaeologist from the antiquarian and the looter.

Only by knowing which elements were found together (from their provenience and association) and by inferring how they got there (from association and context) can the archaeologist reconstruct ancient behavior. So proper excavation records are as crucial to interpretation as proper methods of actual excavation. Of course behavioral reconstruction also depends on determination of what the individual artifacts, ecofacts, and features were used for; this analysis, as we shall discuss further in Chapter 5, is based not only on their provenience and association but also on their form and other attributes.

If we consider the three-dimensional structure of an archaeological deposit, what do the three dimensions represent? We must draw a fundamental distinction between the single vertical dimension (depth) and the two horizontal ones

FIGURE 4.13

Recovery of evidence representing a single moment in time at Ceren in El Salvador. Excavations have exposed the remains of an adobe house and adjacent cornfield buried by a local volcanic eruption that collapsed and carbonized the roof beams and thatch. Later eruptions are represented by the upper deposits of ash. (Courtesy of Payson D. Sheets.)

(lateral extent). The combined horizontal dimensions represent, in an idealized situation, the associated remains of a single point in time. The case of Pompeii, where a whole community was buried and preserved as if in suspended animation, is an extreme illustration. The point is that artifacts and features on the same horizontal surface ideally represent use or discard that is approximately contemporaneous (Fig. 4.13). Over time new surfaces cover the old, and repetition of this process creates a vertical dimension (Fig. 4.14). Thus the vertical dimension in an archaeological deposit represents accumulation through time. This distinction and its implications are crucial in excavation.

Stratigraphy

Archaeological *stratification* refers to the observed layering of matrices and features. These layers or *strata* may be sloping or roughly horizontal, thick or thin. In some cases they are well-defined by contrasts in color, texture, composition, or other characteristics. Just as often, however, boundaries may be difficult or even impossible to see; one stratum may simply grade into another. Whatever the specific characteristics, the layering of stratified deposits reflects the geological law of superposition: The sequence of observable strata, from bottom to

Two contemporary houses at same ground level

One house is abandoned, collapses, and is used as a rubbish dump.

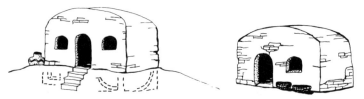

Resulting mound is leveled and a new house is built on its summit, which is now contemporary (although at a higher level) with still-occupied house at right.

FIGURE 4.14

An example of one means by which accumulation of occupational debris results in vertical buildup.

top, reflects the order of deposition, from earliest to latest. Lower layers were deposited before upper layers. The individual strata of an archaeological deposit may represent superimposed formal occupation surfaces, or they may be the result of disposal activities, such as accumulated layers of trash in a midden. Strata may also be deposited naturally, as when floods cover an area with layers of alluvium.

Note, however, that the law of superposition refers to the *sequence of deposition*, not to the age of the materials in the strata. Although the depositional sequence of the material found in stratified matrices usually does reflect relative age, there are exceptions. For example, some stratified matrices may be formed of redeposited material, as when water erosion removes soil from a location upstream and redeposits it in a new location downstream. If this soil contains cultural material, chronologically late artifacts could quite possibly be removed and

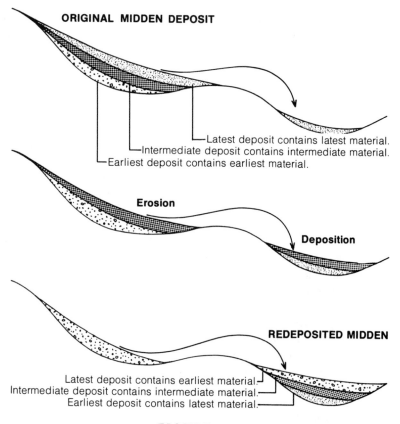

ORIGINAL MIDDEN DEPOSIT

Latest deposit contains latest material.
Intermediate deposit contains intermediate material.
Earliest deposit contains earliest material.

Erosion

Deposition

REDEPOSITED MIDDEN

Latest deposit contains earliest material.
Intermediate deposit contains intermediate material.
Earliest deposit contains latest material.

FIGURE 4.15

Schematic depiction of inverted layering. The uppermost (latest) material in the original deposit erodes first and is redeposited as the lowermost layer downstream.

redeposited, to be followed by redeposition of chronologically earlier artifacts (Fig. 4.15). Thus the redeposited matrix contains later artifacts in its lower strata and earlier artifacts in its upper strata. Note, however, that even in this case of "reversed stratification," the law of superposition holds: The lower layers were redeposited first, followed by the upper layers. The same reversal effect can be caused by human activity, as when stratified deposits are mined for construction fill.

Another reason superposition may not directly reflect age is the presence of intrusive strata. Human or animal pits or burrows may insert later materials into lower levels.

The interpreted significance of stratification is called *stratigraphy*, that is, the archaeological evaluation of the temporal and depositional meaning of the observed strata. In stratigraphic analysis the archaeologist combines the law of superposition with a consideration of context. Since intact archaeological features are invariably in primary context, problems of temporal determination usually arise with portable data, artifacts and ecofacts. The archaeologist must judge whether the artifacts and ecofacts associated with stratified deposits are the undisturbed result of human activity (primary context) or have been rearranged or redeposited by either human agents or natural events (secondary context).

In some cases this judgment is aided by *conjoining studies*, in which fragments of bone, stone, or other material are fitted back together with other pieces from the same original whole. For example, at Site FxJj50 in the Koobi Fora area on the east shore of Lake Turkana, Kenya, conjoining studies linked enough scattered stone flakes to suggest that they represented remains of tool manufacture and use within the 170 m² site. Bone pieces were also conjoined with the same interpretation, and the weathering on the bone suggested it had been exposed to the elements for little more than a year at most, before burial by flood-laid soils. Together these inferences established the 1.5 million-year-old site as a single complex feature, and gave greater weight to behavioral interpretations of the distribution of activities represented.

If, through these or other means, the archaeologist can demonstrate primary context with reasonable assurance—that is, if there is no evidence of redeposition disturbance—the temporal sequence of the archaeological materials within the deposit may be assumed to follow that of the strata. In this way a stratigraphic sequence is established.

Let us consider an example of stratigraphy. In the Lindenmeier Valley of nothern Colorado, bison hunters camped some 11,000 years ago in the area now called the Lindenmeier site. The hunting groups left evidence of their presence in the form of stone tools, toolmaking debris, hearths, and the bones of prey animals. Although each individual group probably spent only a brief time at Lindenmeier, repeated use of the campsite over time led to a gradual accumulation of occupation debris. During this time period, the exact limits of which are unknown, the level of the ground surface was being raised by natural processes: Small depressions would flood with water from a nearby stream, plants would grow in the wet areas, and eventually they would die and decay. The decayed plants would form soil, filling the old depressions, and stream overflow would begin the process in another low area. The new, filled surfaces were used as campsites, and older debris would be buried and sealed in place when a given locale was flooded. In this way, the combined effects of geological buildup and repeated occupation produced a stratified deposit in which the matrix accumulation resulted from natural causes but included and preserved evidence of human occupation. At Lindenmeier the law of superposition is relatively unaffected by disturbing factors: The basic stratigraphy is simply vertical accumulation upward through time, and the relative age of artifactual remains correlates well with stratigraphic position.

The functional dimension of stratigraphy involves distinguishing evidence of natural activity from that of cultural activity. In essence, the archaeologist attempts to determine which layers in the stratified deposit are "features" and which are naturally laid soils. Evidence of past human activity is obvious in some deposits: burials, house foundations, refuse deposits, and so on. In the absence of such clear indicators, however, determining whether a given stratum was produced by human agents may be more difficult. Clues to past human occupation include the presence in the soil of unusually high concentrations of diagnostic residues, such as phosphates, or of pollen from domesticated plants.

Once the archaeologist has distinguished cultural strata from natural ones, a further functional distinction may be made between architectural and nonarchitectural features. Nonarchitectural features include middens, burials, tamped earth floors, hearths, quarries, and so forth. Architectural features include walls, prepared or plastered floors, platforms, staircases, roadways, and the like. Of course nonarchitectural features such as hearths and burials are often associated with architectural units.

Stratigraphic evaluation, then, has both temporal and functional aspects. Combining the law of superposition with assessments of context, the archaeologist interprets the depositional history of the physical matrix. Functional interpretation begins with a distinction between the parts of the sequence that are natural strata and those that are cultural features. On the basis of these evaluations, the archaeologist establishes first a stratigraphic sequence for each excavation and then, by comparing stratigraphy between excavations, an overall or composite stratigraphic sequence for the entire site. This stratigraphic sequence forms the underlying framework on which all further interpretation is founded.

Stratigraphy thus emphasizes sequence and accumulation over time; it is primarily related to the vertical dimension of archaeological deposits. Distribution in the two lateral dimensions—that is, the spread of features and artifacts through a given horizontal layer—associates these data with one another in a single point or span of time. Because horizontally associated materials within a stratum are ideally the remains of behavior from a single unit of time, these lateral distributions fill in the functional picture and provide data to reconstruct the range of activities carried on simultaneously. Taken together, stratigraphy and association—the vertical and the horizontal—constitute the three-dimensional physical structure that excavation attempts to reveal.

Excavation Methods

An archaeological excavation is usually a complicated, painstaking process. The aim of an excavation program is the acquisition of as much three-dimensional data relevant to its research objectives as possible, given available resources. The success of any particular program depends on a variety of factors, the most important of which is the overall organization or strategy of the excavations. This strategy guides the archaeologist in choosing the locations, extent, timing, and kinds of excavation to meet the research goals with maximum efficiency.

Obviously the kinds of problems being investigated, the nature of the site or sites, and the availability of resources are unique to each situation. But the archaeologist's range of choices is limited. To make the best decisions for a given

FIGURE 4.16

View of an earthen structure at Las Tunas, Guatemala, revealed by a trench; a second, smaller trench has now penetrated this structure and its supporting platform. (Verapaz Project, University Museum, University of Pennsylvania.)

project, the researcher must be thoroughly familiar with all the alternatives and the ends they are best suited to accomplish.

The two basic kinds of excavations mirror the two kinds of dimensions in archaeological site formation.

1. *Penetrating excavations* are primarily deep probes of subsurface deposits. Their main thrust is vertical, and their principal objective is to reveal, in cross-section, the depth, sequencing, and composition of archaeological remains. They cut through sequential or adjacent deposits. This category includes test pits, trenches, and tunnels (Fig. 4.16).

2. *Clearing excavations* aim primarily at horizontal investigation of deposits. Their main thrust is outward or across, and their principal objective is to reveal both the horizontal extent and the arrangement of an archaeological deposit. Clearing excavations emphasize tracing continuities of single surfaces or deposits of varying extent (Fig. 4.17).

Archaeologists frequently use a combination of these types of excavations to meet the diverse goals of their research.

Many strategies are clearly possible for excavating an archaeological site. More than one archaeologist has compared the excavation task to solving a three-dimensional jigsaw puzzle. Of course excavation does not attempt to put the

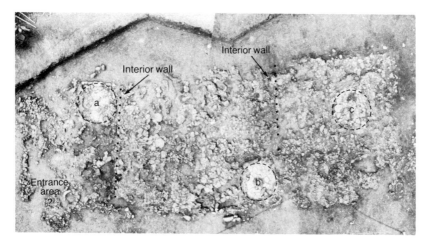

FIGURE 4.17

A labeled photograph of House 14 at Divostin, Yugoslavia. This was the largest dwelling (18 m long) found and cleared at that Neolithic site. Three hearths (a, b, c) and nearly 100 pottery vessels were found on the fired mud-and-chaff floor. (Courtesy of Alan McPherron.)

pieces together; instead it takes them apart. The archaeologist reassembles the pieces later, on paper. To do this the investigator must not only use care in taking them apart (excavating) but also observe and record precisely how they originally fit together. In the following sections we will consider the techniques for controlling and recording excavations—techniques that, when properly executed, enable the archaeologist later to reconstruct and interpret the original three-dimensional site.

Provenience Control

Archaeologists have developed a variety of methods to ensure accurate vertical and horizontal provenience control during excavation. Horizontal location is determined with reference to a site grid. Within each excavation or other data-collection operation, then, the location of artifacts and features discovered can be related to the grid system, either by direct reference to specific grid coordinates or to the edges of the excavation (Fig. 4.18). Vertical location is determined with respect to a known elevation; this may be done with surveyors' instruments or by direct measurement. A leveling instrument or transit may be used to measure relative elevation from a known elevation. Alternatively, elevation above or below a point nearby may be measured with a line level, steel tape, and plumb bob (Fig. 4.19).

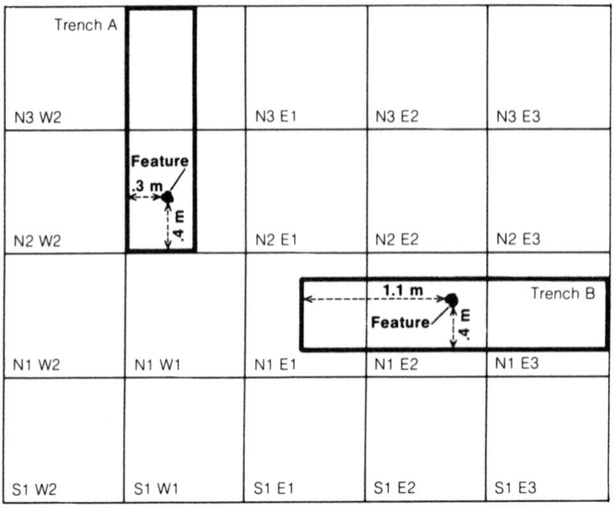

FIGURE 4.18

A site grid may be used to designate the horizontal provenience of excavated features. In Trench A, measurements
are made north and east of the N2 W1 stake, to record the
provenience as "(N2).4m/(W1).3m." In Trench B, horizontal provenience is measured from the excavation limits, as
"1.1 m east of west wall, .4 m north of south wall." The
latter is convertible to a site grid designation as long as the
location of the trench walls in relation to the grid is known.

Provenience control for artifacts and ecofacts is often complicated by their
usual small size and abundance. When artifacts are relatively sparse, or when
they are encountered in primary contexts, the location of each item is usually
precisely plotted. Otherwise provenience can be recorded by reference to a
specified area within an excavation, such as a single stratum. The most common
means of recovering artifacts and ecofacts under such circumstances is by flotation (catching small, especially organic, materials by immersing matrix batches
in water) and screening (trapping small finds by passing matrix through a wire
mesh) (Fig. 4.20). After recovery, artifacts are bagged and taken to the field laboratory for processing. From this point on, of course, they must carry a label
relating them to their provenience.

Recording Archaeological Data

Apart from artifacts and other samples physically removed from their provenience, all data retrieved by archaeologists are in the form of records. Because
the portion of a site that is excavated is thereby destroyed, the manner in which

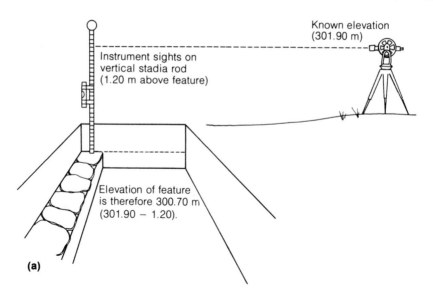

Known elevation
(301.90 m)

Instrument sights on
vertical stadia rod
(1.20 m above feature)

Elevation of feature
is therefore 300.70 m
(301.90 − 1.20).

(a)

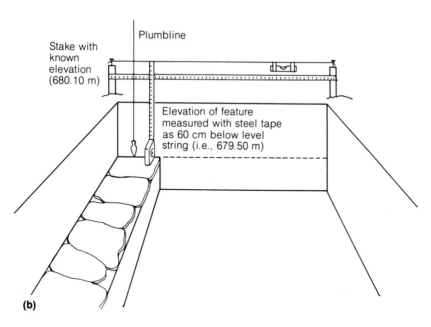

Plumbline

Stake with
known
elevation
(680.10 m)

Elevation of feature
measured with steel tape
as 60 cm below level
string (i.e., 679.50 m)

(b)

FIGURE 4.19

Two ways of determining vertical provenience: In (a) an instrument of known
elevation is used in conjunction with a stadia rod; in (b) an elevation is measured
along a plumb line intersecting a level string of known elevation.

FIGURE 4.20

Screening at Copan, Honduras. This technique is a means of recovering small artifacts and ecofacts that might otherwise be missed during excavation. (Courtesy of the Peabody Museum of Harvard University and Gordon R. Willey.)

archaeological research is recorded is of crucial importance. The only records of the original matrices, proveniences, associations, and contexts of the data are the field notes, scaled drawings, photographs, and computer disks produced by the investigator.

These four kinds of data records are used for all types of data collection, but they are generally more detailed when used to record archaeological excavations. In such cases the most common and important formats remain scaled drawings and photos. Scaled drawings include sections, which depict the vertical or stratified relationships exposed by excavation, and plans, which depict the horizontal relationships of features and other material remains. Sites and features are thoroughly photographed before, during, and after excavation. Initial photos document the appearance of sites and features before excavation disturbs them. Once excavation is underway, a continuous series of photographs is taken to chronicle everything as it is revealed (Fig. 4.21).

DATA PROCESSING

Once archaeological data are collected and recorded in the field, the recovered materials and records must be organized. The processing of these raw forms of data ensures their preservation, security, and availability for study. Although this step seems self-evident, it is an essential prerequisite to any further work. Imagine trying to do research in a library in which books and other publications

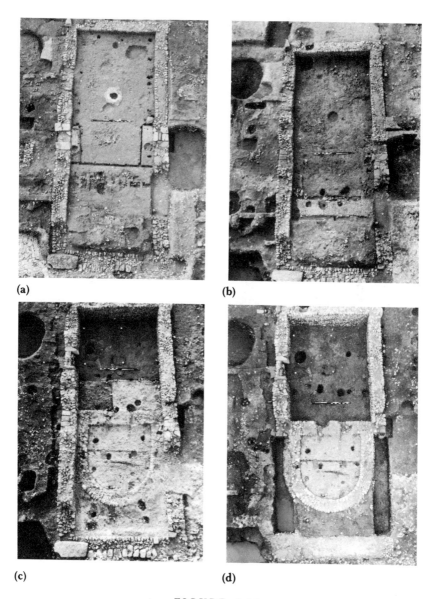

(a) **(b)**

(c) **(d)**

FIGURE 4.21

Views of successive stages, (a) through (d), in the excavation of the Church of St. Mary, Winchester, England. Foundations visible in (a) date from ca. A.D. 1150; those exposed in (d) represent an earlier building dated at ca. A.D. 1000. (Courtesy of Martin Biddle, © Winchester Excavations Committee.)

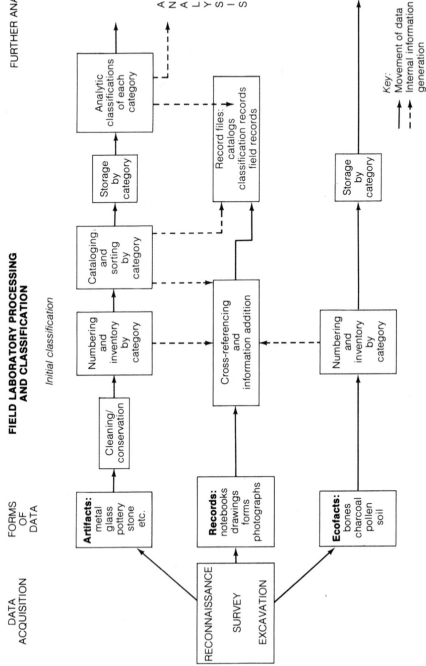

FIGURE 4.22

Flow chart to illustrate the data-processing and analysis stages normally undertaken in a field laboratory.

are simply piled on the floor as they arrive without cataloging. This suggests the importance of orderly processing of all forms of archaeological data for continued use.

Most artifacts and ecofacts are cleaned, labeled by provenience, and sorted into basic categories to prepare them for later analysis. Such processing is usually done during the course of fieldwork so that the archaeologist can evaluate the data as they are recovered and continue to formulate and modify working hypotheses for testing while the research is in progress. For example, if the archaeologist recognizes that the evidence being recovered indicates occupation in an area not consistent with a current hypothesis, further excavation can be carried out to verify this finding. Should this expanded work validate the initial indications, the original hypothesis may be altered or replaced by a new proposition.

Artifacts usually undergo the most steps in processing and are often classified in some way in the field as well. Ecofacts are generally handled more simply and usually must be turned over to a specialist for identification. Features, of course, are not "processed" as wholes, beyond being recorded as they are revealed. Constituents of some features, such as the mortuary offerings in a burial, are of course portable and can be taken to a laboratory to be processed as artifacts and ecofacts. Recorded data such as notebooks and drawings also pass through the processing stage in the field laboratory (Fig. 4.22).

CLASSIFICATION

In all branches of science, classification provides the working basis for further study. As mentioned in Chapter 2, much of the work of early archaeologists was devoted to the description and classification of their collections. Although classification is no longer the archaeologist's major concern, it remains a fundamental analytical step in reconstructing the past.

Before collected data can be analyzed and interpreted, they must be placed in some kind of order. Classification refers to the process of arranging or ordering objects into groups on the basis of shared characteristics called *attributes*. An attribute is any observable trait that can be defined and isolated. Three basic categories of attributes apply to archaeological data (Fig. 4.23).

1. *Stylistic attributes* usually involve the most obvious descriptive characteristics of an artifact believed to reflect choices of its maker: its color, texture, decoration, alterations, and other traits.

2. *Form attributes* include the overall three-dimensional shape of the artifact and aspects of that shape. These include measurable dimensions ("metric attributes") such as length, width, and thickness.

3. *Technological attributes* include the characteristics of the raw materials used to

STYLISTIC ATTRIBUTES

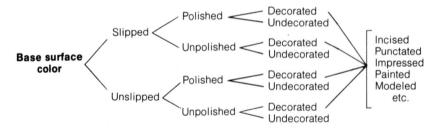

FORM ATTRIBUTES

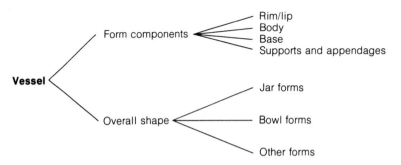

TECHNOLOGICAL ATTRIBUTES

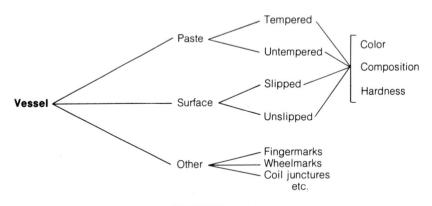

FIGURE 4.23

Classification of pottery: examples of kinds of attributes used to define stylistic, form, and technological types.

make artifacts ("constituent attributes") and any other traits that reflect the manufacturing process.

The kind of attribute selected will, of course, determine the kind of archaeological classification that results. Depending on the kind of artifact and the objectives of the study, the archaeologist uses the selected attributes to define *technological types, form types,* or *stylistic types.* Examples of technological types include Near Eastern metal artifacts where different copper alloys can be distinguished by their constituents, such as brass (copper and zinc) or bronze (copper and tin or copper and arsenic). In defining form types, component shape attributes—for example, the inward or outward curve of a vessel's walls—are especially important in classifying fragmentary artifacts such as pottery sherds; metric attributes such as vessel height are usually more applicable to intact specimens. An example of form types is the common classification of hand-held grinding stones by their cross-sectional shape (round, ovoid, rectangular, and so on). Stylistic types are generally based on color, surface finish, and decorative attributes. Pottery classifications are usually based on such attributes, including types based on the presence or absence of painted decoration and, if decorated, the number of colors and style of painting.

These kinds of classifications are based on directly observable traits. Artifacts can also be classified using inferred characteristics, attributes measurable only by tests such as spectrographic and chemical analysis. Classifications based on these kinds of criteria are seldom carried out in the field, however, since they usually require specialized laboratory facilities and technicians.

All classifications serve a variety of purposes. First and most fundamentally, classifications create order from apparent chaos by dividing a mass of undifferentiated data into groups (classes). Classification thus allows the scientist to organize vast arrays of data into manageable units. As a very basic example, "artifacts" are distinguished from "ecofacts" and "features" in terms of their collection and processing requirements. Artifacts are often further subdivided into gross categories such as chipped stone, pottery, or metalwork. These classes may then be subjected to more detailed classification, breaking them down into kinds of chipped stone artifacts, kinds of pottery, and kinds of metalwork.

The second purpose of classification is to allow the researcher to summarize the characteristics of many individual objects by listing only their shared attributes. Most archaeological classifications result in definition of *types.* Types represent clusters of attributes that occur together repeatedly in the same artifacts. For example, the potsherds and whole vessels in a given pottery type will share attributes such as color and hardness of the fired clay; but other attributes, such as evidence of ancient vessel repair or of ritual vessel breakage, may not be defining traits of the type class. Thus reference to types enables the archaeologist to describe large numbers of artifacts more economically, ignoring for the moment other attributes that may differentiate among members of a single type.

Third, classifications define variability. The explanation of such variability often leads to further understanding of the past. For example, recognition of

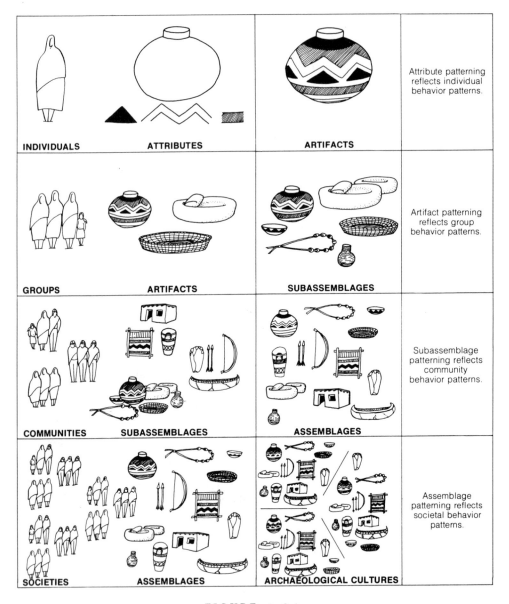

FIGURE 4.24

Behavioral reconstruction based on hierarchical classification, independent of archaeological context. (After *Invitation to Archaeology*, by James Deetz, illustrated by Eric Engstrom, copyright © 1967 by James Deetz. Reprinted by permission of DOUBLEDAY, a division of Bantam, Doubleday, Dell Publishing Group, Inc.)

different pottery styles can reveal distinctions in social status within an ancient society.

Finally, by ordering and describing types, the scientist suggests a series of relationships among classes. The nature of these relationships generates hypotheses that stimulate further questions and research. For instance, the most obvious kind of question that emerges from a classification concerns the meaning of the classification: How did the order originate, and what is its significance? In classifications of artifacts, the described order and relationships among categories or types represent aspects of the artifacts' raw materials, techniques of manufacture, use (function), and decorative style.

The point to remember is that classification is a convenient working tool, organizing artifacts or other archaeological data into manageable and meaningful groups, and facilitating further analysis. There is no single "right" classification. The attributes the investigator chooses to look at depend on the research issues he or she wants to explore. For example, a researcher interested in food storage patterns in different parts of a community or in different time periods would look at shapes and sizes of storage vessels rather than designs used to decorate them.

Some archaeologists seek to reconstruct the past by correlating a series of classifications with various levels of behavior. The most widely cited example of such behavioral reconstruction is that outlined by James Deetz (Fig. 4.24). According to this scheme, the individuals who created artifact types adhered to culturally defined standards. Patterned sets of artifacts used by occupational groups (defined by form and functional attributes), such as the various tools used by farmers or hunters, are called *subassemblages*. Patterned sets of subassemblages, representing the sum of social activities, define the *assemblage* of an ancient community. At the highest level, patterned sets of assemblages are used to define *archaeological cultures*.

The usefulness of this kind of behavioral reconstruction, often based on style and form types, relies on the validity of the assumption that archaeological classifications reflect the structure of ancient cultural patterns. The best test of the utility of this kind of hierarchical classification rests with the context and associations of the data on which it is based.

SUMMARY

Archaeological fieldwork involves the collection and processing of data. Fieldwork may begin with reconnaissance to discover and locate sites. Ground reconnaissance is the oldest and most thorough way to identify sites, but it is often slow and unable to detect deeply buried sites. Aerial reconnaissance provides rapid coverage of wide areas and is efficient for identifying sites that have at least some surface indications. Subsurface detection methods, using mechanical probes or electronic instruments, are slow, but may be the only way to find buried sites.

Once sites are identified and located, surface survey is used to gain representative data without resorting to excavation. Sometimes this may be the only way data are acquired; more often, however, surface survey is a prelude to excavation, aiding in selecting areas to excavate and producing hypotheses to be tested by excavation. Ground survey is the most common method, acquiring data by mapping sites and collecting surface artifacts and ecofacts. Subsurface sensors, like those used to discover sites, may also be used as part of surface survey. Together, ground survey and subsurface detection methods are used to produce maps showing the distributions and densities of features, artifacts, and ecofacts at archaeological sites.

Excavation is used to investigate the three-dimensional structure of buried archaeological data, and to determine the functional and temporal significance of these data. The three dimensions of an archaeological deposit reflect the processes of site formation: Activities that took place at any one time are represented by the horizontal dimensions, while sequential activities are represented by the vertical dimension. Archaeologists, therefore, use stratigraphy—the interpreted sequence of deposition—to determine which data reflect simultaneous (and functionally related) activities and which reflect the sequence of activities through time. These dimensions are reflected in the two basic kinds of excavations: Penetrating excavations cut through deposits to reveal the depth, sequence, and composition of sites, while clearing excavations expose the horizontal extent and arrangement of remains within a single stratum.

Provenience control is crucial to the collection of archaeological data. To reconstruct later how a site was formed, the location of all recovered materials must be accurately recorded. All data from excavations or surface collections are given distinctive labels and plotted with reference to horizontal location and vertical elevation. Data acquisition is a destructive process, so records—field notes, standardized forms, scaled drawings, and photographs (the first two are increasingly preserved in computerized formats)—are essential for later analysis and interpretation.

Both data and records are usually processed in a field laboratory, to ensure that they are preserved, secured, and available for further study and analysis. After this, portable data, such as artifacts and some ecofacts, are classified by the attributes (stylistic, form, and technological) the archaeologist selects to address particular research questions. Classification is a convenient means of ordering, summarizing, relating, and understanding a mass of data, and each classification is only one of many possible organizing schemes. All, however, are useful to the archaeologist in providing a starting point for further analysis and interpretation.

· 5 ·

Analyzing the Past

IT IS NOW TIME to examine the various kinds of studies archaeologists use to analyze each of the categories of archaeological data: artifacts, ecofacts, and features. Since each of these broad categories encompasses a wide variety of archaeological remains, we will emphasize those forms most commonly encountered by archaeologists. We will look at the characteristics that differentiate one kind of data from the others to show the ways each kind can most effectively contribute to an understanding of past behavior. At the same time we must keep in mind that the information gleaned from these remains is influenced by their physical characteristics, their state of preservation, and the specific questions being asked.

ARTIFACTS

We begin by considering the analytic methods most appropriate to each of the major artifactual *industries*. Industries are defined according to both substance and manufacturing techniques. Our discussion will highlight lithic and ceramic industries because stone and fired clay are the most commonly encountered archaeological materials.

Lithic Artifacts

Stone tools were undoubtedly among the earliest used by human societies; in fact, their use predates the evolution of modern *Homo sapiens* by more than a million years. The first stone tools used by the ancestors of modern humans were probably unmodified rocks or cobbles, used only once for tasks such as hammering or pounding. But *lithic technology* has its roots in the first attempts to modify and shape stone to make tools.

There are two basic kinds of lithic technology: One involves fracturing or flaking stone (chipped stone industry); the other is based on pecking and grinding or polishing stone (ground stone industry). Because chipped stone is the oldest preserved form of culture and technology, archaeologists have used it to name the earliest period of cultural development, the Paleolithic ("Old Stone") period. In this traditional scheme, the later development of a stone technology involving grinding signals the advent of the second developmental age, the Neolithic ("New Stone") period. Ground stone tools did not, of course, replace chipped stone; the two technologies coexisted for several thousand years in both the Old and New Worlds. Of the two, chipped stone is usually more commonly encountered by the prehistoric archaeologist, and it will be emphasized in the following section.

Chipped stone technology takes advantage of the characteristics of several hard, nonresilient, and homogeneous minerals, including flint or chert, obsidian (a natural volcanic glass), basalt, and quartz. When struck, these materials fracture in a uniform manner, not according to any natural planes of cleavage in the rock. Shock waves from the blow spread through the struck stone or *core* in a cone-shaped pattern, detaching a fragment called a *flake* (Fig. 5.1). Chipped stone tools are produced either by removing flakes to give a sharp edge to the core (core tools), or by using one or more of the detached flakes (flake or blade tools).

Chipped stone tools may be made by a variety of techniques. Some of these have been inferred from traces left on the tools themselves, others from ethnographic observations of people still manufacturing stone tools, and still others through archaeologists' experiments in duplicating the ancient forms. Some of these techniques are as old as the origins of stone tools; others represent later refinements during the long development of lithic technology. We shall briefly summarize some of the more important techniques.

The shape and size of the flake detached from a core depend on the physical characteristics of the stone itself, on the angle and force of the blow being struck, and on the physical characteristics of the tool being used to detach the flake. Short, rather thick flakes are produced by *direct percussion*, striking the core with a hammerstone or striking the core against a fixed stone called an anvil. The earliest recognizable stone tools, manufactured during the earliest part of the Paleolithic period more than two million years ago, were produced by these methods. Later other materials such as antler were used in direct percussion (Fig. 5.2a).

A refinement of the percussion technique used in forming both core and flake tools is the *indirect percussion* technique, using a punch made of bone or wood between the core and the hammerstone. The punch directs and softens the stoneworker's blow, producing longer and thinner flakes. The usual result of indirect percussion is a series of long, thin, parallel-sided flakes called *blades*. True blades produced from prepared cylindrical cores are typical of the later

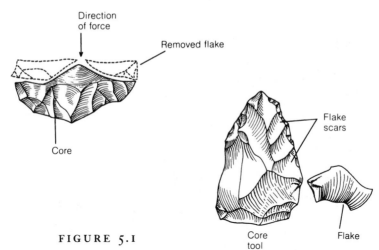

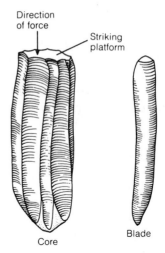

FIGURE 5.1

Terminology used in describing lithic core, flake, and blade tools, reflecting manufacturing technology. (After Oakley, by courtesy of the British Museum [Natural History].)

Paleolithic in the Old World and of much of the pre-Columbian era in the New World.

Once a flake or blade tool has been detached, it may be ready for use as a cutting or scraping tool. In other cases, the tool must be further modified for use. Edges that required strength and durability rather than sharpness, such as those on scrapers, were *retouched* or secondarily flaked. *Pressure flaking*, or detachment of flakes by steady pressure, was developed in the later Paleolithic and allowed finely controlled edge retouch through removal of small, steep flakes (see Fig. 5.2b). Skillful pressure flaking can sometimes completely alter the shape of

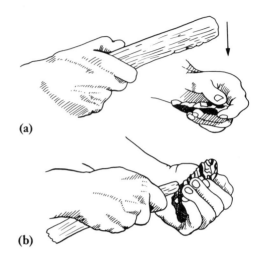

(a)

FIGURE 5.2

Some manufacturing techniques
for chipped stone tools: (a) direct
percussion using an antler,
(b) pressure flaking using an antler.

(b)

a flake, as in production of barbed or notched *projectile points* and miniature
forms (microliths).

Archaeologists have traced the development of chipped stone technology
through a span of more than two million years. During that time, the new techniques and forms that gradually emerged increased both the efficiency of tool
production and the available inventory of tool forms. By the end of the Paleolithic period, however, a new lithic technology was also being developed: the
shaping of harder, more durable stone by pecking and grinding against abrasives
such as sandstone. These tools, which took the form of axes and adzes, had
much longer-lasting edges than their chipped counterparts and were thus more
efficient for such tasks as cutting trees and splitting lumber. Ground stone techniques were also used to shape large basins (*querns* or *metates*) used for grinding
grain and other tasks.

Lithic analysis has traditionally involved classification based on form, often
using direct or implied functional labels such as "scrapers" and "handaxes." The
earliest and best-known classifications of this sort, made in Europe during the
19th and early 20th centuries, are still the basic reference classifications for Paleolithic chipped stone tools. This form classification has recently been refined
to specify more precisely the sets of criteria that distinguish form types.

To a large extent lithic typologies based on overall form have given way to
more-sophisticated attribute analyses based on either manufacturing technology
(technological types) or actual use (functional types). Stone tools are particularly well suited to such analyses and classifications because stone working and
use are progressively *subtractive* actions: Each step in shaping and use permanently removes more of the stone. Clues to most steps in ancient manufacturing
and use are preserved and can be detected in flake scars, striking platforms, and
other identifiable attributes (see Fig. 5.1). By analyzing the full range of lithic

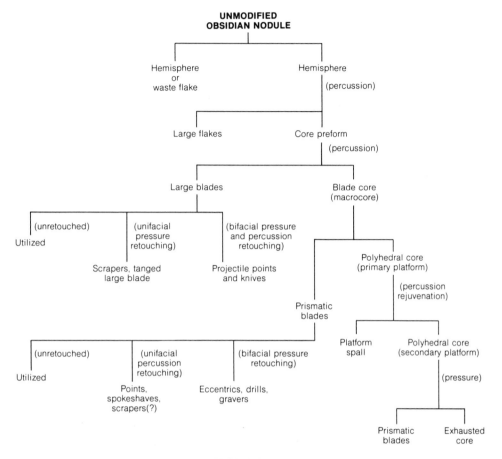

FIGURE 5.3

A technological classification representing manufacturing steps used in production of chipped stone artifacts at Chalchuapa, El Salvador. (Courtesy of Payson D. Sheets.)

material, both artifacts and workshop debris, the archaeologist can often reconstruct most or all of the steps in tool manufacture (Fig. 5.3).

In order to test and refine reconstructions of ancient tool manufacture, lithic specialists such as François Bordes and Don Crabtree have attempted experimental duplication of ancient chipped stone technology. Through these experiments, and through their training of other archaeologists in the techniques used to manufacture stone tools, lithic specialists have increased the precision with which ancient manufacturing practices can be analyzed and have proposed alternative methods that may have been used in the past.

Microscopic or chemical examinations of stone are sometimes useful for establishing the source of the raw material. By microscopically comparing quarry samples with artifact samples, analysts can sometimes identify distinctive quarry "signatures"—particular patterns of constituent minerals that come from one source alone. For example, Herbert Thomas demonstrated in 1923 that the bluestones of Stonehenge had been brought from the Prescelly Mountains of Wales, a straight-line distance of about 130 miles, but actually some 240 miles by a feasible transport route. Diagnostic trace elements within lithic materials such as obsidian can be identified and measured by neutron activation (measuring the material's response to brief and harmless bombardment by neutrons) or similar analyses. The use of these techniques for detection of raw material sources has allowed reconstruction of ancient exchange networks in many parts of the world.

Determination of how stone tools were used requires other approaches. In the past inferred function was often a primary criterion for lithic classifications. One common distinction was between objects that were "utilitarian" (having domestic or household uses) and those that were "ceremonial" (having ritual or nondomestic uses). This categorization could sometimes be supported when applied to artifacts from secure contexts, such as tools from household living floors versus those from burials. But the distinction was often misused by those who automatically associated elaborate forms with ceremonial uses and simpler shapes with utilitarian uses. Most modern archaeologists recognize that even artifacts from secure ceremonial contexts, such as burials, may have served multiple functions, including utilitarian ones, prior to their final deposition in a burial or cache.

More recently, lithic analysts have sought to identify stone tool function through detailed attribute study. They examine specific aspects of form, such as angle of the cutting edge, as well as attributes of wear resulting from use—microscopic fractures, pitting, or erosion of the edge—to establish the range of tasks once performed by lithic artifacts.

These interpretations are based on analogy, comparison of the attributes of the archaeological materials with those of modern forms whose function is known. For example, ancient "arrowheads" and spear points are identified by the similarity of archaeological forms to modern versions. In other cases analogs are provided by imitative experiments in which archaeologists make stone tools and use them to chop, scrape, slice, whittle, or saw various materials such as meat, bone, wood, and so on. After such an experimental tool is used, its edges can be examined microscopically to detect the pattern of wear resulting from each kind of use. Distinctive wear "signatures" can be identified in some cases and can be used to infer ancient tool uses when archaeological specimens show similar wear patterns.

Residues left on working edges may also provide clues to ancient function. A well-known example is the interpretation of silica residue as an indicator that an artifact was used as a sickle to cut grain or other plants containing silica. The presence of such a silica sheen has been sought as evidence of crop harvesting for sites believed to have been occupied during early stages of the development of grain agriculture. And Thomas Loy has found that weapons may preserve traces of the blood that allow identification of animals killed, even after thousands of years.

Ground stone tools can also preserve clues to manufacture and use, but when both of these processes involve grinding, many of the traces are necessarily erased. Examination of residues may reveal what was ground on the implement in question. For example, a quern or mortar could have been used to grind food or pigment materials; only analysis of residues or wear will tell.

Ceramic Artifacts

The generalized term *ceramics* covers all industries in which artifacts are modeled or molded from clay and then made durable by firing. In addition to pottery, this overall category includes a variety of artifacts such as ceramic figurines, musical instruments, and spindle whorls (used for spinning thread or yarn). Although clay figurines—such as the "Venus" figurines from the site of Dolni Vestonice, Czechoslovakia, dating to the European Upper Paleolithic—appear to be the earliest known form of ceramic technology, pottery is undoubtedly the most abundant and widespread kind of ceramics.

Pottery can be defined as a separate ceramic industry because of its unique manufacturing techniques and its specialized function: providing containers for a wide range of solid and liquid substances. Archaeological evidence throughout the world indicates that pottery originated with humanity's first attempts at settled life. In the Near East, East Asia, and South America, pottery developed as part of a more complex, expanding technology fostered by the relative stability of settled village life. Pottery was and still is used to transport, cook, and store a wide range of foods, as well as other supplies. But as societies became increasingly complex, pottery also assumed other specialized functions, including such ritual uses as burial urns and incense burners.

Compared with the age of the chipped stone industry, pottery's 12,000-year history seems short. But the widespread and common occurrence of pottery vessels, combined with extreme durability and capacity for great variety in form and decoration, make pottery one of the most commonly analyzed and useful kinds of artifacts available to archaeologists. The traditional importance of the "infamous potsherd" in archaeological research can hardly be overstressed; at least one unabridged dictionary even defines *potsherd* as "a broken pottery fragment, esp. one of archaeological value."

Pottery technology ranges from simple household hand production to modern factory mass production methods. First, however, the potter must acquire and prepare the proper clay. The moist clay must be thoroughly kneaded (or wedged) to drive out air bubbles and create a uniform, plastic mass. *Plasticity* refers to the capacity to be molded and shaped. As part of the clay processing

(a)

(b)

(c)

(d)

the potter may add nonplastic substances such as sand or ground shell as *temper* to reduce shrinkage and thereby lessen the chance that the completed vessel will break during drying or firing.

Hand forming pottery involves modeling a vessel either from a clay core or by adding coils or segments and welding the junctures with a thin solution of clay and water (Fig. 5.4). Mold forming is commonly used not only to make pottery but also to mass-produce small clay artifacts such as figurines and spindle whorls. Wheel forming is the most common means of mass-producing pottery vessels. In fact, although a relatively recent invention—appearing some-time before 3000 B.C. in the Near East—this technique is now the most common for all pottery production throughout the world. In this technique the potter forms a vessel by manipulating a clay core centered on a vertically mounted wheel, which is rotated rapidly by the potter's hands or feet or by other power sources.

Hand-forming methods undoubtedly represent the oldest kind of pottery technology. They are usually associated with small-scale production by part-time specialists for immediate household uses or, sometimes, limited markets outside the family. Mold- and wheel-forming techniques, because of their poten-tial for mass production, are often associated with full-time specialist potters, who manufacture their vessels for widespread market distribution.

Once the vessel is formed, it is usually smoothed to create a uniform sur-face. An overall coating with a thin clay solution or *slip* may be applied to give a uniform texture and color. Other slips or paints may be used to decorate the vessel in a variety of painted patterns and colors. Specialized slips that vitrify during high-temperature firing are called *glazes*. A vessel may also be further modified or decorated by modeling, either adding clay (welding appliqués) or subtracting clay (incising, carving, cutting, and so on). When dry, the vessel may be polished by rubbing with a smooth hard object such as a beach pebble to compact the surface and give it a shine.

Firing transforms clay from its natural plastic state to a permanent, non-plastic one. During the firing process clay may pass through as many as three stages:

1. Dehydration or loss of water occurs at temperatures up to about 600° C.

2. Oxidation of carbon and iron compounds in the clay takes place at tempera-tures up to about 900° C.

FIGURE 5.4

Selected steps in pottery manufacture: (a) hand-forming vessels (Chinautla, Guatemala); (b) applying a slip (Senegal); (c) decorating the vessel shoulder by incising with a shell (Senegal); (d) firing pottery in an open kiln (Chinautla). (Photos b and c courtesy of Olga F. Linares; photos a and d by author.)

3. *Vitrification*—a complex process at which glass and other new minerals are formed in the clay—occurs at temperatures above about 1000° C. Vitrification fuses the clay making the vessel walls waterproof. The earliest glazed pottery appears to have been produced in China by 1500 B.C.

Pottery analysis uses a variety of approaches; those applied in any given situation depend on the objectives of that study. Each of the three broad approaches discussed earlier—based on stylistic, form, and technological attributes—is frequently used with pottery.

Stylistic analyses of pottery have traditionally received the greatest emphasis by archaeologists. Pottery lends itself to a variety of stylistic and decorative treatments—painting, appliqué, incising, and so on—that have no effect on the vessel's usefulness as a container. Because of this underlying "freedom of choice" in pottery style archaeologists assume that stylistic regularities represent culturally guided choices rather than technological or functional limitations. Pottery styles based on decorative attributes have been used to trace ancient social and cultural links in time and space, and stylistic classification remains one of the most important methods of analyzing ancient pottery collections.

Analysis of pottery on the basis of vessel form is perhaps not as common as analysis based on stylistic attributes. However, form attributes may be combined with stylistic classifications to assist in the definition of types. Because clay can take a wide variety of shapes, differences in form among pottery vessels (beyond strictly functional considerations) should represent the potter's choices rather than technological limits (Fig. 5.5).

Ancient vessel function may be determined in several ways. The archaeologist may recover direct evidence of function in association with the pottery. In such cases skill in excavation and use of analogy in interpretation may enable the archaeologist to reconstruct a great deal about ancient patterns of pottery usage. In most instances, however, direct evidence of function is not present, and ancient use must be inferred from analysis based on vessel form. The use of general shape-function analogs is common in archaeological studies. For instance, vessels with necks are assumed to have been used for storing and dispensing liquids, as they are today; the restrictive neck helps control spills and reduce waste.

Analysis of vessel function can include examination of residues from use. Such remnants may be visible or may be discovered through microscopic analysis. For example, cooking vessels may have identifiable interior residues. In such cases, the archaeologist can not only infer vessel function but also reconstruct ancient cooking practices and food preferences. Other residues, such as incense resins, grain pollen, or unfired clay help identify the function of incense burners, storage jars, or potter's equipment.

The archaeological provenience of pottery may also help the investigator determine past uses. Vessels associated with burials are usually regarded as ritual paraphernalia used in funerary rites. Funerary vessels, however, often show traces of prior use, indicating that they served different purposes before being assigned their final, ritual function. Determination of multiple uses and of re-

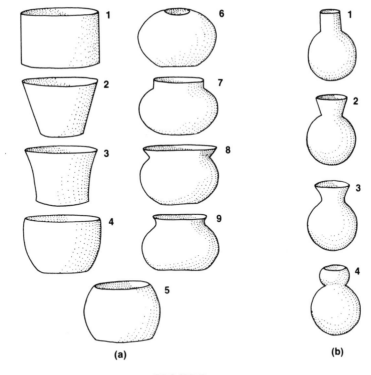

FIGURE 5.5

An example of pottery form classification: (a) nine defined bowl categories,
(b) four defined jar categories. (After Sabloff 1975.)

cycling of pottery vessels is often not possible, but these complicating factors
should be kept in mind in interpreting vessel function.

An analysis of ancient pottery remains may reveal clues about the manufacturing methods used. But in contrast to a subtractive technology such as the
manufacture of stone tools by chipping and flaking, pottery involves a plastic,
additive technology. Manipulation of the clay in the later stages of manufacture
may thus obliterate the diagnostic markings and features left by earlier stages.
The only way to overcome this difficulty is to use analogy with documented
instances of pottery production today. New clues may be recognized in observing actual production procedures and matching them with similar features on
ancient pottery.

Metal Artifacts

Metallurgy refers to the complex technology involved in the extraction of metal
from ores and the production of metal artifacts. The earliest roots of this technology are found in the Old World—specifically in the Near East—where

people began to shape copper into simple tools and ornaments between 8000 and 9500 years ago. These first metal artifacts were *cold hammered*, probably with stone tools. Several millennia later, however, copper was being extracted from ores by heat and then cast into a variety of forms. True metallurgy was underway.

An independent tradition of metalworking appeared in the New World. It was marked by copper use in the upper Great Lakes region by 3000 B.C., and somewhat later by the development of more sophisticated metallurgy in the Andes of South America and in Mesoamerica. Since that time, metallurgy has developed and spread throughout the world, almost completely replacing lithic technology. Today, of course, sophisticated metal technology has become an essential part of our own civilization.

Metal technology originated in the prehistoric exploitation of three hard metals—copper, tin, and iron—and, to a lesser degree, of two rare or precious metals—silver and gold. Because the development of metallurgical technology followed a fairly regular sequence, 19th-century archaeologists found it convenient to classify the "progress" of Old World civilization with labels referring to the successive "ages of metal." The first metal to be used gave its name to the Copper Age, or Chalcolithic. The combination of copper and tin that was produced in later times gave its name to the Bronze Age, which was followed in turn by the Iron Age.

Since the 19th century archaeologists have learned a great deal more about the origin and development of prehistoric metallurgy. As a result, the course of technological innovation can now be traced not only in the Near East but also in Southeast Asia, China, Africa, and the New World. The picture is by no means complete; for instance, recent discoveries at Non Nok Tha and Ban Chiang in Thailand have generated new—if controversial—support for the hypothesis that tin-bronze metallurgy developed in Southeast Asia, independently of the Near East.

The sequence of metallurgical development is still best known for the Near East, however. The first uses of metal in that area, sometime before 7000 B.C., involved cold hammering of copper. Copper is malleable enough to be shaped by hammering, but the progressive pounding cracks and weakens the metal. Annealing—heating and slow cooling—"heals" the cracks and stresses produced by hammering, thus providing renewed strength to the metal tool. Before 4000 B.C., copper was being melted and cast in a growing variety of shapes, from axe heads to spearpoints, swords, and ornaments. At the same time, intense heat was used to *smelt* copper from ores, thereby greatly expanding the range of sources for the raw material.

Another significant advance involved deliberate production of metal *alloys*. Most scholars believe that experimental attempts to remove impurities from copper led to the discovery or realization that some of the "impurities" were beneficial. Most notably, inclusion of small quantities of tin or arsenic in copper forms a new metal combination, or alloy, called *bronze*. Bronze has several advantages over copper: Not only is its melting point lower, but also it cools into a

FIGURE 5.6

A grouping of bronze vessels from the first millennium B.C. found in a tomb chamber at Gordion, Turkey. (Courtesy of the Gordion Project, the University Museum, University of Pennsylvania.)

harder metal capable of retaining a sharper, stronger edge. Further hammering after cooling hardens it more. Bronze was certainly being produced in the Near East by about 3000 B.C. (Fig. 5.6), and as noted above, Southeast Asia has recently yielded some very early bronze artifacts that may date to about the same era. Bronze metallurgy spread swiftly. Some of the most sophisticated products of bronze casting were created in China during the Shang Dynasty, which extended from about 1500 to 1027 B.C.

Iron metallurgy was the next major development in metallurgical technology. Meteoric iron was known and used during the Bronze Age, but in the later part of the second millennium B.C. ironworking displaced bronze casting as the principal metallurgical means of tool production. The change was more than one of material; ironworking is also more complicated than bronze casting. The principal iron output of the Near Eastern furnaces was a spongy mass called a *bloom*, which was then reheated in a forge and hammered by a blacksmith to shape the tool, drive out impurities, and increase the metal's strength. Even so, forged iron is relatively soft. Use of a charcoal fire for the forge, however, introduces carbon and strengthens the iron, producing carburized iron, or *steel*, a much harder and more durable metal. By the end of the second millennium B.C., Near Eastern blacksmiths were making "steeled" iron tools, and the Iron Age was well underway.

Analyses of metal artifacts have varied with the geographical area, in accord

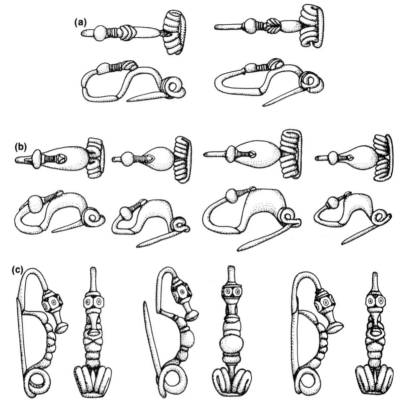

FIGURE 5.7

Three hypothesized stylistic types of bronze fibulae from an Iron Age grave at Münsingen, Germany. (After Hodson 1968.)

with differing research priorities. Because metal—especially molten metal—is a plastic, malleable material, like pottery, it should be well suited to stylistic analyses and classifications. Such studies have been done; one example is the classification of bronze *fibulae*, or safety pin brooches, from La Tène sites of Iron Age Europe (Fig. 5.7). Other studies have focused on the form of metal artifacts and on functional attributions based on formal variation, like the studies done for stone and ceramic artifacts.

But the general focus in metal artifact analyses is reconstruction of ancient technology. Classifications divide the metal industry into subindustries according to the metal being worked. More technical analyses are then performed, including constituent analysis and microscopic examination of the metal structure. These studies help the archaeologist understand the range of technology involved in production, the procurement of raw materials, and the refinement of the final product. Not only can constituent analysis, for example, identify the metals and nonmetallic materials present, but also it may allow specification of the metal sources. Examination of the microstructure of an artifact may yield clues about the precise techniques used in its production: hammering, annealing, quenching, and so on.

A complicating factor in these analyses is that metallurgy, like pottery, is an additive and correcting process in which mistakes can be covered and "smoothed away" by subsequent treatment. Unlike pottery, however, in which firing permanently alters the raw material, metal artifacts can also be melted down and the raw material reused. Such recycling may, for example, account for a relative lack of bronze artifacts early in the Iron Age: To save valuable alloying materials, many whole implements may have been refashioned into a succession of new tools, with only the final version left to the archaeological record.

Organic Artifacts

A variety of artifacts are made from organic materials such as wood, bone, antler, ivory, and shell. Although such items are known to be important or even numerically dominant in the material culture of some modern peoples, such as the Inuit (Eskimo), they are especially susceptible to decay and thus are encountered by archaeologists only under special conditions.

Other kinds of organic materials used to produce artifacts include paper, leather, gourds, and plant fibers. Many of these materials have special technologies, such as basketry or textiles, associated with their production and use. However, we shall restrict discussion here to the most frequently encountered artifact categories: bone and related materials (such as antler and ivory), wood, and shell.

Despite some controversy over the precise origins of bone technology, there is no doubt that by the Upper Paleolithic, people were making artifacts from a variety of animal parts. In both the Old and New Worlds, bone was split and carved with stone tools to form spear points, fishhooks, and other tools (Fig. 5.8). Antler, usually from deer, was split or carved to make projectile points, especially barbed points for spears or harpoons. In the Arctic the prehistoric tradition of carving ivory with stone to make harpoons and other artifacts has survived into historic times.

The technology involved in the production of bone, antler, and ivory tools is subtractive like stoneworking. The simplest such tools involved no form modification, as when an animal bone would be used as a club. The next technological level would be breaking the bone to produce a sharp or jagged edge. Many forms, however, involved working with other tools. The earliest finds suggest that such working was first confined to chipping and cracking, but by the Upper Paleolithic the production of bone, antler, and ivory tools shows great variety, skill, and sophistication; some forms even have engraved decoration.

Because wood is even more perishable than bone, antler, and ivory, the origins of woodworking remain obscure. Isolated finds, particularly from water-

FIGURE 5.8

Bone harpoon heads from Alaska, with flint inserts, illustrate one kind of artifact fashioned from organic materials. (Courtesy of the University Museum, University of Pennsylvania.)

FIGURE 5.9

An example of a Hohokam decorated shell from Arizona (ca. A.D. 800–1200). The design was etched with acid from a saguaro cactus. (Arizona State Museum Collections, University of Arizona.)

logged sites, attest to woodworking by the Lower Paleolithic in Africa and the Middle Paleolithic in Europe. Being a subtractive industry, this technology is preserved in the finished implements themselves, but due to the rarity of their discovery, methods of manufacture are more often inferred indirectly, from woodworking tools made of stone (scrapers, gravers, and so on).

Shell artifacts have been found the world over, even substituting for stone where stone is scarce. Other shell artifact forms include cups, spoons, and fishhooks. Shell working is another subtractive industry; one of the most remarkable ancient means of modifying shell surfaces, a delicate etching by application of a cactus-derived acid, was used by the Hohokam in the American Southwest (Fig. 5.9).

Analysis of organic artifacts yields information about the range of biotic resources exploited by an ancient society and may give clues to communication links with other areas, as when shell artifacts at an inland site are found to be marine (saltwater) species. We will consider the "ecofactual" aspects of organic artifacts in more detail later on.

Most classifications of organic artifacts are based on criteria of form. Sometimes these form taxonomies have stylistic overtones, but more often they involve functional inferences, and the types are labeled with direct or implied functional names. For example, the well-known artifact assemblages of the European Upper Paleolithic include a great variety of barbed bone projectile points, almost always referred to as "harpoons." Such designations provide convenient, easy-to-remember names, but they do not establish the actual function of these artifacts.

ECOFACTS

Because they are "natural" objects, ecofacts yield more indirect information about technology. Ecofacts, however, are no less important than artifacts as clues to understanding past human societies. For example, at the Olsen-Chubbuck site in southeastern Colorado, a series of bison skeletons was found associated with some stone tools, all strewn along the base of a ravine (Fig. 5.10). The site represents the remains of human food procurement behavior some 8500 years ago. The location and arrangement of both ecofacts and artifacts have been used to infer a good deal about hunting strategy (how and from what direction the animals were driven over the ravine edge, including which way the wind may have been blowing), butchering techniques (how the carcasses were dismembered, which bones were stripped of meat on the spot and which were carried off to the presumed campsite), and yield (how much meat and by-products would have been available from the kill).

Ecofacts can also tell us about noneconomic activities such as ritual. Analysis of the heavy concentration of pollen found scattered over Burial IV in Shanidar cave, northern Iraq, indicates that when this Neanderthal man was buried some 60,000 years ago, his survivors covered him with flowers, including daisies, cornflowers, and hollyhocks. Further, because such flowers now bloom locally in May and June, one can infer that the burial probably took place at that time of year.

Most frequently, however, ecofacts are used to reconstruct the environment in which past societies lived and the range of resources they exploited. Grahame Clark and his co-workers analyzed pollen samples from Star Carr, a 10,000-year-old site in northern England, and inferred that the surrounding area was largely covered by forest of birch and pine; the presence of pollen from plants that thrive in open areas pointed to localized clearings, one of which was the site of Star Carr. By examining both the plant remains and the abundantly recovered

FIGURE 5.10

Remains of bison killed and butchered by hunters some
8500 years ago, excavated at the Olsen-Chubbuck site,
Colorado. (Reproduced by permission of the Colorado
State Museum and the Society for American Archaeology,
from *Memoirs of the Society for American Archaeology* 26: ix,
1972.)

antlers of red deer, roe deer, and elk, the investigators could establish the times
of year the site had been occupied. This was done by comparing the distribution of antlers broken from the animals' skulls with those that had simply
been collected after being shed naturally and correlating the data with the known
seasonal cycles of deer antler growth and shedding. The work at Star Carr was a
landmark, showing the wealth of interpretation that could be gained from ecofactual data.

As with artifacts, the first step in analysis of ecofacts is classification.

Clearly, however, the classification of ecofacts must use different criteria from those used for artifacts, borrowing schemes from botany, zoology, and geology. Once these preliminary steps are completed, ecofacts may be classified in many specific ways, according to properties that might relate them to past human societies. For example, some plants and animals are available for harvesting only at limited times of the year; these, as the Shanidar and Star Carr cases indicate, may be used to determine seasonality of exploitation. Animals can be studied in terms of the amounts of meat they would yield and therefore the size of the human population they could support. Soils can be classified as to their relative potential fertility under given kinds of agricultural exploitation.

Floral Ecofacts

Floral remains in archaeological contexts fall into two basic categories: microspecimens and macrospecimens. Microspecimens include pollen as well as the more durable silica bodies formed in plants (phytoliths). Macrospecimens include seeds, leaves, casts or impressions, and so forth. Both categories require technical identification. As part of this process many plants (and animals) are identified as wild or domesticated. The domestication of plants and animals in the Old and New Worlds was a significant cultural development that gave people more direct control over the quantity and quality of their food supply. A good deal of study has been done concerning when, where, and how the domestication process was carried out. Critical to such study, of course, is the ability to identify wild and domesticated forms. Since domestication is a gradual result of repeated selection for desired traits—as when larger or quicker-growing strains are deliberately replanted and nurtured—there is no single "original" domesticated maize cob or wheat kernel. Rather one can discern trends in form from "fully wild" to "fully domesticated" (Fig. 5.11).

Another dimension in the study of floral ecofacts is the context in which they are found. The Shanidar IV context is one of ideological or symbolic use of plants. On the other hand, the only sure indication that a plant fragment was a food resource is contextual, from its occurrence in the digestive tracts of mummies or bog corpses or in human *coprolites* (preserved feces). Food remains and residues may also be found adhering to the interiors of food storage vessels or to preparation surfaces such as grinding stones.

Faunal Ecofacts

Faunal remains in archaeological contexts take a number of forms, from whole specimens, such as mummies, to partial ones, such as bones or coprolites. Bones and teeth, the most commonly recovered forms, have received the most attention.

A basic question of faunal studies is: What kinds of animals were being exploited? Archaeologists attempt not only to identify the species distinctions but also to establish the proportions of adult versus juvenile and, for some adult animals, male versus female. Tallies of this kind have been used as evidence for the

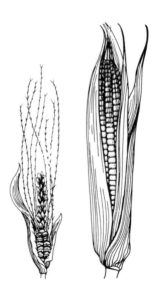

FIGURE 5.11

Comparison between a reconstructed view of wild maize (now extinct) on the left, and domesticated maize on the right. Over time, selection favored more and longer rows of kernels.

very beginning of animal domestication, before bone changes due to selective breeding can be detected. In this case the presence of large numbers of young-animal remains may indicate direct access to and control of a herd, or selective culling before breeding age to "weed out" certain characteristics. In other cases the presence of immature animals may point to use of the site in the season when the young animals would have been available. In contrast, changes in bone mass of sheep and goats of the third millennium B.C. in Israel suggested that older females were more numerous in later occupation levels: From this shift in herd composition, analysts inferred a rising emphasis on milk production.

Archaeologists can also examine the parts of animals present at a site. At Star Carr the occurrence of stag frontlets as well as detached antlers gave evidence not only of the season of occupation of the site, but also of the range of antler raw materials that were desired by or acceptable to the site's occupants. At Olsen-Chubbuck, study of the presence or absence of various skeletal elements led to inferences about butchering techniques by indicating which parts of the animals were taken back to the residence area for more leisurely consumption.

Special characteristics of particular animals may lead to specific interpretations. Some small animals, such as snails, are very sensitive to climate and thus can serve as indicators of local climatic change or stability. An increase in white-tailed deer could signal an increase in cleared areas or a decrease in local forest cover. The presence of large mammals as prey often suggests organized group hunting practices, and herd animals require different tactics from solitary animals. Ideological interpretations may also be made from faunal evidence.

Contextual associations can be related to various kinds of human-animal relations. For example, the occurrence of mummified cats in ancient Egypt and of jaguar remains in elite Maya burials reflect the high symbolic status enjoyed by those animals in the two societies. Bones found in middens, on the other hand, are usually interpreted as remains of food animals and/or scavengers.

As part of the consideration of context, the archaeologist must distinguish, as far as possible, which animals are related to human presence and exploitation and which are not. For example, burrowing animals, such as gophers or opossums, found in graves may have gotten there on their own, independent of the ancient burial. Other animals, such as the bats roosting in abandoned Maya temples, may simply have taken advantage of the shelter provided by occupation areas. As an example of how critical such a determination can be, consider the debate over Makapansgat, an early site in South Africa. Raymond Dart used the pattern of occurrence of the nonhuman bones—how they were broken, what elements were present, and how they were deposited—to argue that these bones include tools, as well as ecofacts, used by early human ancestors two million years ago. Other scholars, however, argue that the bones are neither artifacts nor ecofacts: Recent studies indicate that the Makapansgat bones are like those accumulated by modern carnivores, and are thus the result of animal not human activity.

Human Remains

Human remains are the domain of one entire branch of anthropology—physical anthropology. More than anything else encountered and studied by archaeologists, human remains raise significant ethical issues. This is most apparent when living descendants of the dead express their concerns about the excavation and analysis of skeletal remains. We will consider the professional responsibilities of the archaeologist in the treatment of human remains in our final chapter. Here we shall simply review some of the ways in which human remains from an archaeological context may further the understanding of the extinct society being investigated. Forms of human remains include mummies, fragmentary bones and teeth, and coprolites. Bones and teeth are most often preserved, and they will receive most attention.

Analysis of human remains begins with identification of the particular elements (bones, teeth) present and of the number of individuals represented. Since people are often buried in individual graves, this may not be a difficult task, but mass graves or reused ones present special problems. Once the elements are identified, however, an assessment is made of each individual's sex and age at death. Some skeletal elements are more reliable or easier to interpret in these assessments. For example, sex can be most readily judged from the pelvis. Age can be assessed by a variety of means, including eruption sequence and degree of wear on teeth, fusion between bones of the skull, and fusion of the ends (epiphyses) to the shafts (diaphyses) of limb bones.

Once age and sex identifications are made, a number of other studies can be done. Paleodemographic analysts examine the structure of the ancient population under investigation, including determination of the sex ratio and life expectancy (Fig. 5.12). Human remains also yield information on the health and

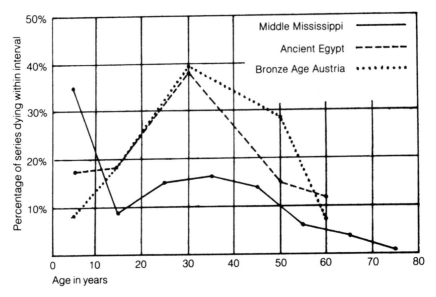

FIGURE 5.12

Comparative mortality profiles from selected ancient populations. Middle Mississippians, of the southeastern United States after A.D. 1000, were two to three times as likely to die before 10 years of age than were ancient Egyptians or Austrians of the Bronze Age several thousand years earlier. Once past childhood, however, members of all three groups reached a peak death rate between ages 25 and 35. (From Blakeley 1971; courtesy of Robert L. Blakeley and the *American Journal of Physical Anthropology*.)

nutrition of the population. Not all diseases or injuries affect the skeleton, but many do. Obvious examples are bone fractures and tooth caries; other maladies, including arthritis, yaws, and periodontal disease, leave tangible marks. (Of course, if mummified bodies are available for study, analysis can be much more complete, like a regular autopsy.) These diagnostic traces make ancient human remains important to the study of the origins and development of diseases such as tuberculosis. Human bones also offer clues on ancient social standing. William Haviland has attributed differences in male stature at the Maya site of Tikal, Guatemala, to social class and accompanying wealth differences. The taller males, found in richer tomb burials, were probably also richer in life and thus able to secure better food than their shorter counterparts buried in less well made and furnished interments.

Some cultural practices also leave their mark on skeletal remains. One example is cranial deformation, practiced in pre-Columbian times in North, Central, and South America. According to this custom the head is tightly bound until it takes the desired form (Fig. 5.13). The Chinese practice of binding girls' feet to make them smaller is comparable.

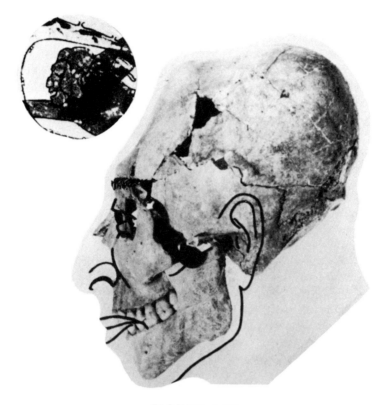

FIGURE 5.13

Photograph of an artificially deformed skull from the Classic Maya site of Altar de Sacrificios, Guatemala, with a superimposed reconstruction of the individual's profile in life. The inset shows an individual with a similarly deformed skull painted on a pottery vessel from the same site. (Courtesy of Dr. Frank P. Saul, Medical College of Ohio.)

Inorganic Remains

Inorganic remains include one of the most important categories of ecofacts: the various soils uncovered by excavation. The soil in an archaeological deposit is more than just a matrix in which culturally relevant materials may be embedded. It is only in the last quarter century or so, however, that the full importance of archaeological soils has begun to be recognized. Two principal aspects of soil should be examined: how it was deposited and its composition.

Deposition of soil layers can be the result of human activities or natural geological processes. It is basic to stratigraphic evaluation to distinguish between natural and cultural origins for all deposits encountered. But in some cases the soils have a particularly dramatic story to tell. For example, Alan Kolata has found water-laid soils capping the occupation levels at 750-year-old sites on the south shore of Lake Titicaca in Bolivia. He suggests that the soils account for the sudden decline in this part of the ancient Tiwanaku state: Flooding and a rise in the lake level may have waterlogged and thereby ruined what had been a productive agricultural landscape.

Even more dramatic is the fate of the island of Thera (now called Santorini) in the Aegean, where an earthquake destroyed the town of Acrotiri in about 1500 B.C. In Chapter 3, we discussed the explosion of the volcano on that island, and the way this event completely disrupted local human occupation. However, excavations at Acrotiri have established that a considerable time elapsed between the earthquake and the volcanic explosion, since a thin humus layer (the result of natural, gradual soil formation processes) was found between the remains of the fallen abandoned buildings and the ejecta from the volcano. Indeed, two distinguishable eruptions apparently took place: a small one followed by the catastrophic destruction. The "warning" provided by the smaller eruption probably allowed most of the residents of Thera to leave. The finds at Thera are relatively lacking in human remains compared, for instance, to Pompeii, where many residents had no time to flee before the eruption of Vesuvius in A.D. 79.

Soil characteristics were observed by ancient inhabitants as well as modern investigators. Soil surveys in many areas of the world have indicated that, for example, occupation by agriculturalists correlates well with the distribution of well-drained and fertile areas. Fertility potentials must be tested, however, and not simply assumed. For example, volcanic ash is generally a fertile parent material for agricultural soils, but Payson Sheets and his associates showed that the eruption around A.D. 200 of Ilopango volcano in what is now El Salvador blanketed the area with an infertile layer of ash that would have decreased local agricultural production capacities for as long as several centuries.

FEATURES

Features, like artifacts, owe their form to human intervention, so it is not surprising that analysis of features is similar to that for artifacts. Formal, stylistic, and technological analyses are all appropriate approaches to the study of features. But artifacts can be moved, whereas features are fixed and thus destroyed by removal. Two particular characteristics of features are important in analysis: location and arrangement. For example, when a multistory house collapses, features from the upper floors, such as hearths or grain-grinding bins, may still be inferred from their disarrayed component parts (Fig. 5.14). But the original form, placement, and arrangement of the feature can only be estimated.

As when dealing with artifacts, the archaeologist attempting to understand the significance of a particular feature makes use of provenience, association, and context. The difference is that intact features can directly indicate the origi-

(a)

FIGURE 5.14

Features may often be
identified, even after disturbance: (a) an intact
mealing bin, where
stones were set for grinding grain, in a pre-
historic pueblo from the
southwestern United
States; (b) a feature presumed to be a collapsed
mealing bin, the distur-
bance seemingly result-
ing from destruction of
the building's roof or
upper story. (Photo a by
author; photo b by
M. Thompson, Arizona
State Museum, Univer-
sity of Arizona.)

(b)

nal makers' and users' intentional placement, while the locational aspects of artifacts are used to infer (by determination of context) whether a use-related placement has been preserved. Features are most valuable in understanding the distribution and organization of human activities, for they represent the facilities—the space and often some stationary equipment—with which these activities were carried out.

We shall discuss features in two categories that have possible behavioral implications: constructed features and cumulative features.

Constructed Features

Constructed features were built to provide space for some activity or set of activities. Examples range from simple windbreaks to elaborate houses and temples, from burials and tombs to roadways and fortification walls, and from artificial reservoirs and stone-lined hearths to agricultural terraces and irrigation canals. The important criterion is that there is some construction that formally channels the ongoing use of space.

Classification and analysis of constructed features may examine attributes of form, style, technology, location, or some combination of these. Technological analyses include consideration of the materials used in the construction and the ways they were put together. When complex architecture is involved, as in the construction of imposing features such as the Egyptian pyramids, analysis may require intricate study. The technological analysis of such features usually yields data not only about the physical act of construction, such as the use of particular materials and the sequence of their incorporation in the growing structure, but also about related social aspects of the construction process. For instance, in the prehistoric Moche Valley in Peru, adobe bricks from large structures were marked with distinctive labels. Michael Moseley concluded that each mark represents a separate group of brick producers (a little more than 100 of these marks were identified). Each work force responsible for supplying a certain number of bricks could thus have verified that its proper contribution had been made.

Even unimposing and partially perishable structures can yield complex data about construction methods and materials. For example, remains of one of the earliest known structures, revealed at the site of Terra Amata in Nice, France, indicated some of the constructional considerations of its builders 300,000 years ago. Although the structure was a temporary, seasonal shelter, its builders showed concern for its stability and strength by bracing the stake walls with stones (Fig. 5.15). In addition, some protection from prevailing winds was provided by the location of the entry and by erection of a windbreak for the hearth.

Internal arrangement, elaboration, and orientation of features are often important attributes. A good example of this is the range of features now being studied as astronomical observatories. Gerald Hawkins has published a number of analyses of the astronomical alignments found in the component parts of Stonehenge, interpreting the range of observations that could have been made

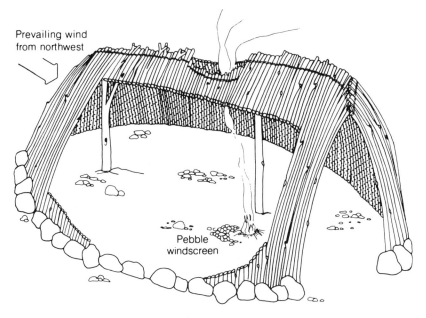

Prevailing wind
from northwest

Pebble
windscreen

FIGURE 5.15

Cutaway view of a reconstructed Paleolithic hut built of stakes braced by an
outside ring of stones, found at Terra Amata, France, representing one of the
earliest constructed features thus far discovered. (After "A Paleolithic Camp at
Nice" by H. de Lumley. Copyright © 1969 by Scientific American, Inc. All
rights reserved.)

from this Bronze Age station. Inspired at least in part by Hawkins' work, other
scholars are examining other monuments to see if their arrangements suggest
similar use. The kinds of features under investigation range from the Big Horn
Medicine Wheel in northern Wyoming, to entire communities that may incor-
porate astronomical layouts.

Location of constructed features can also be informative for particular research questions. For example, location of burials in special mortuary structures
or elite areas, such as the North Acropolis of Tikal, Guatemala, or the Great
Pyramids of Egypt, may indicate special social status and privilege. Study of the
locations of features may also suggest factors involved in siting or placement decisions, such as preference for elevated ground or proximity to water sources in
locating houses. With the increased use of quantitative methods and the adoption of analytic techniques from fields such as geography, archaeologists are beginning to study locational attributes more thoroughly and to specify more
rigorously whether the locational choices observed are due, in fact, to human
preferences and decisions or to chance.

Cumulative Features

Cumulative features are those that are formed by accretion rather than by a pre-planned or designed construction of an activity area or facility. Examples of such features include middens, quarries (which "grow" by subtraction of the exploited resource, sometimes accompanied by an accumulation of extracting tools), workshop areas, and so on. In Chapter 4 we saw how conjoining studies helped define a cumulative workshop feature at Koobi Fora.

Although stylistic analysis is rarely appropriate here, cumulative features can be analyzed according to attributes of form, location, and sometimes technology. Formal attributes include, for example, size and content. Because we are dealing with accumulated entities, size can indicate either the duration or the intensity of use. For example, a trash deposit will be larger not only if it is used longer but also if it is used more frequently. It is not always possible to distinguish the relative importance of these two factors in cumulative features. But when long-term stratified middens are identified, they are particularly valuable to the archaeologist because they yield evidence concerning the temporal span of occupation at a site.

Analysis of the location of cumulative features may give information on the distribution of ancient activities. For example, distribution of quarries relative to habitation sites might indicate how far people were willing to travel to obtain stone raw materials, and the location of workshop areas reveals the distribution of manufacturing activities within or among settlements.

Although cumulative features are unplanned accretions of artifacts and other materials, they may still yield technological information. For example, quarries may preserve extraction scars as well as abandoned mining tools and thus may indicate how the raw materials were removed. The ancient copper mines of Rudna Glava, in eastern Yugoslavia, attest to heat extraction of ore there 6000 years ago. Similarly, study of the debris from stone-chipping stations may help in reconstructing chipping technology, and artifacts from a midden— molds, bowl sherds containing unfired clay or pigments, and so on—may indicate the nearby presence of a pottery production area and aid in outlining the technology involved in its use.

SUMMARY

In this chapter we have reviewed the analysis of the three categories of archaeological data: artifacts, ecofacts, and features. Analysis of these remains is influenced by their physical characteristics, their state of preservation, and the specific questions being asked.

Artifacts are divided into industries based on shared raw materials and manufacturing techniques. The industries most commonly encountered by archaeologists are those of stone (lithic) and fired clay (ceramic). Lithic industries involve subtractive production processes that often preserve evidence of the steps taken during manufacture. This makes technological analysis, especially with chipped stone tools, rewarding for understanding this kind of ancient behavior. Functional analysis of lithic artifacts is also useful in reconstructing past activities when based on detectable wear and residues.

Ceramic industries, such as pottery, are made by additive processes that often destroy evidence of manufacturing steps, so technological analysis is more difficult. But since clay is a plastic and easily manipulated substance that can be shaped and decorated in a variety of ways, it lends itself to stylistic classifications that define variations in both time and space. Pottery vessel shapes and the identification of residues are used to infer function as a way to reconstruct past activities.

Metal artifacts also possess characteristics that allow technological, stylistic, and functional analyses. Artifacts made from organic materials are usually classified by form as a basis for functional inferences. Constituent analyses of most kinds of artifacts can identify raw material sources and allow the reconstruction of past trade and distribution networks.

The various categories of ecofacts—plant, animal, human, and inorganic remains—can be analyzed to yield culturally meaningful information. Floral remains include both microspecimens (pollen and phytoliths) and macrospecimens (seeds, plant fragments, and impressions). Faunal remains include mummified, skeletal, and coprolite materials. Once identified as to species, both floral and faunal samples can yield information on ancient environments and subsistence activities, as well as medical and ritual behavior. Human remains provide direct evidence about ancient nutritional and health status, which is vital to our understanding not only of the past but also of the present (as in the origins and evolution of human disease). Examination of inorganic remains, especially the analysis of soils, can yield clues to the presence or absence of past human activity and information about ancient land use and environments.

Features preserve in their form and location a record of the spatial distribution of past human activities. Some features are deliberately constructed to house activities; others represent cumulative activities (additive or subtractive) that modify the environment. Constructed features usually represent attempts to channel the use of space. Their analysis allows reconstruction of past technologies, while their attributes of form and location allow inferences about ancient behavior and culture. In addition, variations in building or decorative style provide important markers of age or cultural identity. Cumulative features are the result of gradual accumulation of artifacts and ecofacts, as in workshops or middens, or progressive removal of materials, as in mines or quarries. Both provide important clues to ancient technology and other forms of behavior.

· 6 ·

Dating the Past

BEFORE WE CAN BEGIN to reconstruct the past, we must be able to control the time dimension. That is, we need to determine which remains are from the same period and which are from different periods. Only then can we examine behavior systems at single points in time and the ways these systems change through time.

Throughout much of their discipline's history, archaeologists have been preoccupied with establishing the age and proper sequence for their evidence. As a result, a variety of methods has been developed for determining the date of remains from the past. Recent advances in chemistry and nuclear physics have greatly expanded the inventory of dating techniques, which has freed archaeologists from their traditional concern with dating. The "radiocarbon revolution" of the 1950s has been followed by development of a series of newer age determination methods, all of which allow the archaeologist to focus on behavior-oriented studies rather than chronological issues.

Before we discuss a few of the specific techniques, however, we should consider some basic definitions. First, age determination may be direct or indirect. *Direct dating* involves analysis of the artifact, ecofact, or feature itself in order to arrive at its age. *Indirect dating* considers analysis of material associated with the artifact, ecofact, or feature being studied to evaluate its age. For example, an obsidian blade found in a tomb might be dated directly by the obsidian hydration method (explained later); other artifacts found in the same tomb, and the tomb feature itself, can then be dated indirectly by assigning them the same age as the obsidian blade with which they were associated. Of course the reliability of indirect age determination depends on the security of the context—in this

TABLE 6.1

Major Archaeological Dating Techniques

RELATIVE METHODS	ABSOLUTE METHODS
Seriation	Obsidian Hydration
Sequence Comparison	Dendrochronology
Stratigraphy	Radiometric (radiocarbon,
Geochronology	potassium-argon, etc.)
Bone Age	Archaeomagnetic

case the evidence that the obsidian and the other materials were deposited at the same time.

The second distinction to be considered is that between *relative* and *absolute* dating methods (Table 6.1). The first term refers to methods that evaluate the age of one item of data relative to other data; for example, artifact A is older than artifact B. The second term refers to methods that place the age of a sample on an absolute time scale, usually a calendrical system (artifact A was used from ca. 400 to 300 B.C.), and therefore assign an age in years. Absolute methods are seldom absolutely precise, however. Instead, as the example above indicates, most absolute methods assign an age expressed as a time span or range and often include a statement of the degree of statistical probability that the "true" age of the sample falls within that range (expressed by a ± symbol).

An exception to this may be found in dealing with artifacts or features inscribed with calendrical notations, even if these refer to a calendar different from the one in use today. For instance, most coins minted during the Roman Empire carry at least one reference to a specific year in the reign of a particular Emperor. And in the New World most monuments carved by the Maya of the Classic Period (ca. A.D. 250–900) are inscribed with one or more dates in their calendrical system. In both of these cases the ancient calendrical system can be correlated to our own, so the Roman and Maya notations can be assigned to a date in our system—to the month and day in the Maya case. Materials such as these can thus be used to provide indirect absolute dates for clearly associated remains.

Relative dates lead to definition of chronological sequences. By determining the age of a multitude of samples relative to each other, and arranging them in chronological order, the archaeologist defines a time framework that can be used to organize all subsequent data. There are various ways of finding relative ages and thereby constructing chronological sequences. Establishing such sequences has been one of the prime objectives of prehistoric archaeology since they enable archaeologists to reconstruct the order in which ancient events took place. In many areas of the world these sequences are well defined, and newly discovered data can simply be placed in the existing scheme. In other areas, however, basic chronologies have yet to be established and are therefore still a prime objective.

In the following section we shall briefly discuss the most important methods used by archaeologists to determine age and chronological sequence. Most of these methods, however, have limits or built-in inaccuracies of some sort, so archaeologists are wary of temporal schemes that rely on a single method or just a few dated samples. A sequence based on a dozen dated samples is obviously better than one based on two or three. And the greatest degree of confidence in any chronology arises from agreement among results of several different dating methods.

SERIATION

Patterns of human behavior change continually, and as behavior changes, so do its material products. We have all observed how changes through time in design and style alter familiar objects in our own society. Many of us can identify the trends of change well enough to place any particular item in its approximate time period. For instance, when shown several automobiles of varying ages, many of us can arrange them in rough chronological sequence (Fig. 6.1); similar sequential changes are noticeable in our clothing styles, art, music, and so on.

The artifacts and features of the past also exhibit changes through time, and by observing and studying various attributes archaeologists can usually discover these trends. By identifying the attributes that are most sensitive to change—

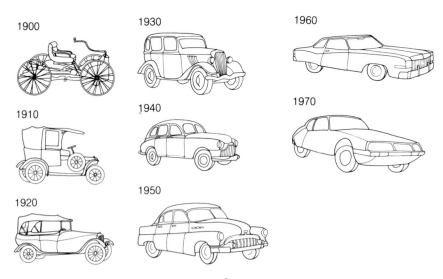

FIGURE 6.1

Gradual changes in design are clearly evidenced in familiar aspects of our own culture, such as automobiles.

ARBITRARY SEQUENCE DATES

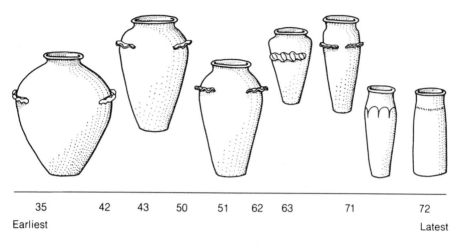

| 35 | | 42 | 43 | 50 | 51 | 62 | 63 | 71 | 72 |
| Earliest | | | | | | | | | Latest |

FIGURE 6.2

One of the earliest applications of stylistic seriation was Petrie's chronological ordering of tombs at Diospolis Parva, Egypt, based on changes in associated pottery vessels. (After Petrie 1901.)

that is, which traits change most rapidly—the archaeologist can construct a sequence that will most accurately reflect the passage of time. Surface decorative or stylistic attributes generally shift most rapidly and freely and tend to be the best chronological indicators because they are least affected by functional or technological requirements. For example, a water storage jar must be deep enough to hold water and should have a restricted mouth to lessen evaporation and spills, but it can be any color or design. Artifacts made from such plastic materials as clay or metal are usually good sources for deriving temporal sequences, because they are amenable to decorative manipulation.

Seriation is a relative dating method derived from these cultural regularities. It refers to a variety of techniques that seek to order artifacts "in a series" so that adjacent members in the series are more similar than members farther apart in the series. Seriation has two basic applications: stylistic seriation and frequency seriation.

Stylistic Seriation

Stylistic seriation is a technique by which artifacts and attributes are ordered according to similarity in style (Fig. 6.2). In this case the variation may reflect either temporal change or spatial distance. It is therefore up to the archaeologist to determine whether time or space (or both) caused the stylistic variation observable in each situation. Generally the more limited the source area of the artifact in question, the more likely the seriation reflects the passage of time.

One of the first studies to use stylistic seriation successfully was the Diospolis Parva sequence outlined by Sir Flinders Petrie at the close of the 19th century. Petrie was faced with a series of predynastic Egyptian tombs that were not linked stratigraphically, but had each yielded sets of funerary pottery. He ordered the pottery by its shape (Fig. 6.2) and assigned a series of numbers to the seriated pots. The numbers, of course, did not relate to a calendar of years but indicated the relative age of the materials within the series. Nonetheless this technique allowed Petrie to organize the pottery chronologically and, by association, to order the tombs as well.

Petrie's study also provides evidence that the archaeologist cannot assume that the trend of change is always from simple to complex or that it implies "progress" as our own culture defines that term. In the Diospolis Parva sequence, the vessel handles began as functional attributes and ended as decorative lines mimicking handles. Thus, for a sequence to be valid, the archaeologist must ensure that it is free from presumptions of "progress," increasing complexity, or other ethnocentric biases. Of course, one must also have some idea of which end of the resulting seriation is "up"—that is, which is the earlier end and which is the later. In most cases, links with other dating methods (usually absolute) will provide this information.

Frequency Seriation

Frequency seriation is a method that is more strictly oriented to chronological ordering. It involves determining the sequence of sites or deposits by studying the relative frequencies of their artifact types. This analysis is based on the assumption that the frequency of each artifact type follows a predictable career, from the time of its origin to an expanding popularity and finally to total disuse. The length of time and the degree of popularity (frequency) varies with each type, but when presented diagrammatically most examples form one or more lenslike patterns known as *battleship-shaped curves*. The validity of this pattern has been verified by plotting the frequencies of artifact types from long-term stratified deposits and by testing historically documented examples. The best-known historical test is that by James Deetz and Edwin N. Dethlefsen, involving dated tombstones from 18th- and early 19th-century New England. This study demonstrated that the popularity of various decorative motifs on the headstones did indeed show battleship-shaped distribution curves over time (Fig. 6.3).

If seriation is not feasible, the archaeologist has another recourse in order to construct a temporal sequence. If other well-documented artifact sequences exist in the geographical area being investigated, the artifact classes in question may be compared to those already defined from nearby sites, and placed into a temporal order corresponding to those already established. This comparative method, however, makes the assumption that some past cultural connections, such as trade, did exist and that the resemblances are therefore not accidental. Furthermore, even if connections can be documented, two similar types may not be exactly the same age. The work of Deetz and Dethlefsen, for example,

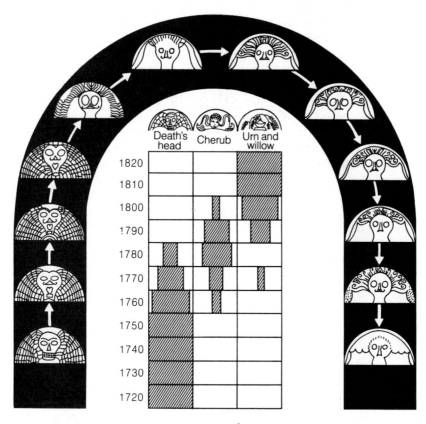

FIGURE 6.3

A study of dated New England tombstones shows that the changes in popularity of particular styles is aptly described by battleship-shaped curves, and it supports assumptions used in both stylistic seriation and frequency seriation. The outer ring shows the gradual change in one motif, the death's head. (After *Invitation to Archaeology* by James Deetz, illustrated by Eric Engstrom, copyright © 1967 by James Deetz. Reprinted by permission of DOUBLEDAY, a division of Bantam, Doubleday, Dell Publishing Group, Inc.)

showed that even among colonial communities as close together as Plymouth, Concord, and Cambridge, Massachusetts, the time ranges in which particular tombstone motifs were used were rather variable. Because of these difficulties, the comparative method is usually the weakest means for inferring a local chronological sequence; it is usually used only when other means are impossible.

Sequence comparison is very useful, however, for building broad area chronologies. By matching sequences already established for individual sites or regions, archaeologists produce the time–space grids important to cultural historical reconstruction, as discussed in Chapter 8. These time–space grids allow identification of trends and regularities in cultural change and stability across broad expanses of space and time.

STRATIGRAPHY

The age of archaeological materials can sometimes be assessed by their association with geological deposits or formations. Often these assessments are relative, as in cases based on the rule of superposition, which states that materials in lower strata were deposited earlier than those in higher strata. As stated in Chapter 4, *stratigraphy* refers to the archaeological interpretation of the significance of stratification. We have also seen how archaeological stratigraphy may represent a combination of both behavioral and natural transformation processes (as in a midden composed of alternating strata of materials in primary context and redeposited alluvium). As long as the context—and, therefore, the temporal order—of a stratified deposit is clear, the archaeologist can use stratigraphy to determine the relative age of artifacts and other materials in the deposit.

GEOCHRONOLOGY

Many methods have been developed for determining the absolute age of geological formations. Since the earth existed for billions of years before humans appeared, however, only a few techniques of geochronology apply to the relatively recent span of archaeological deposits. Nevertheless, when geologists have determined the absolute age of geological formations using radiometric or other techniques (discussed below), the archaeologist can assign an indirect date to artifacts found in these matrices.

The effects of long-term geological processes, such as glacial advance and retreat or fluctuations in land and sea levels, can sometimes be quite useful in dating archaeological remains. If the chronology of the geological events is known, associated archaeological materials can be fitted into that scheme. For example, the successive formation of post-Pleistocene shorelines at Cape Krusenstern, Alaska, provided J. Louis Giddings with a means of ordering sites chronologically. As the beach expanded seaward through time, people continued to locate their camps near its high water limit. In this progression the younger beaches—and, through association with them, the more recent sites—are those located closer to the current beach front. More than 100 old beach lines are discernible at Cape Krusenstern, representing some 5000 years of accumulation (Fig. 6.4). Through this beach sequence—which some have called *horizontal stratigraphy*—Giddings arranged the sites in temporal order. By applying other dating techniques he then converted the relative dating to an absolute scheme.

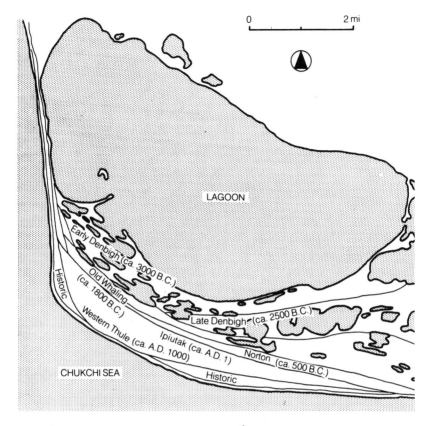

FIGURE 6.4

This map of Cape Krusenstern, Alaska, emphasizes some of the series of ancient beach ridges that have been related to particular periods of occupation during the last 5000 years. (Redrawn from *Ancient Men of the Sea* by J. Louis Giddings. © estate of J. Louis Giddings, New York: Alfred A. Knopf, Inc., 1967.)

OBSIDIAN HYDRATION

In 1960 Irving Friedman and Robert L. Smith announced a new age determination technique based on the cumulative *hydration*, or adsorption of water, in obsidian. Over time the water forms a hydration layer on the exposed surfaces of obsidian (see Fig. 6.5). The thickness of this layer is measured in microns ($1\mu =$ 0.001 mm) and is detectable microscopically. Since the hydration layer penetrates deeper into the surface over time, the thickness of this layer can be used to determine the amount of time that the surface has been exposed. In other words, the age of manufacture or use—either of which could fracture the obsidian, exposing a new surface for hydration—can be calculated if the rate of hydration is

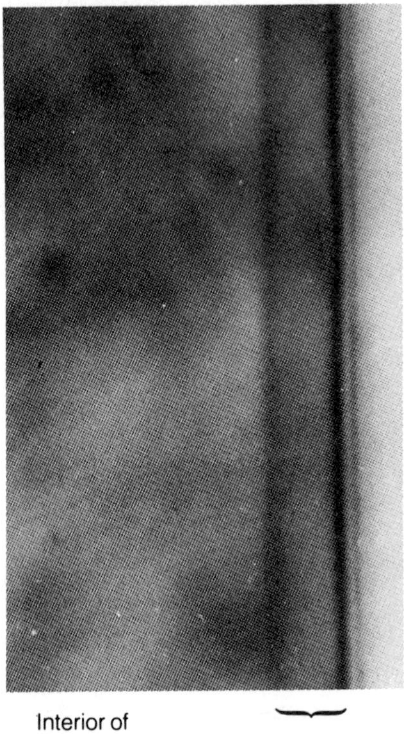

FIGURE 6.5

In this magnified view, the 3μ-wide hydration zone appears as a wide band at the edge of the obsidian. (From Michels 1973; by permission of the author and Seminar Press.)

Interior of
obsidian
specimen

Hydration
zone

known. Once this rate is established, the thickness of the hydration layer from any obsidian sample can be compared to a chronological conversion table to provide the sample's age.

Since the method was originally applied, problems have emerged that have had to be corrected to furnish reliable dates. First, we now know that the hydration rate varies with the composition of the obsidian, which differs from one source deposit to another. Second, the hydration rate also changes through time and space, in response to variations in the temperature of the matrix in which the obsidian was deposited. As long as the correction factors for these variations are known and applied, obsidian hydration can still be a simple, accurate, and inexpensive means for directly dating obsidian artifacts.

FLORAL AND FAUNAL METHODS

Several dating methods rely on floral and faunal remains. We will discuss two of the most commonly used techniques.

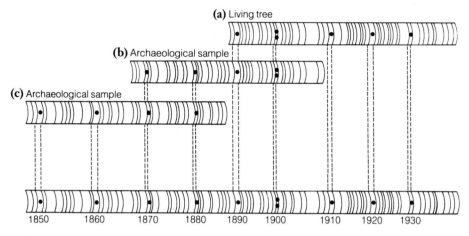

FIGURE 6.6

A master dendrochronological sequence is built by linking successively older specimens, often beginning with living trees (a) that overlap with archaeological samples (b, c), based on matching patterns of thick and thin rings. Provided the sequence is long enough, specimens of unknown age can be dated by comparison with the master sequence. The rings are marked with dots at 10-year intervals for ease of reading. (After Bannister 1970).

Dendrochronology

Dendrochronology is the best-known method of directly determining absolute age for floral materials. This approach, also called tree-ring dating, is based on counting the annual growth rings observable in the cross-sections of cut trees and has been known for centuries. For instance, in 1848 Squier and Davis reasoned that the minimum age of mounds in the Mississippi valley could be ascertained from the age of the oldest trees growing on the ruins. Assuming that trees would not be allowed to grow on mounds before abandonment of the site, one could say that if the oldest tree growing on a site were 300 years old, the site itself could be no more recent than that.

The modern method of dendrochronology involves a refinement of such growth ring counts. The basic refinement is the cross-linkage of growth ring patterns among trees to extend a sequence of growth cycles into the past, far beyond the lifetime of a single tree (Fig. 6.6). The compilation of a long-term sequence of growth ring patterns was first established by an astronomer, A. E. Douglass, working in the southwestern United States in the first decades of the 20th century. Douglass's original research was aimed at relating past climatic cycles—as reflected in cycles of wider and narrower growth rings—to sunspot cycles. Although variations in growth rings do provide valuable clues to past climatic cycles, the additional usefulness of this method in establishing an absolute chronological sequence was soon realized. By counting back from the known starting point, the growth ring sequence could be projected back for thousands of years; a given tree segment could be dated by matching to part of the known sequence. In the case of the bristlecone pine in southeastern California, the record spans more than 8000 years.

Although it seems potentially useful anywhere in the world where trees were used by prehistoric peoples, dendrochronology has in fact been applied in only a few parts of the world: the southwestern United States, Alaska, northern Mexico, Germany, Norway, Great Britain, and Switzerland. The method is limited by its dependence on four conditions that cannot be met everywhere:

1. The proper kind of tree must be present: The species must produce well-defined annual rings and be sensitive to minute variations in climatic cycles. Many species of trees produce roughly uniform rings regardless of small changes in climate.
2. The growth ring variation must depend primarily on one environmental factor, such as temperature or soil humidity.
3. The prehistoric population must have made extensive use of wood, especially in construction.
4. Cultural and environmental conditions must allow for good archaeological preservation of tree segments.

Dendrochronology determines the age of a tree by placing its last or outermost growth ring within a local sequence. This represents the cutting date; if the outermost ring is missing from the sample, the cutting date cannot be assessed. But even with a cutting date, the validity of an archaeological date based on dendrochronology also depends on correct evaluation of the archaeological context and association of the wood. Specimens that form parts of construction features—and are therefore in primary context—are more reliable. Even so, Bryant Bannister has listed four types of errors in interpreting tree-ring dates:

1. The wood may be reused and therefore *older* in date than the construction in which it was used.
2. Use of the construction feature—house or whatever—may have extended well beyond its construction date, so that the wood is *older* than this use date.
3. Replacement of old, weakened beams by newer, stronger ones may result in the wood being *younger* than the original construction.
4. Wooden artifacts or ecofacts found within a construction feature—such as furniture or charcoal in a house—may be *younger or older* than the building date for the feature.

To help offset these problems, the archaeologist tries to recover multiple samples for dendrochronological analysis. The dates from the various specimens can then be used to check each other. Good agreement among several samples relating to the same feature creates a strong presumption that the date is correct.

Bone Age

Bone age techniques enable the archaeologist to see if bones found in the same matrix were indeed deposited together. The basic premise is that a bone loses organic components, principally nitrogen, and gains inorganic components, such as fluorine and uranium, at the same rate as other bones buried at the same time in the same deposit. Since the rates of nitrogen loss and fluorine gain differ with such local environmental conditions as temperature and humidity, the rates vary from one deposit to another. Thus the method cannot be used to establish absolute dates.

The classic applications of these relative dating techniques involved human skeletal remains of disputed antiquity. The most dramatic of these was the exposure of the great Piltdown hoax. The Piltdown finds, unearthed between 1911 and 1915, revealed an apelike jawbone apparently paired with a modern-looking human cranium. The two were anatomically mismatched overall, but the apparent geological evidence, combined with the uniformly discolored appearance of age in all the bones and some human characters in the otherwise apelike jaw, soon convinced all but a few disbelievers that "Piltdown Man" represented a significant new discovery that altered conceptions about the course of human evolution. The skeptics held out, however, and finally prevailed. In 1950 Kenneth Oakley tested the bones for fluorine content and later for nitrogen; he found that the jaw was much younger than the cranium (Table 6.2). Uranium tests reinforced these findings. Further examination showed that the "human" aspects of the jaw were due to deliberate alteration of a modern ape jaw.

TABLE 6.2

Fluorine, Nitrogen, and Uranium Content of Piltdown and Related Bones

REMAINS	PERCENTAGE OF FLUORINE	PERCENTAGE OF NITROGEN	URANIUM PARTS PER MILLION
Fresh bone	0.03	4.0	0
Piltdown fossil elephant molar	2.7	—	610
Piltdown cranium	0.1	1.4	1
Piltdown jaw	0.03	3.9	0

SOURCE: *After Oakley 1970, Table B, p. 41.*

RADIOMETRIC METHODS

Several dating techniques exploit the principle of radioactive decay—transformation of unstable radioactive isotopes into stable elements. These methods are all termed *radiometric techniques*. Although they can sometimes be used to date archaeological materials directly, they more frequently provide indirect age determinations. The radiometric technique most commonly used by archaeologists is *radiocarbon dating;* the following discussion will emphasize this particular technique. Most other radiometric techniques are applicable to extremely long time spans (Table 6.3), beyond the time range of human existence. They are used mainly by geologists to determine the age of geological formations.

The physical properties of radioactive decay can be used for dating purposes only if three facts are known: (1) the original amount of the radioactive isotope present at the onset of decay; (2) the amount now present; and (3) the rate of radioactive decay. In most cases the first factor must be computed indirectly. The amount of the radioactive isotope now present is "counted" directly, using different methods according to the isotope being measured. Since the decay of any unstable isotope is a random process, there is really (except for directly counted radiocarbon) no strictly determinable rate; it is possible, how-

TABLE 6.3

Half-Lives and Utility Ranges of Radioactive Isotopes

ISOTOPES	HALF-LIFE (IN YEARS)	LIMITS OF USEFULNESS FOR ARCHAEOLOGICAL DATING
$^{14}C \rightarrow {}^{14}N$ (Radiocarbon) (Cambridge half-life)	$5,730 \pm 40$	Normally 100,000 years and younger
$^{40}K \rightarrow {}^{40}Ar$ (Potassium–Argon)	$1,300,000,000 \pm 40,000,000$ $(.04 \times 10^9)$	100,000 years and older
$^{235}U \rightarrow {}^{207}Pb$ (Uranium-235–Lead)	ca. 700,000,000	Too slow to be of archaeological value
$^{238}U \rightarrow {}^{206}Pb$ (Uranium-238–Lead)	ca. 4,500,000,000	Too slow to be of archaeological value
$^{232}Th \rightarrow {}^{208}Pb$ (Thorium–Lead)	ca. 14,000,000,000	Too slow to be of archaeological value
$^{87}Rb \rightarrow {}^{87}Sr$ (Rubidium–Strontium)	ca. 50,000,000,000	Too slow to be of archaeological value

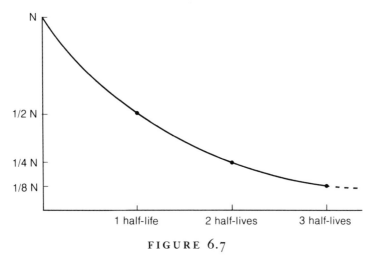

FIGURE 6.7

The decay rate of a radioactive isotope is expressed by its half-life, or the period after which half the radioactive isotopes will have decayed into more stable forms. After two half-lives, only one quarter of the original amount of radioactive isotopes will remain, and by the end of the third half-life, only one eighth ($\frac{1}{2} \times \frac{1}{2} \times \frac{1}{2}$) will remain radioactive.

ever, to calculate the statistical probability that a certain proportion of the isotope will disintegrate within a given time (Fig. 6.7). This disintegration rate is usually expressed as the *half-life* of the isotope: the period required for half the unstable atoms to disintegrate and form the stable daughter isotope. It is important to remember that the half-life of any radioactive isotope represents not a fixed rate but a statistical average with a specified range of error.

Radiocarbon

Radiocarbon dating is the most important radiometric technique for archaeologists. Carbon dioxide enters plants through photosynthesis, and the plants are in turn eaten by animals. Thus all living things constantly take in both ordinary carbon (^{12}C) and radioactive carbon (^{14}C). The proportion of ^{14}C to ^{12}C in an organism remains constant until its death. At that point, however, no further C is taken in, and the amount of radioactive carbon present at that time begins to decrease through radioactive decay. Thus measurement of the amount of ^{14}C still present (and emitting radiation) in plant and animal remains enables us to determine the time elapsed since death.

Any archaeological specimen of organic origin is potentially appropriate for direct radiocarbon dating. Charcoal from burned materials, such as is found in ancient hearths or fire pits, is most commonly used, but unburned organic materials such as bone collagen, wood, seeds, shells, leather, and so forth—sometimes even the carbon in worked iron—can also be dated. Most of the latter materials require larger sample amounts because they contain a smaller proportion of carbon.

In the original method developed in the late 1940s by Willard F. Libby, the amount of ^{14}C is detected by Geiger counters, which are used to measure the rate of decay emissions from the sample, usually for a period of 24 hours. A more recently developed procedure using a tandem accelerator allows the physicist to measure directly the amount of ^{14}C in a sample. Although equipment for the new technique is available in fewer laboratories, such direct measurement does offer a significant advantage because it can obtain dates from samples, such as seeds, that are too small for the traditional method.

Radiocarbon age determination has revolutionized archaeological dating. It provided the first means of relating dates and sequences on a worldwide basis because, unlike other methods available at the time, it did not rely on local conditions. The great wave of enthusiasm led, however, to uncritical acceptance and overconfidence in the precision of radiocarbon "dates." Although radiocarbon age determination is still the most popular method and among the most useful of all dating techniques available to the archaeologist, it does have a number of limitations.

The first limitation lies with the archaeologist. Any radiocarbon date is only as meaningful as the evaluation of the archaeological context from which it came. Charcoal from disturbed deposits—that is, from secondary contexts—will furnish dates, but these may have no bearing on the ages of associated materials. To use charcoal to date associated materials indirectly, the archaeologist must establish that all were deposited together.

The second limitation derives from the small amount of ^{14}C available for detection. The third is the built-in statistical uncertainty inherent in all radiometric techniques, since both the decay rate and the half-life are averages. Thus a radiocarbon age expressed as 3220 ± 50 years B.P. (before present, which for radiocarbon dating means before 1950) does not mean that the analyzed sample died 3220 years ago but that there is a 67 percent probability that the original organism died sometime in the 100-year span between 3170 and 3270 years before A.D. 1950. The probability that a reported range includes the right date can be improved to 97 percent by doubling the ± range—in this case from 50 to 100 years on either side of the central date.

A fourth limitation to the radiocarbon technique is the documented fluctuation of past levels of ^{14}C on earth. Measurements of radiocarbon dates for wood samples with ages determined by dendrochronology demonstrate these fluctuations. The result is that before about 1500 B.C. radiocarbon age determinations furnish dates that are increasingly out of line (Fig. 6.8). At 1500 B.C., radiocarbon age determinations are about 150 years too recent; by 4000 B.C. radiocarbon dates are about 700 years too young. The solution to this problem has emerged from the same source that exposed the error: dendrochronology. Extensive radiocarbon testing of known-age samples of wood has yielded a calibration formula that allows a date calculated in "radiocarbon years" to be corrected to a more

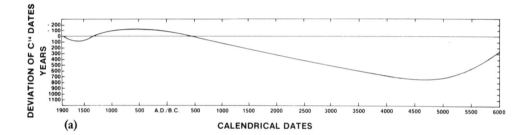

(a)

DEVIATION OF C¹⁴ DATES
YEARS

CALENDRICAL DATES

(b)

FIGURE 6.8

(a) A representation of the discrepancy between the ideal ¹⁴C chronological scale
(straight line) and a plotted series of samples, dated by radiocarbon analysis,
whose age was independently determined by dendrochronology. The discrepancy is due to past fluctuations in the amount of ¹⁴C on earth. (After Michael
1985). (b) The bristlecone pine, found in the White Mountains of California, is
the longest-living tree species known and is the key to increasing the accuracy of
age determinations using the radiocarbon method. (Photo by Henry N. Michael,
courtesy of the Museum Applied Science Center for Archaeology, University
Museum, University of Pennsylvania.)

accurate time value. The correction tables are limited by our ability to secure known-age samples of wood, but use of the oldest living tree, the bristlecone pine found in southeastern California, has enabled scientists to extend the correction range back more than 8000 years.

Recent revisions and refinements in radiocarbon dating have provided what Colin Renfrew has called the "second radiocarbon revolution." The first revolution was the development of this dating method, giving a uniform means to develop absolute chronologies applicable anywhere in the world. The second one has been the realization of the archaeological implications, particularly in the Old World, of the dendrochronological calibrations that have revised many of the most ancient radiocarbon determinations, making them older still.

Before radiocarbon dating was available, archaeologists used dating techniques based on stylistic and form comparisons to interrelate European and Near Eastern sequences. Whenever a question arose about the source of an invention or innovation, such as copper metallurgy or the construction of megalithic (monumental stone) tombs, the usual assumption was that it had come from the "civilized" Near East to "barbaric" Europe. The first sets of radiocarbon dates seemed to support the chronological links based on these assumptions. Now, however, calibrated radiocarbon dates indicate that many of the interrelated elements, such as megalithic architecture, which had been thought to be the result of Near Eastern influence, actually occurred earlier in Europe! The traditional belief in a Near Eastern monopoly on innovation and cultural advance has been tossed aside, and archaeologists are now seriously reexamining their interpretations of the long-distance communication in the Old World in the last few millennia B.C.

Potassium-Argon

Potassium-argon age determination is based on the radioactive decay of a rare isotope of potassium (^{40}K) to form argon (^{40}Ar) gas. The half-life of ^{40}K is 1.31 billion years, but the method can be used to date materials as recent as 100,000 years old. The technique is used principally to determine ages for geological formations that contain potassium. The basic principles of radiometric age determination, already described for the radiocarbon method, are used with a rock sample to measure the ratio of ^{40}K to ^{40}Ar. A recent refinement of the potassium-argon technique allows several age determinations to be made from each sample, thus increasing the reliability of the date.

The potassium-argon technique has been particularly helpful in dating geological formations associated with the remains of fossil hominids (human ancestors) and Lower Paleolithic tools. When Louis and Mary Leakey found the remains of *Zinjanthropus*, an early hominid (now included in the genus *Australopithecus*), they were able to assign the bones an age of about 1.75 million years on the basis of potassium-argon dating of the volcanic strata in which the remains were found. More recently potassium-argon dates have been determined for formations associated with early hominid finds in the Lake Turkana/

Omo Valley area on the border between Kenya and Ethiopia, extending the chronology of hominid existence back more than two million years.

ARCHAEOMAGNETISM

Dating by *archaeomagnetism* relies on the fact that the earth's magnetic field varies through time, shifting in the horizontal plane (expressed as declination angle) as well as vertically (expressed by dip angle). The course of these shifts over the past few hundred years has been determined from compass readings preserved in historical records. Certain mineral compounds, such as clay, contain iron particles that may align to magnetic north just as a compass does. This occurs most readily when clay is heated above its curie point: the temperature at which the particles lose their magnetic orientation. When the minerals cool again, the new magnetic alignment of the iron particles is "frozen" in the clay body. Thus if a sample of baked clay is not disturbed, it will preserve the angles of dip and declination from the time when it was heated. By using known-age samples of fired

(a)   (b)

FIGURE 6.9

Age determinations based on archaeomagnetism: (a) Careful collection and recording in the field are essential. One sample has been removed and preserved in the small square container to the left (above the leveling device); another is about to be removed (behind the compass). (b) The specialist measures and analyzes magnetic alignments in the laboratory later by replicating the original orientation of the sample. (Photo (a) Santa Bárbara Project, Honduras; photo (b) M. Leon Lopez and Helga Teiwes, © 1967 National Geographic Society.)

clay, such as hearths dated by radiocarbon associations, archaeologists have traced the location of the magnetic pole into the past. When enough cross-dated archaeomagnetic samples have been analyzed, the variations in dip and declination can be matched to a time scale, thus allowing newly discovered fired clay samples to be dated directly, using the archaeomagnetic data alone (Fig. 6.9).

There are numerous dating methods beyond those we have discussed, and new techniques are being developed all the time. But most of these are less frequently used or more limited in their application than the ones considered here. Nonetheless some of these additional methods are well established and accurate, such as calendrical dating (using deciphered ancient calendars), varve analysis (using strata deposited annually in lakes by retreating glaciers), and other radiometric techniques (fission track and uranium dating). Others remain more experimental, such as thermoluminescence (used to date ceramics) and aspartic acid racemization (used to date bone).

SUMMARY

Control over the dimension of time is crucial; reconstruction of the past depends on the ability to distinguish contemporaneous and sequential events. Various techniques are used to determine the age of recovered data, either directly (by dating the artifact, ecofact, or feature itself), or indirectly (by association with other remains that can be dated). Absolute dating refers to age in calendrical years or years before present (B.P.). Relative dating refers to age in relation to another date (older, younger, or the same age).

Archaeologists have long used relative dating techniques based on provenience, such as stratigraphy, or based on the characteristics of the remains, such as stylistic or frequency seriation. Geological associations may also provide dates for archaeological evidence, as in the use of geochronological sequences. Obsidian hydration yields direct and absolute dates for obsidian artifacts. Floral and faunal remains can be dated by several means, including absolute age from tree growth ring sequences (dendrochronology) and relative age from detection of chemical changes in bones. Radiometric methods are based on radioactive decay of unstable isotopes, the most useful being radiocarbon dating, since it relies on an isotope of carbon (^{14}C) present in all living tissue. Potassium-argon dating determines the age of geological deposits and can provide indirect dates for associated archaeological remains. Traces of ancient magnetism, preserved in features such as hearths, can be dated by correlation to known-age magnetic sequences (archaeomagnetism).

The varied methods of age determination now available can lead to accurate control of the time dimension for archaeological data, provided the archaeologist is aware of each method's limits and whenever possible cross-checks the sequence with two or more methods to produce an internally consistent chronological order.

· 7 ·

Reconstructing the Past

Now that we have described how archaeologists control the time dimension of their data, we will describe the ways these data are used to reconstruct the past. Just as analysis means breaking down the data into essential elements and their relationships, reconstruction means putting these elements back together to form a meaningful whole.

Of course there is no definite line between analysis and reconstruction. As we noted in discussing research design in Chapter 3, the collection and analysis of archaeological data often overlap in time, and the archaeologist is always looking for new ways to answer the questions formulated as research progresses. Even in examining the tiniest bit of evidence—such as a decorative motif on a painted sherd—the archaeologist works with an eye to how this might bear on the larger questions the investigation is attempting to answer. This chapter will consider how the archaeologist uses analogy and the spatial patterning of data to reconstruct the past.

ANALOGY

There is a basic paradox in archaeology: The archaeological record exists in the present, while the archaeologist is interested in the past—specifically the past conditions and human behaviors that created that record. Since events in the prehistoric past cannot be observed directly, the archaeologist's behavioral reconstructions are based on *analogy*—a form of reasoning whereby the identity of

137

FIGURE 7.1

Manufacture of chipped stone tools in
Ethiopia. Lithic technology survives
today in several parts of the world,
providing analogs for understanding
similar technologies in the past. (Photo
by James P. Gallagher.)

unknown items or relations may be inferred from those that are known. Everyone uses this kind of reasoning, but its application in archaeology merits a more
detailed consideration at this point. Reasoning by analogy is founded on the
premise that if two classes of phenomena are alike in one respect, they may be
alike in other respects as well. In archaeology analogy is used to infer the identity of and relationships among archaeological data by comparing similar phenomena documented in living human societies.

On the most basic level, it is analogy that allows the archaeologist to identify
the remains of past human behavior as archaeological data at all. For example, the
archaeologist does not observe the ancient human activity that produced chipped
stone implements. But hunters and gatherers in several remote parts of the
world have continued to make and use similar chipped stone tools into this century. This behavior has been recorded by ethnographers and other observers.
Because of the similarity in form between the artifacts and the ethnographically
observed examples, analogy has identified many of the ancient tools and, by ex-
tension, has allowed reconstruction of relevant manufacturing and use behavior
associated with them (Fig. 7.1).

This is not to say that analogy underlies all archaeological reconstruction.
Historical archaeology often relies on documentary sources to identify archaeological remains. In protohistorical situations, later historical information is sometimes projected back in time to assist archaeological reconstructions. But in
clear-cut prehistoric situations, without direct links to historical information,
the archaeologist must rely on inferences using analogy.

In many cases the archaeologist's use of analogy to identify a familiar artifact or feature such as a building foundation or a burial is not a conscious process. An automatic association takes places from everyday experience relating, for instance, masonry foundations that support modern buildings to an archaeological feature that looks similar. But often the archaeologist encounters features or artifacts that are not familiar; in such cases identification by analogy becomes most clearly a conscious, rational process.

A good example of detailed analogical reasoning is Lewis Binford's study of a certain category of pits encountered in sites of the middle and lower Mississippi valley and adjacent areas after A.D. 1000. The pits in question are always fairly small, averaging about 30 cm or less in length and width and slightly more than that in depth. They contain charred and carbonized twigs, bark, and corncobs, and are found around houses and domestic storage areas, never near public buildings. The one sure interpretation concerning these pits was that the charred contents had been burned in place, in an oxygen-starved atmosphere that must have produced a lot of smoke. So the pits were labeled "smudge pits." Further interpretations offered for these features, however, ranged from "corncob offerings" to facilities for creating smoke to drive away mosquitoes!

In seeking a firmer interpretive base from which to establish the nature of these smudge pits, Binford went through the ethnographic literature on modern Native American groups in that area. These accounts included descriptions of hide-smoking procedures in which an untanned deerskin was tied as a cover over a small hole. A smoldering, smoky fire was then set in the hole and allowed to burn until the hide was dry, tough, and ready to be sewn into clothing. Binford pointed out that whenever the ethnographic accounts offered details on the form and contents of the hide-smoking pits, these details corresponded well with equivalent attributes of the archaeological smudge pits. Because there was a high degree of correspondence in form between ethnographic and archaeological examples, because the geographical areas involved were the same, and because a good case could be argued for the continuity of practices in that area from the archaeological past (after A.D. 1000) to the time of ethnographic observations (1700–1950), Binford argued, by analogy, that the archaeological smudge pits represented facilities for smoking animal skins.

More precisely Binford offered the analogical interpretation as a hypothesis to be tested. If this identification were correct, other ethnographically described aspects of hide-smoking activities should also be found associated with the archaeological smudge pits. For example, since the ethnographic accounts describe tanning activities as occurring between, rather than during, peak hunting seasons, the sites with these kinds of smudge pits should be spring-summer camps, not hunting camps. The more correspondences there are between the ethnographic and the archaeological data, and the more strictly the specific attributes identified refer to a particular kind of feature—in this case, hide-smoking pits rather than any other kind of smudge pits—the stronger the analogical interpretation.

	Stage		Examples of associated technological innovations
	Civilization		Alphabet and writing
BARBARISM		Upper	Iron tools
		Middle	Plant and animal domestication
		Lower	Pottery
SAVAGERY		Upper	Bow and arrow
		Middle	Fishing and fire
		Lower	Fruit and nut subsistence

Direction of unilineal evolution ↑

FIGURE 7.2

Lewis Henry Morgan's unilinear stages were used to equate past and present societies on a scale of evolutionary progress.

Abuse of Analogy

Before examining in more detail the kinds of analogy that exist and the ways they should be used, we should first understand some of the errors that have resulted from improper use.

In the 19th century, when anthropology was dominated by the theory of unilinear cultural evolution (as we saw in Chapter 2), living "primitive" societies were often equated directly with various postulated stages of the proposed evolutionary sequence (Fig. 7.2). These stages were defined largely by technological attributes (Stone Age, Iron Age, and so on), and each stage had its own corresponding developmental level of social system, political organization, and religious beliefs. By means of these combined technological, social, and ideological attributes, living societies could be ranked with respect to their progress along the evolutionary scale.

It should be obvious that this kind of analogy is suspect, since it is dominated by only one criterion—technology—and ignores other variables such as time and space. In linking the Australian Aborigines with the European Paleolithic, for instance, the analogy disregards a temporal separation of more than 10,000 years and a spatial separation of over 10,000 miles. In a 1966 conference, 75 scholars spent four days discussing and debating the nature of cultures and societies that shared a single stated trait—hunting and gathering as a means of subsistence. The published report of that conference, a volume called *Man the Hunter*, makes it clear that although some regularities of social structure and cultural organization can certainly be recognized, one cannot use the single trait of "hunting" to predict the forms the rest of the culture will take. Yet this is essentially what the 19th-century unilinear evolutionists attempted to do.

Because of such simplistic reliance on limited criteria—usually technological—the wide-ranging analogies associated with the 19th-century unilinear cultural evolutionists are generally not accepted today. However, simplistic analogies are not confined to the literature of the previous century. Similar careless equations between living cultures and those of the past may be found in some archaeological publications of the 20th century. And the general analogy between the hunters of the European Paleolithic and certain contemporary peoples still occurs; for instance, popular accounts of the discovery of the Tasaday of the Philippines, in the 1970s, described this isolated society as a "Stone Age tribe."

The obvious abuses of analogy in reconstructing the past have led to reactions, both by cultural anthropologists and by archaeologists, against the use of this method of reasoning. Much of the criticism of analogy has been concerned specifically with the use of ethnographic studies as analogs for archaeological interpretation. However, as we shall see below, the use of analogy in archaeology involves a wider range of analog sources, including historical accounts and modern experimental techniques.

Specific and General Analogy

A useful distinction can be made between specific and general analogy. *Specific analogy* refers to specific comparisons within a given cultural tradition, while *general analogy* refers to generalized comparisons that can be documented across many cultural traditions.

Specific analogy has rich potential for detailed interpretation of archaeological remains. But to use this kind of analogy, the archaeologist must be prepared to defend its appropriateness on three grounds (all of which were controlled in Binford's interpretation of the Mississippi valley smudge pits):

1. Cultural continuity. In the southwestern United States, for instance, there is considerable evidence that the contemporary Native American societies documented by ethnographic and historical accounts are the direct descendents, both culturally and biologically, of local prehistoric occupants (Fig. 7.3). This link allows the archaeologist to draw frequent and reasonable analogies on the basis of living societies in order to interpret Southwestern prehistory.

2. Comparability in environment. This is the premise that an analog drawn from a society living in an environment different from that of the prehistoric society will be less reliable than one based on a society in a similar environment.

3. Similarity of cultural form. This involves several considerations, including relative cultural complexity and the degree to which traditional behavior is maintained by the analog society. For example, in Southeast Asia, conservative highland tribal groups prove more likely analogs for local prehistoric reconstructions than do their urbanized neighbors in Bangkok.

Not all archaeological situations can be interpreted by specific analogies, however. Difficulties in using living societies of hunters and gatherers as detailed analogs for Paleolithic groups have already been cited. Rather than throwing up

(a)

(b)

FIGURE 7.3

Cultural continuity, in the southwestern United States, for example, is an important criterion for using ethnographic studies as specific analogs for understanding ancient societies. The photographs above were taken around the turn of the century and show (a) an overall view of Oraibi Pueblo, Arizona, and (b) a room with equipment for preparing meals. Compare (b) with the mealing bin in Fig. 5.14. (Courtesy, Field Museum of Natural History, Chicago.)

their hands in dismay, however, archaeologists have responded in recent years by developing general—that is, more widely applicable—analogies, each usually involving a narrow range of activities. Much of this has been accomplished through *actualistic studies*, where "actual" behavior can be tied to diagnostic material remains, regardless of the cultural setting. These studies range from observing modern trash disposal patterns to examining how humans differ from other hunters in consuming their prey. In all cases the keys are rigorous specification both of the material traces of behavior and of the range of conditions under which certain kinds of behavior would be expected—and therefore might turn up in archaeological contexts.

Sources of Analogs

The analogs used in archaeological interpretation come from various sources: historical accounts and documents that describe societies in the past, ethnographic studies that describe present societies, and actualistic studies that attempt to duplicate conditions that existed in the past.

Historic sources include the full range of past records, including studies written by professional historians, and descriptions made by other observers such as travelers, merchants, soldiers, or missionaries. In the New World much of our understanding of the pre-Columbian cultures of Mesoamerica and the Andes rests on documents from the Spanish Conquest in the 16th century (Fig. 7.4).

Ethnographic studies of living human societies are probably the most common source of archaeological analogs. Written by professional anthropologists, ethnographies are generally more focused and useful to the archaeologist than other sources. However, professional ethnography is less than a century old, and most has been conducted among people influenced to some degree by European customs for far longer than that. Moreover, since ethnographers pursue their studies for their own theoretical interests, the data are often not presented in ways that relate behavior to material remains—that is, in ways that facilitate archaeological analogy. As we said earlier, actualistic studies are undertaken to resolve precisely this dilemma, either through ethnoarchaeology or experimental archaeology.

Ethnoarchaeology refers to ethnographic research done by archaeologists. That is, archaeologists are increasingly taking such research into their own hands, so that the information emphasized in recording will be useful to understanding the past as well as the present. Many human ecological studies fall, at least in part, within this category. For example, studies of the !Kung San of Namibia and Botswana have been oriented toward understanding the interrelationships among population size, social structure, subsistence methods, and environment. Other ethnoarchaeological research is more specific, such as Robert Wauchope's study of the construction and use of modern Maya houses. A recent trend in these studies has directed attention to material diagnostics of behavior

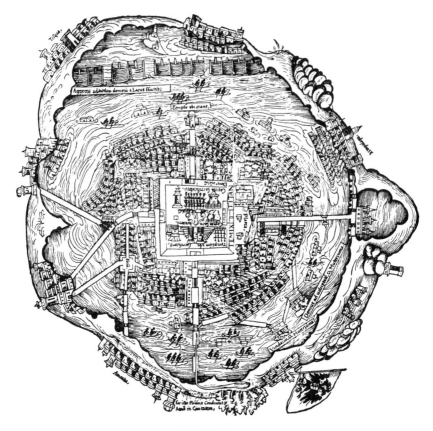

FIGURE 7.4

This 16th-century map of the Aztec capital of Tenochtitlán, Mexico, is illustra-
tive of Spanish records that are used to complement the archaeological record of
pre-Columbian societies. Although, in this case, spatial relationships are shown
differently from those of modern maps, the document provides valuable information, such as means of access (causeways and canoes) to the city and planning of
its central plaza. (By permission of the British Library.)

more likely to be otherwise invisible in the archaeological record, such as ideology or ethnicity.

Experimental archaeology is another aspect of actualistic studies done by archaeologists. Although experiments have a long history in archaeology, only
recently have they begun to be used as a fundamental source for past reconstructions. Early examples often involved using actual archaeological materials or
replicas, such as cutting tools and musical instruments, in an attempt to discover
their ancient functions. Similar experiments continue, but in many cases experimental archaeology has been reoriented to provide analogs for a broader range of

FIGURE 7.5

The Colonial Pennsylvania Plantation is an example of experimental archaeology where past conditions and behavior are recreated to understand more fully what life was like in the past. (Courtesy of the Colonial Pennsylvania Plantation, Edgmont, Pa.)

behavior—acquisition, manufacture, use, and disposal—associated with archaeological materials.

Experimental work with stone artifacts is particularly well known. Don Crabtree and François Bordes were leaders in reconstructing the techniques used to manufacture ancient stone tools by experimental stone chipping to duplicate the archaeologically recovered forms. S. A. Semenov and Lawrence Keeley pioneered in studying the wear patterns produced on stone tools by various kinds of use (slicing, chopping, and so on).

The most elaborate experimental studies—and the least often manageable—involve reconstruction and maintenance of a community under ancient conditions. Archaeologists dealing with recent, historically documented periods are in a better position to do experiments of this kind. Plimouth Plantation in Massachusetts and Colonial Pennsylvania Plantation in eastern Pennsylvania are examples of "reconstituted" colonial American communities (Fig. 7.5). In these projects, crops have been raised, food cooked, buildings heated, and tools produced, all according to colonial customs. The experience provided by these cases is comparable to that of archaeological ethnography, for the archaeologist has the opportunity to observe and record the behavior associated with the material "remains."

An important category of experimental archaeology involves study of what happens to archaeological materials after disposal. These experiments consider the taphonomic and other transformational processes discussed in Chapter 3. Although these processes do not always involve human behavior, they are relevant to the interpretation of human behavior. For example, Glynn Isaac and his colleagues have sought to outline details that will help in distinguishing whether stone tool scatters in riverbank locations are intact sites or just the cumulative effects of artifacts being washed downstream from their original deposition points. To accomplish this, they set out a series of systematically arranged artifact scatters in the valley of a stream feeding into Lake Magadi, Kenya; they then returned annually to chart changes in artifact positions in these experimental analogs.

SPATIAL ORDER AND BEHAVIOR

Spatial distributions and associations are often readily observable; plotting finds on plans and maps, for example, is an essential part of data collection. But until the artifacts, ecofacts, and features are described, analyzed, and sorted in time, archaeologists do not know which parts of the spatial picture are remains of related activities. Past behavior cannot be reconstructed until the archaeologist knows whether bits of evidence go together in time or are from different periods. The former give information about behavior and human interaction in one span of time, while the latter allow the archaeologist to look at continuity and change in behavior through time.

In the following discussion, we will adopt the threefold division of culture commonly used by archaeologists in reconstructing ancient behavior:

1. *Technology* is the means by which human societies interact most directly with the natural environment. It consists of the set of techniques and the body of information that provide ways to procure raw materials and convert them into tools, to obtain and process food, to construct or locate shelter, and so on. Because technology relates so closely to the natural environment, our discussion of technology will also examine the ways archaeologists reconstruct ancient environments.

2. *Social systems* assign roles and define relationships among people. Kinship organization, political structure, exchange networks, and the like are all facets of the way people organize themselves and their social interactions. We shall consider settlement patterns and evidence of exchange systems as examples of frameworks for reconstructing ancient social systems.

3. *Ideology* encompasses the belief and value systems of a society. Religious beliefs come most readily to mind as examples of ideological systems, but art styles, writing, and other records also provide information about the ways human groups have codified their outlook on existence.

The divisions among these three categories of human activity should not be taken as inflexible boundaries. For example, exchange systems move tools and raw materials, thus acting as part of the technological system, as well as reflecting and affecting social relations. The categories simply represent broad distinctions among general kinds of cultural behavior that relate people to the physical environment, people to one another, and people to ideas.

Technology

In Chapter 5, we presented specific information about the technologies involved in production and use of various kinds of artifacts. This information, focusing on the analysis of individual artifacts, enables the archaeologist to answer specific questions about how stone tools or pottery vessels were made. At this point we want to ask different questions. Most broadly we want to know what technologies were available to a given group for producing tools, facilities, and other manufactured products. In a specific research project, the question is usually phrased in more concrete terms, such as: Was metallurgy practiced by the occupants of this site (or region)? To answer such a question we must ask another: What is the evidence that indicates the presence of a given technology? An archaeologist usually forms a working hypothesis about the technologies the prehistoric people being studied were likely to have used and tests it against the recovered evidence.

Projectile points, for instance, are usually taken as evidence of hunting; discovery of these points in association with the bones of slaughtered animals, as in the Olsen-Chubbuck, Lindenmeier, or Folsom sites mentioned previously, clearly reveal the prehistoric subsistence technology. Other hunting technologies, however, leave little in the way of artifactual traces. Trapping equipment, for example, is seldom preserved; the technology in such a case is usually reconstructed by analogy with modern hunting techniques used in the same or a similar area.

One extremely valuable form of technological evidence is provided by remains of workshops. These are particular, activity-specific clusters of artifacts, sometimes including specially constructed features, such as kilns, that preserve a variety of details about manufacturing processes. There are as many kinds of workshop features as there are different manufacturing technologies, and how formalized the area is depends on how specifically isolated the activity was. For example, flint knapping might have been carried out at various locations over time, so that a number of casual chipping stations might be found in a given area of occupation. Activities that require specialized facilities, however, such as iron metallurgy with its need for intense and controlled heat, are more likely to have easily identifiable areas set aside as workshops. In a workshop, one would expect to find some or all of a variety of manufacturing remains, including raw materials, partially finished artifacts, mistakes (such as pottery vessels that cracked during firing), debris (such as stone fragments), and of course any special tools or facilities needed for production.

Technology mediates human interaction with the environment in many ways. People build shelters and make clothing to protect themselves from heat, cold, rain, wind, and snow. They make baskets to help in plant collecting, fashion spears and arrows to kill food animals, and dig irrigation ditches to provide water for crops. The precise techniques and equipment used for a given task in a given time and place depend on past accumulation of technological knowledge. But they also depend on the nature of the environment and the raw materials it supplies. The Inca, for example, built roads to unite their far-flung empire. They often needed bridges to link road segments, and when the rivers and other gaps were narrow, the bridges were made of stone and timber. Where gaps were wider than those materials could span, however, they used other resources (plant fibers) and existing technology. The results were suspension bridges of stout rope, bridges so strong the Spanish could later cross them on horseback.

Environment does not determine culture, but it provides a flexible framework within which a culture operates. Similarly culture does not determine environment, but cultural values and technological capacity may define the extent to which available resources are exploited. These principles are at the heart of one of the current theoretical frameworks in anthropology, cultural ecology.

Cultural ecology includes interaction with a social environment—neighboring human groups—as well as the natural environment. Furthermore the relations between technology and environment are themselves complex and interactive. For example, an innovation in technology may redefine the nature of the exploitable environment: Irrigation ditches have made gardens in the desert. The ecological questions asked by archaeologists center on which aspects of the range of environmental resources a prehistoric society exploited and which available resources it used. To answer these questions, archaeologists must reconstruct not only the nature of the techniques and equipment used by the past society but also the nature of the environment that could be exploited. In terms of research the most common meeting ground for these approaches is the study of subsistence technology: What resources were available for food? What did the society choose to eat and how did it obtain these resources?

How can the archaeologist discover what the ancient natural environment itself was like? Archaeologists seek two kinds of data in order to reconstruct ancient physical environments. The first is observation of the modern landscape, including topography and the range of biotic and mineral resources. The second is collection of ecofactual data, either from archaeological deposits or from other deposits within the zone under study. Such data give the archaeologist evidence about whether, and how, the available resources in the area may have been different in ancient times. We have seen an example of this with the Star Carr study described in Chapter 5. And pollen studies have proven especially useful as sensitive indices of paleoenvironments. Combining these kinds of approaches, archaeologists attempt, usually in consultation with other specialists, to reconstruct the nature of the ancient environment in which the past society lived.

Examples of studies using both ecofactual collection and modern observational approaches are easy to find. For instance, in the Tehuacán Archaeological-

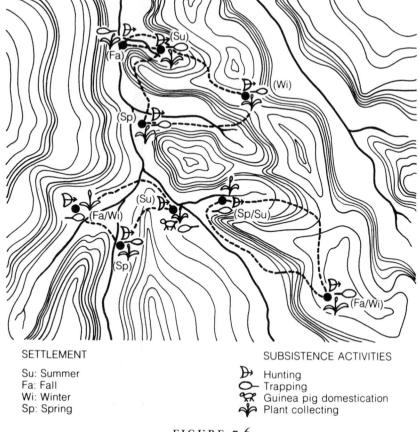

SETTLEMENT

Su: Summer
Fa: Fall
Wi: Winter
Sp: Spring

SUBSISTENCE ACTIVITIES

Hunting
Trapping
Guinea pig domestication
Plant collecting

FIGURE 7.6

Synthesis of archaeological data from the Ayacucho Valley of Peru has led to postulation that ancient populations moved seasonally among sites to exploit different subsistence resources. (After MacNeish, Patterson, and Browman 1975.)

Botanical Project, the resource area recorded was the same as that in which archaeological remains were recorded. The overall goal of the project was to trace the development of agriculture in the New World. The Tehuacán Valley, in the Mexican state of Puebla, was chosen as the research location partly because it contained a number of dry caves that seemed to promise the climatic conditions under which maize (corn) and other domesticated plants would be preserved. At the same time, however, Richard MacNeish and his colleagues needed to determine the range of food resources available to the ancient residents of the Tehuacán Valley, in order to outline the conditions under which they increasingly chose food production over food collection as their subsistence base. To get this information, the investigators divided the Tehuacán Valley into four microenvironmental types, each with its own set of seasonally or perennially available resources. Combining this information with analysis of ecofactual materials recovered from the various archaeological sites, MacNeish and his coworkers were able to reconstruct the subsistence-related migrations of ancient human populations within the valley, postulating their movements in search of shifting food resources as the seasons passed. In a later project, MacNeish and his colleagues conducted a similar study in the Ayacucho Basin of Peru (Fig. 7.6).

Social Systems

All societies distinguish among their members by various assigned roles and statuses. The most fundamental distinctions are those based on age and sex differences, but most human groups organize social interaction along a number of other lines as well. Kinship studies, a well-known part of anthropological research, have revealed the great variety of ways people have developed for naming relatives, reckoning descent, governing what family members one lives with, and so on. The principles of social organization extend beyond consideration of family organization, however, to include such other things as the ways power is channeled (political organization) and who controls production and distribution of wealth and other resources (economic organization).

As recorded by ethnographers and social anthropologists, much of the evidence of social structure is intangible, such as attitudes of respect or kinship terminologies. Especially in recent years, however, archaeologists have tried to recognize how aspects of material remains might be clues to past social organization. In this section we shall discuss two different approaches to reconstructing past social relationships and social structure: settlement archaeology and exchange systems.

Settlement archaeology is the study of the spatial distribution of ancient human activities and occupation, ranging from the differential location of activities within a single room to the arrangement of sites in a region. Because they are concerned with locational information, settlement studies use features and sites as their principal data bases. This does not mean that individual artifacts and ecofacts are not considered. However, since the focus is on understanding the distribution of ancient activities, the archaeologist doing settlement studies needs the locational information preserved by primary context, and features and sites retain such information intact.

Because they place sites and features in space, settlement studies clearly have much potential relevance for examining ancient exploitation of the environment. In the Tehuacán Valley, for example, MacNeish and his colleagues not only examined ecofactual evidence of specific food use but also looked at the distribution of occupational sites or base camps. The latter allowed them to reconstruct the seasonal cycle of shifting residence and food procurement. In this section, however, we shall focus on the ways settlement archaeology can elucidate past social systems.

The assumption underlying settlement archaeology is that the spatial patterning evident in the distributions of archaeological remains results from and reflects spatial patterning in ancient human behavior. Archaeologists tend to analyze spatial patterns on three levels: (1) activities within a single structure or on a single occupation surface, such as a cave floor; (2) arrangement of activities and features within a settlement or site; and (3) distribution of sites within a region. We shall consider some studies on each of these levels.

At the smallest level of human settlement, archaeologists reconstruct the spatial organization of activities within a single structure—a dwelling or some other kind of building—or within a comparably small unenclosed space. Such a study can consist of identifying areas in which various activities were carried out, such as distinguishing food preparation areas from other areas. What went on in the archaeological space is inferred by comparison of the archaeological remains with material remains of known activities. For example, hearths, fire-blackened jars, and grinding stones would indicate a cooking area. At this smallest level of settlement analysis, then, the archaeologist attempts to understand how the prehistoric society divided space into areas appropriate for particular activities.

At this "microsettlement" level of analysis, one of the most frequently studied features is the dwelling. A number of scholars have examined the potential determinants for house form. Bruce G. Trigger's list of such factors includes subsistence strategy (whether the society is sedentary or migratory), climate, available building materials, family structure, wealth, incorporation of special activities such as craft production, ideology, security, and style. Although a number of these factors are related to environmental variables, several have to do with the social system of the culture being studied. For example, societies in which people live in extended families (several generations of a family residing together) tend to have larger house structures than those in which nuclear families (parents plus children) are the usual household unit. In fact, study of households has been emphasized in recent archaeological research because these are fundamental organizational units of society.

The next level of settlement analysis is settlement layout. Here, the site is the unit of analysis, especially sites that are considered to be residential communities (as opposed to kill sites, for example). At this level, archaeologists consider how individual microunits fit together to form the larger whole; this allows them to examine aspects of prehistoric social systems from a number of perspectives.

Social stratification, for example, is frequently inferred partly on the basis of evidence from settlement analysis. At the Maya site of Tikal, Guatemala, archaeologists have found that houses are consistent in form throughout the site but range considerably in size, decoration, and the relative use of perishable versus stone construction materials. Larger, more substantial houses are assumed to have housed people who had more wealth or other means of controlling and acquiring goods and labor.

Aspects of social control can also be inferred from the regularity of settlement layouts. The site of Teotihuacán, Mexico, with its gridded streets and its orientation to the cardinal directions (see Fig. 4.12) is a striking example of im-

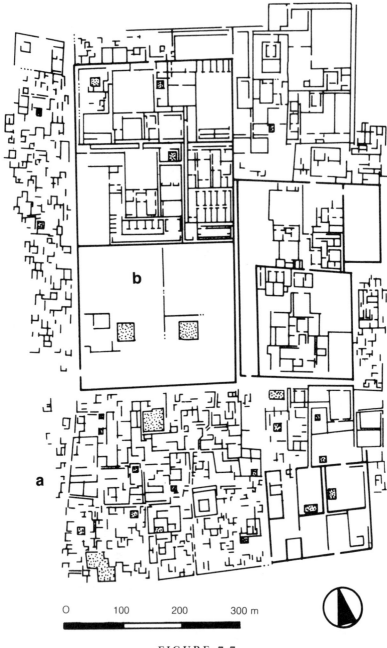

FIGURE 7.7

This portion of the map of Chan Chan, Peru, shows remains of (a) commoner residential areas contrasting with (b) one of the ten royal walled enclosures with restricted access from the outside. (After Moseley and Mackey 1974.)

posed planning. This implies the presence of a powerful elite able to command and direct the placement of structures and facilities over this broad expanse of land. Ancient Chinese political centers were also laid out according to a plan, the basis of which was partly religious but whose execution required effective social control.

Concerns with privacy or security can also be detected. For instance, the complex urban center of Chan Chan, in the Moche Valley of Peru, can be divided into three component parts: houses of the poor, intermediate buildings, and monumental structures. The three categories reflect differences in both complexity and regularity of arrangement; the "monumental structures" are the most complex and regular of all. These comprise a set of ten enclosures (Fig. 7.7) that have been interpreted as royal residential compounds. Given this interpretation, the relations between the ruling groups and commoners at Chan Chan can be partially examined by looking at how the residences relate, or were allowed to relate, in space. The poorer areas were clearly segregated even from the areas of intermediate wealth, but the monumental compounds were the grandest and most exclusive of all. Although they encompassed great amounts of space, each had only one or two entrances, allowing its occupants to control strictly with whom they would interact.

At the broadest level of settlement analysis, archaeologists consider the distribution of sites within a region. This can be approached in two ways. One is to reconstruct the function of each component in the settlement system and then look at the various ways in which they may have been organized into an interacting social network. The same settlement pattern can reflect a number of different systems of social relationships (Fig. 7.8). MacNeish's Tehuacán subsistence cycle is one example of a particular view of settlement systems. A different example is provided by analysis of Paleolithic sites, in France and elsewhere, having a Mousterian stone tool assemblage. These sites have been categorized in a number of Mousterian "types." François Bordes, a leader in delineating variation in Mousterian artifacts, argued that the different sites reflect occupation of adjacent locales by contrasting social groups who used different styles of tool manufacture. Lewis and Sally Binford, however, used statistical analysis of some of the tool assemblages to support their contention that the variability represents, not "ethnic" differences, but simply contrasts in tasks being carried out. The Binfords' analyses led them to propose that some of the occupations represent residential "base camps," while others represent hunting-butchering or other work camps. The contrast in the kinds of social interaction implied by the two interpretations is clear. In one view the Mousterian occupations represent distinct human social groups doing similar things; in the other, a single overall group was simply dividing up activities according to appropriate locales. Again the nature of individual parts of the settlement system must be examined in order to reconstruct the social system involved.

Economic geographers have developed a set of approaches that have proven useful to archaeologists; together these approaches are termed *regional analysis*. Many of the actual techniques are called, more specifically, *locational analysis*,

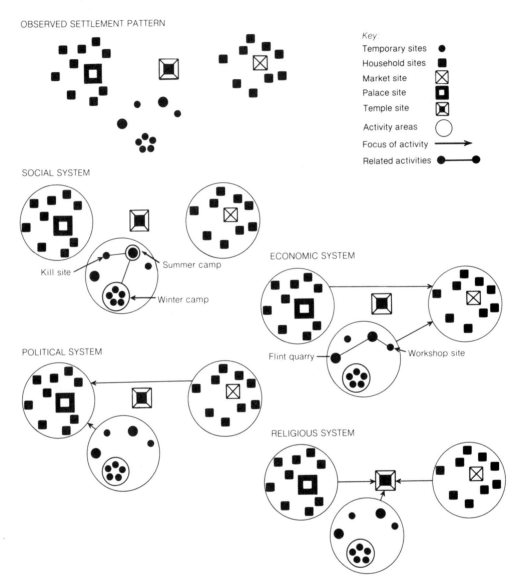

FIGURE 7.8

A single settlement pattern may be the physical expression of a number of systems of social relations, each of which can be studied at several scales. For example, within the region, some households may live permanently in one place while others move seasonally from one place to another. Although the diverse people of the region may all be governed from a single political capital, it need not be located in the same place as the economic hub or the ritual center. (Redrawn from K. C. Chang, *Settlement Patterns in Archaeology*. © 1972 by The Benjamin/Cummings Publishing Company, Philippines copyright 1972 by The Benjamin/Cummings Publishing Company.)

and a particularly important analytic model is one called *central place theory*. Underlying the latter—and other models derived from economic geography—is the assumption that efficiency and minimization of costs are among the most basic goals involved in spatial organization of human activities. For instance, an individual settlement will be located in a position where a maximum number of resources can be exploited with the least effort; these resources will include not only aspects of the natural environment but also communication with neighboring groups. As the landscape fills with people, settlements will tend to space themselves evenly across it, and central places—settlements providing a wider variety of goods and services than their neighbors—will arise at regular intervals within the overall distribution. The most efficient pattern for spacing of communities is a hexagonal lattice. This is all in theory, of course; in practice landscape variables such as steep topography or presence of uninhabitable areas—swamps and the like—break up the predicted pattern. Still, a reasonably close approximation of the hexagonal lattice pattern has been observed in a number of both modern and ancient situations, including Ian Hodder and Mark Hassall's study of Romano-British towns (Fig. 7.9).

A good example of analysis combining all the foregoing levels is David Clarke's study of an Iron Age settlement at Glastonbury, England. On the smallest level, many kinds of individual activity areas were discerned, where cumulative workshop features marked the locations of wool spinning, leather working, iron smelting, carpentry, weaving, milking, and animal husbandry. Seven residential compounds were also identified (Fig. 7.10), each with multiple separate houses. Individual dwellings were associated with distinct work and storage features; carpentry, metalworking, and small corral areas seem to define male subdivisions of the compounds, while baking, spinning, and granary areas suggest female working and living areas.

Study of the overall site layout gives an idea of the distribution of activities within the community, including social concerns about channelling traffic and protecting privacy. The settlement as a whole consisted of the seven residential compounds plus paths and intervening open spaces that connected them, an encircling palisade with guard houses at the entrances, and a small pier linking the east entry to the adjacent river. Distinctions among the seven Glastonbury compounds indicated wealth and status differences: The compound of the wealthiest residents was associated with a locally unique array of luxury and imported artifacts such as jewelry and fine pottery; the same compound (of House 1 on Fig. 7.10) apparently had long-standing importance, for it had provided the pivot around which the small community grew. Adjacent neighbors in Houses 2 and 3 also had sizable compounds but, unlike House 1, lacked both wealth and status goods and facilities for the production of metal and other commodities, thus indicating something of the social hierarchy present even within such a small community.

On a more inclusive scale, Clarke described a series of three larger regions defined beyond the site proper. The smallest of these regions was a territory of 10-mile radius around the site, embracing diverse economic resources such as pasture land, sources of potting clay or chipping stone, and fishing areas, as well

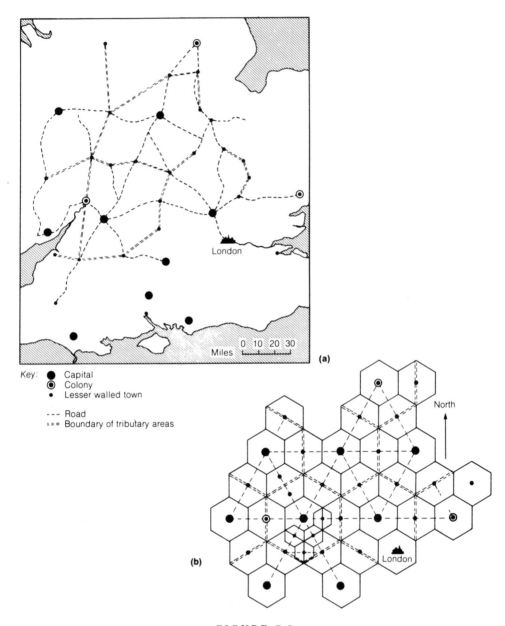

Key: ● Capital
       ◉ Colony
       • Lesser walled town

       --- Road
       ꞊꞊꞊ Boundary of tributary areas

FIGURE 7.9

Romano-British settlement in the third century A.D.: (a) plotted on a conventional map, and (b) fitted to an *idealized* hexagonal lattice demonstrating central place theory. (After Hodder and Hassall 1971, by permission of the Royal Anthropological Institute of Great Britain and Ireland.)

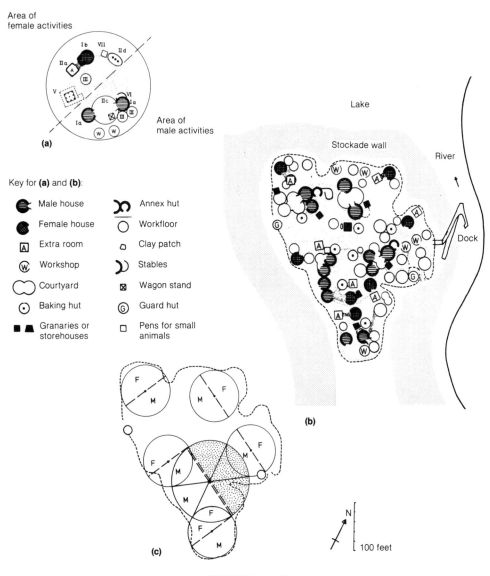

FIGURE 7.10

Iron Age Glastonbury illustrates several levels of settlement archaeology. (a) An idealized household compound shows the kinds of activity areas these contain. (b) The site of Glastonbury at the peak of its growth, showing the location of houses and other features. (c) A schematic version of (b) identifies individual house compounds, each with male-associated (M) and female-associated (F) areas. The large, partly shaded compound at the lower right contains both the wealthiest (1) and the poorest house units (2 and 3) in the ancient community. (After Clarke 1972.)

as neighboring settlements. The larger regions incorporated sites and resources up to 20 and 30 miles from Glastonbury, comprising areas with which its ancient residents were less constantly involved, but which still contributed social, political, and economic settings important to their lives. All in all, Clarke's was a well-integrated analysis of social (and other) influences on settlement features across the widest possible range of scales.

Exchange systems are established so that people can acquire goods and services not normally available to them locally. Trading ventures and institutions arise to facilitate cooperative and peaceful exchanges between two or more parties. Of course, there are other means of acquiring nonlocal goods and services. For example, foraging expeditions collect materials from distant sources, and raids or military conquest often plunder foreign lands for wealth and slaves.

The archaeologist may have difficulty in distinguishing trade goods from those acquired by other means, but the distinction is important for at least two reasons. First, the recognition of trade in the archaeological record leads to the reconstruction of past economic systems and thus contributes to a fuller understanding of the organization of entire ancient societies. Second, since cooperative exchange between individuals and between societies provides a primary means for the transmission of new ideas, recognition of trade helps lead the archaeologist to an understanding of culture change.

While human exchange systems involve transfer of goods, services, and ideas, archaeologists deal directly only with the tangible products of trade, usually recovered as artifacts and ecofacts. These data are traditionally divided into two classes. The first category, utilitarian items, refers to food items and tools for acquiring, storing, and processing food, as well as other materials such as weapons or clothing. The second category, nonutilitarian items, includes the remainder of exchanged commodities, including gifts and ritual and status goods.

By considering such distinctions, the archaeologist attempts to reconstruct both the inventory of trade goods and the mechanism of exchange, examining how much was traded as well as where it came from and where and to whom it went. Such reconstructions are based on the archaeologist's ability to separate trade goods from local goods in the archaeological record and to distinguish ancient acquisition, manufacture, and use behavior (Fig. 7.11).

These data allow the archaeologist to reconstruct ancient trade and its accompanying social interaction by examining spatial patterning from several perspectives, including simple presence or absence of certain trade items as well as quantitative patterns in their occurrence. Simple presence/absence plots show the distributions for one or more categories of traded artifacts and their identified raw material sources. Such maps may suggest quite readily the spatial range and even routes used in ancient trade systems (Fig. 7.12).

Ideological Systems

The final and most difficult area of archaeological reconstruction involves ideology. Ideological systems are the means by which human societies codify beliefs about both the natural and supernatural worlds. Through ideology people struc-

(a)

(b)

FIGURE 7.11

Some nonlocal artifacts can be distinguished as imports because of their style. These two seals are both about 4000 years old and are similar in style. Each depicts a humped bull with a brief inscription above its back. Seal (a), however, comes from the Indus site of Mohenjo-daro, in Pakistan, where this style of seal is common and where stylistically related artifacts are also found. Seal (b) was discovered at Nippur, in Mesopotamia, where it is stylistically unusual, leading to the inference that it was imported. (Photo (a) courtesy of George Dales; photo (b) courtesy of McGuire Gibson.)

ture their ideas about the order of the universe, their place in that universe, and their relationships with each other and with things and beings around them. Ancient ideologies are preserved through *symbols*, which are their material expression. The difficulty in reconstructing ideologies lies not in discovering symbolic representations but in recognizing them as such and assigning them an appropriate meaning. For example, artifacts classed as ceremonial appear to offer the kind of information needed to reconstruct ideologies; too often, however, the class is simply a catchall for forms whose utility is not immediately apparent.

Archaeologists have traditionally given scant attention to ideology for two reasons:

1. Since the foundation of archaeology is material remains, it has often been assumed that the realm of ideas lies beyond the reach of archaeological inquiry.

2. Archaeology studies the processes of culture change, and ideology, especially religious ideology, has usually been ignored, considered a conservative force that resists the trends of change.

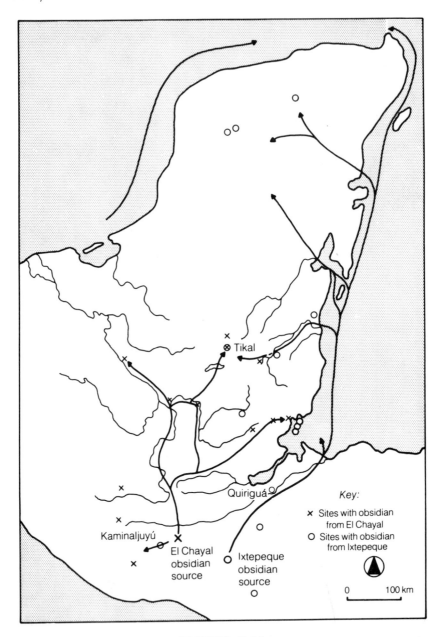

FIGURE 7.12

Obsidian from two known sources in highland Guatemala is distributed among lowland Maya sites in a pattern that suggests an overland route for exchange from the El Chayal source and canoe-oriented routes for transport from the Ixtepeque source. (After Norman Hammond, from *Science*, vol. 178, p. 1093. Copyright 1972 by the American Association for the Advancement of Science.)

FIGURE 7.13

A San rock art scene that was traditionally interpreted as people crossing a bridge but has been reinterpreted as a curing ritual, based on ethnographic information. (After Lewis-Williams, in *Current Anthropology*, published by the University of Chicago Press, © 1986 by the Wenner-Gren Foundation for Anthropological Research.)

The latter argument depicts ideologies as passive rather than causal forces in culture change. It is often assumed that ideology can be safely disregarded because it is both difficult to deal with and not important to the concerns of archaeology. While not denying the difficulty of inquiry into past ideologies, we believe it has become increasingly clear that the assumption that ideology is unimportant is false.

Fortunately archaeological interest in past ideological systems has expanded greatly in recent years. Today most archaeologists agree on the importance of research into this realm, for if ancient ideologies are ignored, our understanding of the past will remain woefully biased and incomplete.

Symbol systems may be preserved in the material remains that archaeologists deal with every day. But it is one thing to discover a symbolic representation and another to interpret its intended meaning. Even when an interpretation seems obvious, it may not be correct. As an example, consider the rock art of southern Africa. The paintings come from areas once occupied by San hunter-gatherers, but the San of today have no surviving tradition of painting. Non-San analysts frequently interpret the pictures as representing life among the ancestral San, and the scene in Figure 7.13 is usually said to show people crossing a rope bridge. J. D. Lewis-Williams argues, however, that if we can step outside our own culture for a moment, and look from the perspective of San customs, the scene can be reinterpreted (and probably more accurately deciphered) as a curing ceremony like those known among the San today. In this view, the individuals in the center have entered a trance. The lines above their heads represent their spirits leaving their bodies, while the dashed lines in front of one figure symbolize an active nosebleed (a frequent side effect of trance). Other features of the painting also fit the trance interpretation. Even the "bridge" (whose end spikes face the wrong way to support a bridge) probably represents two curers facing each other with outstretched arms, the exaggerated length and hairs of which correspond to sensations experienced in the trances. Whether these interpretations are completely correct in detail, they illustrate how easily misled we may be in interpreting archaeological symbols unless we consider them within their own cultural context. Interpretation is possible, but it must be done with caution.

One of the categories of archaeological data most frequently subject to symbolic interpretation involves burial practices and mortuary goods. Much attention has focused recently on funerary customs as indices of social organization: Chiefs are frequently buried in areas separate from paupers, while grave goods in individual interments are often a gauge of the kinds of possessions the deceased had in life. As described at the beginning of this book, Emperor Qin of China was buried with a full inventory of retainers, including an armed force— made of ceramics, to be sure, but life sized and complete down to horse trappings and weapons (see Fig. 1.1). These are symbols of his retinue in life, placed with his tomb to accompany him after death. They thereby signify not only aspects of the social order of the living but also beliefs about continuity of that order into the afterlife. Interestingly, Emperor Qin was apparently the first ruler in China to break with the tradition of sacrificing and burying actual human retainers; he appears instead to have chosen accompaniment by life-size clay figures as symbolic substitutes.

Writing systems provide the most regularized means of codifying symbols (Fig. 7.14). With writing archaeologists enter the realm of historical documentation, vastly increasing the wealth of their interpretive resources. Writing systems were developed by many ancient societies all over the world, and not all have been decipered. Only in recent years have Maya hieroglyphic inscriptions been read with any facility. The earliest writing in the Near East dates to at least 3500 B.C., and people were carving inscriptions in stone in Mesoamerica by the first millennium B.C. In both cases the earliest records archaeologists have unearthed pertain to counting—in the Near East, to accounting records for commercial transactions, and in Mesoamerica, to counts of time. Alexander Marshack has proposed that the earliest known notational records belong to a far earlier era. Marshack examined the scratches and marks on a series of Upper Paleolithic bone artifacts. These marks had been ignored by other scholars, but Marshack detected regularity in such characteristics as angle of nicking or spatial patterning of groups of marks. From this he argued that the marks represent the beginnings of notation—the precursors of writing.

FIGURE 7.14

The earliest known written records are in cuneiform (wedge-shaped) characters, on clay tablets that first appeared in southwest Asia in the fourth millennium B.C. (Courtesy of the University Museum, University of Pennsylvania.)

Marshack has further suggested that the subject of Upper Paleolithic notation was time, the passage of lunar months, seasons, or other observable time periods. This theme raises an area of archaeological inquiry that has seen a great deal of investigation in recent years: *archaeoastronomy*, the study of ancient astronomical knowledge from material remains. As noted in Chapter 5 many archaeological sites and features throughout the world have been identified as ancient astronomical observatories used to chart the cyclical movements of sun, moon, and other celestial bodies. One of the most fascinating of these is the so-called sun dagger of Fajada Butte, in Chaco Canyon, New Mexico (Fig. 7.15), where two artificially focused shafts of light play against spiral rock carvings. The longer shaft, or dagger, pierces the center of the larger spiral at midday on the summer solstice, filling it with light and warmth. The paired daggers skirt the edges of the same spiral at winter solstice, leaving it cold and empty of light. For these and other reasons, the feature as a whole has been interpreted as a solar tracking station. In this case, as in many others, however, the age and inferred purposes of the features remain hypothetical. In the case of Fajada Butte, it has been recently proposed on the basis of ethnographic and astronomical data that

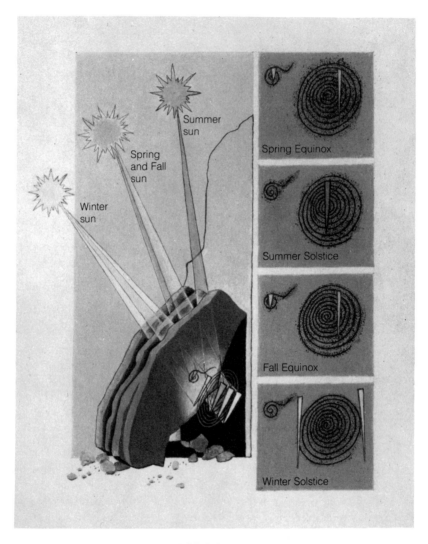

FIGURE 7.15

At Fajada Butte, Chaco Canyon, New Mexico, spaces separating three stone slabs allow two dagger-shaped sunlight patterns to strike spiral designs engraved on the face of the butte. The diagrams show the position of the "sun daggers" at the solstices (June 21 and December 21) and equinoxes (March 21 and September 21). (Christopher A. Klein, © 1982 National Geographic Society.)

this site functioned as a shrine dedicated to the sun, but not as a solar calendrical observatory.

But let us return to writing, which is obviously useful for more than counting. It has been used to describe and record all aspects of human existence. Some of its other early uses include accounts of the origins of the world and human society. The Bible and the Epic of Gilgamesh record ancient and venerated ideologies about the nature of creation. Both anthropologists and archaeologists have increasingly drawn on these and similar records for the wealth of descriptive data they contain, including many details of daily life, social and political relationships, and ideological information that otherwise would remain far beyond the reach of archaeology. As noted in Chapter 1, however, archaeology complements such texts in the kinds of data provided and balances the documentary bias toward affairs of only certain privileged social groups.

We have already mentioned the obvious difficulties in reconstructing ancient ideologies from material remains, which has helped support the assumption that these systems were unimportant in affecting the course of culture change. But this assumption has been successfully challenged by a series of studies combining archaeological and historical data that document the active role played by various ideological systems in the evolution of past societies. An excellent illustration is the rapid rise of the Mexica, or Aztec, nation of central Mexico in the 15th century, just prior to the Spanish Conquest.

Geoffrey Conrad and Arthur Demarest have argued that several interrelated changes in the traditional religious ideology were instrumental to the success of two pre-Columbian societies: the Aztecs of Mexico and the Inca of Andean South America. We will discuss the Aztecs and their expansion from a small tributary of several more powerful states to the dominant power in central Mexico. According to Conrad and Demarest the change of Aztec fortunes was sparked by a reworking of their ideological system in the early 15th century. The ideological reforms were initiated by a few individuals within the ruling elite of Aztec society and were directed toward creating a new and unified cult organized and controlled by the state. This cult combined economic, social, and religious systems and provided a strong motivation for military conquest. At its core the cult created a new view of the universe and of the destiny of the Aztec people. According to this revised view, the sun (the Aztec patron deity and source of all life) was engaged in a daily struggle against destruction by the forces of darkness. Only by constantly feeding the sun with the source of its strength, the lives of human warriors, could the Aztecs save the universe from extinction. To support this new ideology and demonstrate that they were the chosen saviors of the universe, the history of the Aztec people was rewritten and their myths explaining the cosmos were altered.

Since the essential food for the sun could only be secured by the taking of warrior captives and sacrificing them, Aztec society became perpetually mobilized for conquest. Of course the practical benefits from this military expansion included considerable wealth, for tribute was extracted from their vanquished enemies. But an essential motivation and key to the Aztecs' success as conquerors was ideological. Although both militarism and human sacrifice were practiced by all peoples of ancient Mexico, the Aztecs were unique in intensifying the scale of both to an unprecedented degree. Convinced that they were chosen to perpetuate the universe, Aztec warriors fought with a fanatic zeal, believing that they could not fail. In the face of this fanaticism many of the Aztecs' enemies lost their will to resist and succumbed in terror.

The Aztecs' conviction of their destiny was reinforced by their initial successes. But soon these very successes produced an internal crisis. The huge increases in wealth and power gained from conquest led to greater economic and social distinctions within Aztec society, and this led to internal resentment and conflict. Flaws in the new ideological system itself produced an even more insidious problem. The view of the universal struggle between sun and darkness assumed an infinite supply of enemy warriors, but the availability of this "nourishment for the sun" was soon threatened as the numbers of opponents diminished. In effect the Aztecs compensated for this by encouraging rebellions against their authority, since they did little to impose their control over conquered peoples. The uprisings this policy produced gave the Aztecs new opportunities to capture additional warriors for sacrifice. But the consequences of inevitable defeats on the battlefield were more damaging to Aztec society. As the demands for human life and tribute mounted, determination to resist the Aztec terror increased. Eventually the Aztecs confronted enemies that could not be conquered and enemies that inflicted devastating defeats on their armies. These events meant that the Aztec universe was threatened, since the sun was being weakened by fewer human sacrifices. Compounding this threat, each military disaster weakened the confidence and will of the entire society as military failures challenged the Aztecs' belief in their role as saviors of the universe. In sum, the ideology that led to a cycle of victories and confidence eventually yielded a cycle of defeats and demoralization.

Conrad and Demarest's interpretation illustrates how crucial ideology can be in the organization and motivation of human society. The Aztec ideological system guided and justified a military, economic, and political expansion that eventually dominated central Mexico. This development was due largely to a reformulated religious ideology created by a handful of leaders. This is not to say that ideology should be viewed as the only or even the prime cause of culture change. Economic and other factors played a role in both the rise and decline of the Aztecs. But history is full of similar examples of ideologies that have made significant contributions to the direction and development of society, including the rise and fall of nations. Archaeologists must heed the lesson of these examples. They cannot ignore the role of ideology if they wish to reconstruct the past as fully as possible.

SUMMARY

This chapter has examined the use of analogy and of the spatial order of archaeological data as avenues for reconstruction of past human behavior.

Because past activities can never be directly observed, similarities between these data and the material correlates of living societies (either observed directly or recorded in historical or ethnographic accounts) are the basis for reconstructing the past. Reasoning by analogy has not always been correctly applied in archaeology, but use of logical guidelines can reduce or eliminate inaccuracies. For specific analogy these guidelines are based on continuity of occupation, similarity of environmental setting, and comparability of cultural forms between the archaeological situation and the proposed analog. For general analogy actualistic studies define links between particular behaviors and their material traces. The more analog links that can be established—using sources such as history, ethnography, and actualistic studies done by archaeologists—the more secure the proposed reconstruction.

Analogy is paired with examination of spatial order in archaeological data to reconstruct the varieties of ancient behavior. Human activities can be divided into three broad areas: technology, social systems, and ideology.

Technology is the behavior most closely related to the environment and is best understood through the concept of cultural ecology. This relationship is complex, for each environment provides a range of resources, and each culture defines, through capabilities and choices, which of these resources are actually used. As a result understanding ancient technology requires study not only of cultural remains but also of the environment in which they were used.

Past social systems—the various kinds of human organizations that channel human behavior—are reconstructed in various ways. Settlement archaeology relies on the spatial distribution of archaeological remains as reflections of the full range of human behavior, from single activity areas, to households, to sites, and to entire regions. At this broader end of the scale, archaeologists study ancient exchange systems—the means used by all human societies to procure nonlocal goods and services. These studies rest on methods of determining which artifacts or ecofacts are nonlocal and thus may reflect exchanges with other places, such as stylistic and compositional analyses. Reconstruction of these organizations rests on analogies drawn from ethnography, economics, geography, and other sources.

Ideological systems, the means used by human societies to codify their knowledge and beliefs, are the most difficult to approach archaeologically, since this kind of behavior is often marked by relatively fewer (or more enigmatic) material remains. Identification and study of material symbols provide one approach. Although the archaeological record is full of such symbols, their proper interpretation is often difficult. Writing systems, when present, provide the most direct evidence of ideological systems for, if deciphered, they allow reading of messages. Other notational forms, such as counts of astronomical or other events, also provide clues to ancient belief systems. Since belief systems are central to guiding the course of human societies, archaeologists have increasingly come to appreciate that culture change cannot be comprehended without understanding the role played in this process by ideology.

· 8 ·

Understanding the Past

IN THIS CHAPTER WE complete the final step in archaeological research: finishing the reconstruction and interpretation of the past. We began this process in Chapters 6 and 7, where we considered how the archaeologist combines analyses of different data categories (artifacts, ecofacts, and features) across dimensions of time, space, and function to interpret those data. Those chapters involved interpretation in a descriptive sense, in attempts to answer questions about *what* happened in the past, *when* it happened, and *where* it happened. In this chapter we turn to a more explanatory aspect, to address the questions of *how* and *why* it happened.

To illustrate the differences, let us examine the cultures that successively occupied the Great Plains of the United States, each exploiting a different aspect of the region's varied resources. The *what* of our understanding of the sequence consists of the material and historical data pertaining to these cultures. The same sources describe *when* the cultures existed, and *where* within the Great Plains. But *how* did a new culture take the place of the old? And *why?*

Prehistoric occupants of the Plains were limited in their day-to-day mobility. The remains of stone weapons, campsites, bones of game animals, and plants tell us that those who hunted and gathered for their food exploited a wide variety of subsistence alternatives (hunting small game, occasionally hunting large game, gathering wild plant foods, and so on) in small localized groups. Some groups took up cultivation of maize (originally derived from Mexico) and other plants late in the first millennium A.D. In the 17th century some groups adopted a new technology—hunting on horseback, the horses having been introduced by the Spanish—and thereby gained enough mobility, speed, and

168

transport capability to specialize in the hunting of large game animals (bison). Their specialization made these same groups vulnerable to outside invaders (Euro-American colonists) with a different technology, including the repeating rifle, which was used to decimate the herds of bison and thereby destroyed the subsistence base of the mobile Plains societies. The new technology also included the plow, which allowed the invading settlers to harness a previously unexploited portion of the environment for extensive agriculture. What had been a land of hunters became a land of hunters and horticulturalists, then a land of plow farmers, and later a land of industrialized farmers. In the 20th century, of course, a still newer technology has led to the industrialized exploitation of yet another portion of this same environment: the vast deposits of fossil fuel located beneath the surface of the Plains.

It is easy to describe the what, when, and where of this simplified sequence of Great Plains cultures. But how and why did the changes take place? Some of the mechanisms of change—the "how"—are evident: adoption of ideas from other cultures, invasion, migration. Why the ideas took hold in the new culture and why the mass movement of people took place (either the peaceful forms or the warlike ones) are more difficult and controversial questions.

In this chapter we will discuss the principal models archaeologists have used to answer the questions of how and why things happened as they did. These models have been grouped in two categories, those of cultural history and those of cultural process. Archaeologists use these models to complete their investigations—to reconstruct, describe, and explain human behavior in the past.

CULTURAL HISTORICAL RECONSTRUCTION

Cultural historical reconstruction is based on an inductive research methodology and a normative view of culture. The normative view holds that a culture is a set of rules or *norms* that govern behavior in a particular society. These rules are passed from one generation to the next; each new generation learns the norms of behavior within the family (parent to child), schools (teacher to student), occupations (master to apprentice), peer groups, and similar situations. The transmission of rules is not perfect, so a degree of change in the normative system is inevitable. Some behavior, of course, is idiosyncratic—unique to the individual—and may not be perpetuated. In any given culture a range of behaviors is tolerated for each situation; what the norms specify are the ranges and their limits.

The archaeologist often makes use of this view of culture to describe and reconstruct behavior in the past. Those who take this view assume that the material remains of ancient cultures represent past behavioral norms. For instance, pottery is a good indicator of culturally controlled behavior. Although the methods for making and decorating pottery are many and varied, each society uses only a few of these techniques, learned by each potter as an apprentice. Departures from these manufacturing norms are usually discouraged by social and economic sanctions. Archaeologists can therefore infer the ancient rules governing pottery making by studying the regularities in the surviving ceramics.

Within this conceptual framework, the cultural historical approach emphasizes the goal of outlining the sequence (time dimension) and geographical distribution (space dimension) of past cultural norms. Once this is done, interpretation proceeds, through analogy, to apply descriptive models, usually drawn from ethnography and history, that outline the mechanisms most likely to have been involved in stability and change. The culmination of the interpretive process is thus a chronicle of events and general trends of cultural change and continuity in the prehistoric past. In fact, a cultural historical approach is well suited to outline the temporal, spatial, and even functional dimensions of prehistory. It is less suitable, however, for documenting the causes of cultural development and change.

The Cultural Historical Method

The research method associated with the cultural historical approach is inductive, beginning with specific data from individual sites and combining them in increasing degrees of generalization and synthesis. The specific techniques used to collect, process, and analyze archaeological data have been discussed in previous chapters. Here we will briefly recount the steps normally followed in conducting inductive archaeological research as it might be used in a previously uninvestigated area.

Once the zone of archaeological research has been selected, a reconnaissance program identifies archaeological sites, and surface survey provides the initial round of data collection. The archaeologist selects the material cultural traits that seem most sensitive to temporal change and that will therefore best allow these collections to be arranged in a tentative chronological sequence, using seriation or other methods. The traits used may be attributes of features, such as architectural form or style; more commonly, however, they are attributes of pottery or stone tools.

Once the preliminary chronological scheme is worked out, excavations are undertaken to test the sequence and to provide data for its refinement. Other goals may also be pursued in excavation, but the first goal in the cultural historical approach is usually to discover and investigate stratified deposits that enable the archaeologist to perfect or further document the tentative time scheme.

Correlating sequences of data categories, the archaeologist next defines chronological *periods* for the site as a whole. The time scale for ordering them may be either relative or absolute, depending on the nature of associated age determination evidence. Whether or not absolute dating is possible, however, the study is based on a firm chronology, relying primarily on evidence recovered from stratified deposits to verify typological sequence.

The next step in the procedure is to expand the synthesis beyond the individual site to wider geographical areas. This enlargement of scope is accom-

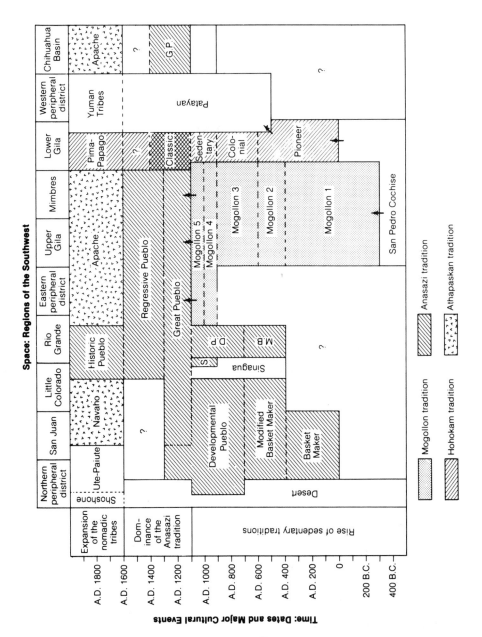

FIGURE 8.1

The cultural historical approach leads to the development of time-space grids, like this one for the southwestern United States, to summarize ancient events and cultural relationships. (After Rouse 1962.)

FIGURE 8.2

Cultural attributes combined with geographical factors are used to define culture areas, in this case, those of North America.

plished by repeating the research procedures outlined above at sites adjacent to those already investigated. Newly acquired data can be compared to extant sequences. This not only refines the cultural chronology but also enables the archaeologist to begin to plot the spatial distributions of artifact and feature types. As more and more sites are investigated and the number of known prehistoric cultural sequences grows, the process of temporal and spatial synthesis expands to cover ever-widening areas. These temporal and spatial syntheses are often termed *time-space grids* (Fig. 8.1).

As a rule, the working unit of cultural historical synthesis is the *culture area*, a conceptual unit based on ethnographically defined cultural similarities within a geographical area (Fig. 8.2). Various archaeologists working within a given culture area usually attempt to facilitate the process of temporal and spatial synthesis by using common terminology and classificatory concepts in order to make information from different sites comparable. The first cultural historical synthesis of an entire culture area in the New World was that of the American Southwest. Since that time other prehistoric culture area syntheses have been worked out in both the New World and the Old.

As the explicitly inductive cultural historical approach began to be used to create broader and more general syntheses in the New World, it became increasingly obvious that some kind of overriding interpretive model would be necessary. Such a framework was worked out in the mid-20th century; it represents an inductively derived temporal-spatial synthesis for the entire New World (Fig. 8.3). The terminology is distinct from that used in the Old World, and the resulting scheme is explicitly *not* founded on cultural evolutionary theory. Yet the New World synthesis implicitly suggests a course of cultural development from simple to complex, certainly not identical with, but clearly parallel to, the course of Old World prehistory.

This New World model, developed by Gordon R. Willey and Philip Phillips, is based on the complementary concepts of tradition and horizon. *Tradition* refers to cultural continuity through time, while *horizon* deals with ties and uniformity across space at a single point in time (see Fig. 8.3). Applying these concepts to data from all areas of the Americas, Willey and Phillips defined a series of five developmental stages, or, as they have been more commonly applied, chronological periods. The exact temporal boundaries for each stage differ from area to area, but overall Willey and Phillips's scheme represents a cultural historical synthesis for the entire New World.

Cultural Historical Interpretation

The formal interpretation process follows the temporal and spatial synthesis of the archaeological data. As already noted, the analogs used for cultural historical interpretation usually presuppose a normative view of culture, describing idealized rules or "templates" for the ways things were done—how pottery was made, what house forms were prescribed, and so on. These models are primarily descriptive, not explanatory, since they identify and describe the elements and

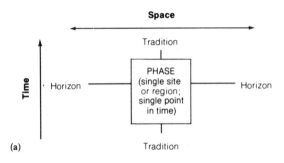

DEVELOPMENTAL STAGES	ATTRIBUTES		
	Technological	*Social*	*Ideological*
Postclassic	Metallurgy	Complex urbanism, militarism	Secularization of society
Classic	Craft specialization, beginnings of metallurgy	Large ceremonial centers, beginnings of urbanism	Developed theocracies
Formative	Pottery, weaving, developed food production	Permanent villages and towns; first ceremonial centers	Beginnings of priest class (theocracy)
Archaic	Diversified tools, ground stone utensils, beginnings of food production	Beginnings of permanent villages	?
Lithic (or Paleo-Indian)	Chipped stone tools	Nonsettled hunters and gatherers	?

(b)

FIGURE 8.3

Willey and Phillips comprehensively outlined New World cultural history by
(a) integrating the dimensions of time and space through the concepts of tradition
and horizon (a *phase* represents the form or content of a particular tradition on a
particular horizon) and (b) summarizing the inductively documented course of
cultural development through five generalized stages. (After Willey and Phillips
1958; part (a) copyright 1958 by The University of Chicago Press.)

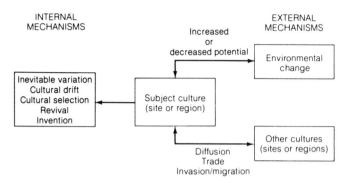

FIGURE 8.4

Cultural historical interpretation is based on models that describe cultural change as proceeding from either internal or external mechanisms.

trends within situations of culture change but do not attempt to describe the relationships among elements or identify the specific causes of change.

Because the cultural historical approach emphasizes chronology and cultural change, most of the interpretive models used are diachronic, identifying and describing change in the archaeological record. A distinction can be made between models that emphasize internal sources of change and those that focus on external stimuli (Fig. 8.4).

Internal cultural models describe mechanisms through which change occurs within a given culture. The most general of these mechanisms is *inevitable variation*, which follows the simple premise that all cultures change through time. One particular version is that all cultures experience growth and development analogous to that of a living organism; they grow, mature, and eventually die (the rise and fall of civilization). But the inevitable variation model is so simplistic and general that it is of little use in archaeological interpretation. We do not increase our understanding by saying that a civilization like Rome fell apart because it was destined to collapse. Of greater benefit to archaeological interpretation are internal cultural models that identify specific variables with which to describe the mechanisms of culture change.

How does this change come about? The human species is inquisitive and innovative. *Cultural invention* is the result of these human qualities; the term refers to new ideas that originate within a culture, either by accident or design. But to attribute to invention the appearance of a given trait in the archaeological record at a particular place, the archaeologist must demonstrate that the trait was not introduced from outside by trade or some other external mechanism. A specific example is the controversy over the early occurrence of bronze metallurgy in Southeast Asia. Proponents of an independent invention model point out that cast bronze artifacts now being found in Thailand rival those of the Near East in age. The counterargument is that the Near East exhibits a full

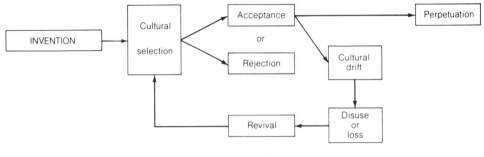

FIGURE 8.5

Internally induced cultural change is affected by the filtering mechanisms of cultural selection, cultural drift, and revival.

range of evidence for the local development of metallurgical technology, including evidence of workshops as well as local sequential evidence of gradually increasing sophistication in metalworking techniques. In order to establish that Southeast Asia was indeed an independent center for the invention of metallurgy, archaeologists are seeking evidence equivalent to that in the Near East, documenting the *local prototypes* and *developmental steps* leading to the invention of bronze metallurgy.

To contribute to cultural change, an invention must be accepted in a culture. Two general models, both founded on loose analogies to biological evolution, have been offered to describe mechanisms of acceptance, perpetuation, or rejection of cultural traits (Fig. 8.5). The first, *cultural selection*, mirrors the biological concept of natural selection. According to the cultural selection model, cultural traits that are advantageous to members of a society are accepted or retained, while those that are useless or actively harmful tend to be discarded. This tendency creates gradual and cumulative change through time. Selection can act on any cultural trait, whether in the technological, social, or ideological realm of culture. Whether a given trait is advantageous depends ultimately on whether it contributes to—or hinders—the survival and well-being of those who adopt it. For example, investment of power in a central authority figure may increase efficiency in food production, resolution of disputes, and management of interactions with neighboring societies. If such centralization of authority leads the society in question to prosper, the trait of power centralization is advantageous and selection will favor its perpetuation. If, however, the society falls on hard times as a result of power centralization—perhaps because of inept leadership—authority is likely to become more dispersed again.

Selection also acts against traits that are inconsistent with prevailing cultural values or norms. Generally speaking, technological inventions are more likely to be accepted than social or ideological ones, because they are less likely to conflict with the value system. A new form of axe head, for instance, usually has an easier path to acceptance than a revised authority hierarchy or an innovative religious belief.

A related model, often labeled *cultural drift* (see Fig. 8.5), describes a mechanism complementary to that of cultural selection. Like selection, this process causes change through time. But this process is a random one; the reason for trait loss is chance rather than active selection against a characteristic. Cultural traits are transmitted from one generation to the next by learning. Cultural drift, then, results from the fact that cultural transmission is incomplete or imperfect; no individual ever learns all the information possessed by any other member of the society. Hence cultural changes through time have a random aspect. Sally Binford and others suggested that cultural drift may be responsible for some of the variations in artifacts of early Paleolithic tool assemblages. That is, the accumulation of minor changes gives a superficial impression of deliberate stylistic innovation, but only after about a million years of development in these tool traditions can consistent styles be discerned.

Another source for cultural change is *revival* of elements that have fallen into disuse. A number of stimuli may lead to revival of old forms, including chance discovery and reacceptance of old styles, reoccurrence of specific needs, and duplication of treasured heirlooms. One particular model relates revival to a coping response to stressful situations. Some kinds of stress elicit technological responses: For example, townspeople construct a fortification wall as a defense against seige. But sometimes societies deal with stress by social or ideological means. Cultural anthropologist Anthony F. C. Wallace has developed a model that describes rapid and radical cultural change in the face of stress. This revitalization model refers to situations in which members of a society perceive their culture as falling apart and unable to provide them with an adequate standard of living. In revitalization a leader revives old symbols associated with earlier periods of well-being, squashes those identified with the stressful situation, inspires positive and prideful identification with the society, and promises renewed prosperity if people adhere to the new rules that are set down.

External cultural models describe change by the introduction of new customs from outside a particular society (Figs. 8.4 and 8.6). When a custom, such as one resulting from the acceptance of an invention, has become established within one society, its utility or prestige may allow it to spread far beyond its place of origin. The spread of new ideas and objects is a complex process. Various modes of dispersal are well documented by both history and ethnography and are often used as models for cultural historical interpretation. They include the spread of ideas (diffusion), the dispersal of material objects by exchange or trade, and the movement of human populations through migration and invasion or conquest.

Diffusion occurs under a variety of circumstances: Any contact between individuals from different societies involves the potential transmission of ideas from one culture to another. When a given society is exposed to a new idea, that idea may be accepted unchanged, reworked or modified to fit the accepting culture, or completely rejected.

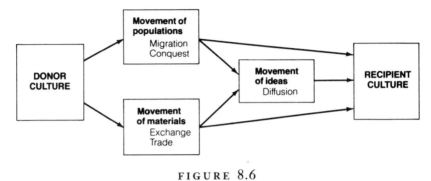

FIGURE 8.6

Externally induced cultural change, or acculturation, includes the mechanisms of diffusion, trade, migration, invasion, and conquest.

The archaeological record contains numerous examples of ideas that have diffused over varying distances with varying degrees of acceptance. The pre-Columbian 260-day ritual calendar of Mesoamerica is found in a wide range of cultural contexts. Although specific attributes such as day names vary from one society to the next, the essential unity of the system reflects a long-term exchange of calendrical ideas over a wide area.

Diffusion is a well-documented mechanism of culture change in historically and ethnographically known societies. Because diffusion is so common, and because evidence of more specific mechanisms, such as trade, migration, invasion, and invention, is sometimes difficult to find, cultural historical interpretations have relied heavily on diffusion as a model. All too often, however, the concept is used uncritically, with any observed similarity between cultures attributed to diffusion. An extreme example of abuse of this concept is found in the diffusionist school of anthropology in the early 20th century, especially the branch that traced all world civilizations to roots in dynastic Egypt. Proponents of this model, such as Sir Grafton Elliot Smith, argued that such widespread traits of civilization as divine kingship and pyramid construction were diffused from a single Egyptian source. When applied in less extreme ways, however, use of the concept of diffusion rests on documenting how and why the cultures involved were in communication with each other.

Although diffusion is often an elusive mechanism, easy to invoke and difficult to substantiate, contact and communication via *trade* can frequently be demonstrated. Trade involves the exchange of material objects; the less perishable of these may be recovered by the archaeologist as artifacts and ecofacts, as discussed in Chapter 7. Once trade goods have been identified, archaeologists may be able to reconstruct ancient trade routes by plotting both the distribution of sources of material and the observed distribution of products from these sources. The important implication of trade distributions for culture change is that archaeologists can use them to demonstrate contact between groups. When an obsidian trade route is reconstructed, for example, a minimal inference is that obsidian was available to people who could add obsidian tools to their cultural inventory. More broadly, however, the observed distribution of obsidian is concrete evidence of contact between groups—a reflection of the transmission of a potentially much greater array of materials and ideas, some of which may leave no material trace in the archaeological record.

Another mechanism of culture change is actual movement of populations in both *migrations* and aggressive *conquests*. Cultural historical interpretations often cite these movements to account for evidence of widespread and rapid change. Emil W. Haury presents four conditions that must be met for an archaeologist to argue that migration has occurred:

1. A number of new cultural traits must appear suddenly, too many to be feasibly accounted for by diffusion, invention, or trade, and none having earlier local prototypes.

2. Some of the form or style of local materials should be modified or used in a different way by the newcomers.

3. A source for the immigrant population must be identified—a homeland where the intrusive cultural elements do have prototypes.

4. The artifacts used as indices of population movement must exist in the same form at the same time level in both the homeland and the newly adopted home.

As an example, Haury notes that new sacred and secular architectural styles, as well as very specific ceramic attributes, appear suddenly in one particular sector of the prehistoric site of Point of Pines, Arizona. At the same time level, some distinctively "foreign" design elements are found on locally made pottery vessels also recovered in this one sector. These two conclusions supply the first two kinds of evidence needed to postulate a migration. Looking for a source for these cultural traits, he finds the same elements in association at sites in northern Arizona on an equivalent time level. Finally he notes that independent evidence points to a population decline in the proposed homeland at the appropriate time.

The concept of peaceful migration as one means of introducing new culture traits into an area can be contrasted with its more violent counterpart, conquest. This, too, involves population movements, but with presumably more drastic effects on the way of life of the recipient society. Elements cited as evidence of conquest include massive burning or other destruction of buildings in a settlement, usually accompanied by large-scale loss of human life (Fig. 8.7).

The change brought about by conquest may, of course, be simple annihilation of the existing population, sometimes with no replacement by the intruders. In many cases, however, part of the original population survives and stays on, often under new political domination. The invaders may bring in new cultural elements, but even historically documented conquests show up rather in-

FIGURE 8.7

Evidence of culture change through conquest can take dramatic forms. This photograph shows human skeletal remains sprawled among the remains of burned buildings in the walled palace compound of Hasanlu, Iran, the result of the ninth century B.C. destruction of the city. (Courtesy of Robert H. Dyson, Jr., and the Hasanlu Project, University Museum, University of Pennsylvania.)

consistently in the archaeological record. A case in point is the Spanish Conquest of the Americas in the 16th century. Both European and native chronicles of the period attest to the extent and severity of the changes wrought by the Spanish. Even so, archaeologists working in a number of the affected areas, including Mexico, Guatemala, and Peru, have sometimes had difficulty in identifying archaeological evidence of the Spanish arrival. At some sites, European artifacts do appear, but local pottery inventories often remain unchanged for long periods after the conquest. With reference to Haury's criteria, then, archaeologists can positively identify some prehistoric population movements, but the example

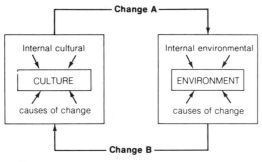

Key:
A: Environmental change caused by cultural factors
B: Culture change caused by environmental factors

FIGURE 8.8

The cultural historical approach stresses a simple interaction between culture and environment, based on the capability of each to modify the other (compare with Fig. 8.12).

just given argues rather strongly that not all such movements—violent or peaceful—can be accurately detected in the archaeological record.

Environmental change is used in cultural historical interpretation as an external factor (see Fig. 8.4), independent of culture, that nonetheless may affect the destiny of human society. This model describes rather general environmental sources of culture change. In most cases, cultural historical models of culture and environment hold that each has the potential to modify the other (Fig. 8.8). A dramatic example of the cultural impact of an environmental change can be seen in the effects of the eruption of Sunset Crater, near Flagstaff, Arizona, sometime in the middle of the 11th century A.D. The initial effect of the eruption was to drive away all residents in the approximately 800 square miles blanketed by the black volcanic ash. A century later, however, the area was resettled by a diverse population that apparently took advantage of the rich mulching action of the volcanic soil. By A.D. 1300, however, the environment had changed again; wind had converted the ash cover to shifting dunes and exposed the original hard clay soil. Once again the human settlers moved away.

Culture also changes environment. A change in technology may redefine the environment by increasing or decreasing the range of exploitable resources. Agricultural overuse may exhaust local soils; the clearing of trees on hillsides may foster erosion, landslides, and ultimately—by increasing the load deposited in a stream bed by erosional runoff—flooding. Alteration of the natural environment by cultural activities is not an exclusively modern phenomenon; the alterations today may be more extensive than before, but they are part of a long, global tradition of cultural impact on the natural world.

CULTURAL PROCESSUAL RECONSTRUCTION

The second major approach to reconstructing the past is cultural processual interpretation. This approach is based on ecological and evolutionary views of culture.

The ecological view portrays culture, and especially technology, as the primary means by which human societies adapt to their environment. Whereas the normative view emphasizes regularities and rules, the ecological view highlights the variation evident in cultural forms (for example, spear points for hunting or distinct horticultural implements for cultivating different crops), seeing the range and variety as potential clues to how the society in question dealt with its environment as a whole. Change stems from alteration of this adaptive relationship between culture and environment, as reflected archaeologically in new forms or new frequencies of particular artifacts, ecofacts, and features.

It must be stressed that cultural ecology does not imply that the environment determines the nature of culture. On the contrary, through time on a global scale the physical and biological components of the environment have become increasingly determined by human culture. We need only look at our own environment to see the changes our culture has wrought in the landscape and the composition of our water, food, and air. The example of changing cultures on the Great Plains, described at the beginning of this chapter, illustrates how changing technology can alter the range of environmental resources a culture can use, essentially "redefining" the environment. By viewing the archaeological record from a cultural ecological perspective, the archaeologist can detect shifts in adaptation that suggest causes and consequences of change rather than merely describing changes in norms.

Cultural processual reconstruction also takes an evolutionary view of culture. Unlike 19th-century unilinear evolutionary theory, however, current cultural evolutionary theory is not locked into a rigid scheme of developmental stages through which all societies must inevitably pass. The prevailing evolutionary concept, like cultural ecology, is *multilinear;* that is, it assumes that each human society adapts to its own environment via its culture, primarily through technology and secondarily through organizational and ideational subsystems. What suits one society to one environment won't necessarily be adaptive elsewhere. What further distinguishes the evolutionary concept from the ecological model is an emphasis on the degree of success or efficiency reached by each culture, as measured by survival or growth. A particular society, such as the Inuit, may be well adapted to its environment, achieving a stable balance or equilibrium, in which change is minimal and survival is the measure of adaptive efficiency.

In other cases human societies become involved in growth cycles. For example, changes originating either from the environment or from within the society may trigger changes in the technological system (and in the organizational and ideational systems as well). If these technological changes increase food production, and if the organizational and ideational changes allow for increases in population size, a process of growth may begin. Continued growth will eventually place new strains on technology (amount of food produced), organization (management of people), and ideology (the belief system justifying the other two systems). This pressure may trigger further changes in technology to increase food production or in social and political organization to mobilize the population, and the cycle may continue. Such a growth spiral is evident in the archaeological record of the development of civilization in both the Old and New Worlds.

These ecological and multilinear-evolutionary concepts of culture allow prehistoric archaeologists to explore the patterns and dynamics of growth within human societies. While cultural historical reconstruction emphasizes identification of cultural interaction and change through description of a sequence of events, cultural processual reconstruction is concerned with discovering the causes of interactions and change. That is, the cultural processual approach seeks not only to identify and describe similarities and differences across time and space but also to explain the observed distributions.

The Cultural Processual Method

How does the cultural processual approach attempt to identify the causes of change and thereby explain the processes involved in prehistoric cultural dynamics? In contrast to cultural historical reconstruction, the study of cultural processes uses a deductive research methodology in which, at the outset of research, hypotheses specify the working model of change (or interaction) and the kinds of data that will support or refute each hypothesis. Competing hypotheses are then tested against the archaeological data in order to eliminate those that are not supported by the evidence. Hypotheses that are supported in the first test are retested and redefined by further research to isolate the factors involved in a given situation of prehistoric cultural change. In the cultural processual approach, then, interpretation refers to the selection and refinement of specific hypotheses that best delineate cultural processes.

Of course the cultural processual approach is rooted, either directly or indirectly, in cultural historical reconstruction. A direct link may be apparent when the hypotheses tested by deductive procedures have been derived from the inductively developed cultural historical models. However, *all* cultural processual interpretation is indirectly built on a cultural historical foundation, since the latter approach has provided the temporal and spatial frameworks of prehistory. These frameworks furnish the analytical controls without which cultural process cannot be discerned. The cultural processual approach well illustrates application of the scientific method in prehistoric archaeology. Initial inquiry based on the application of inductive reasoning allows the formulation of questions that can be investigated deductively.

For example, in a study of the ancient society of the Ulua valley around Santa Bárbara in west-central Honduras, initial cultural historical research suggested that two adjacent valley pockets had quite different developmental sequences. One of them, Gualjoquito, had a sizable elite center during the Classic

Period, between about A.D. 200 and 900, but seemed to lack earlier or later evidence of localized leaders. Initial survey in the other pocket, Tencoa, yielded a comparable center, but that one pertained to an earlier period, probably 400 B.C. to A.D. 200. Tencoa has better agricultural resources, but Gualjoquito occupies an obvious crossroad position and Tencoa does not. Gualjoquito's period of peak development seemed to coincide with that of the major Maya center of Copán, to the southwest along one of the routes linked by the crossroads.

Based on these data several models were proposed to be tested against new data. One of these models linked Gualjoquito's rise and fall to external alliances, specifically with Copán. Since the valley pockets are small, the model included the further hypothesis that, when the crossroads was not in active use, the pocket with more natural subsistence resources (Tencoa) would be the seat of local power. If the model were correct, further survey should reveal no further elite centers in the two periods cited, and should yield evidence of a return to power in Tencoa after A.D. 900. Survey and excavation should also turn up more Classic Period imports, especially those likely to be owned by society's leaders, in Gualjoquito, and the homes and possessions of those same leaders should show strong links with the culture and styles of Copán. These deductive predictions are derived from logical expectations about a particular situation.

The next step in the cultural processual approach involves assembling all the data relevant to rigorous testing of hypotheses under consideration. Hypothesis testing in archaeology, as in any scientific discipline, must follow an explicit, fully documented procedure. In many sciences, from physics to psychology, hypotheses are tested by repeatable *experiments*. For example, the hypothesis that explains how a barometer works holds that the weight of the earth's atmosphere—atmospheric pressure—supports the column of mercury. An experiment to test this hypothesis might involve moving one barometer to a new altitude while a second remained at the first altitude as a check against change in weather conditions. This experiment is controlled: It rules out interference by other factors (in this case weather). It is also repeatable: It can be performed any number of times. In some cases, as in the experimental archaeology examples discussed in Chapter 7, archaeologists use controlled experiments to test specific findings, such as use wear signatures.

But archaeologists cannot rely on controlled, repeatable experiments to test most of their hypotheses. The archaeological record already exists; those who study it cannot return to the past and manipulate situations to test their reconstructions. This observation highlights a fundamental distinction between the physical sciences (such as physics and chemistry) and the historical sciences (evolutionary biology, geology, and archaeology). In the words of Stephen Jay Gould, "historical sciences are different, not lesser. Their methods are comparative, not always experimental; they explain, but do not usually try to predict; they recognize the irreducible quirkiness that history entails" (1985:18). Archaeologists and other historical scientists can, however, test their reconstructions by explicitly and clearly stating the conditions and expectations of their hypotheses and then collecting and analyzing the data specified by the expectations.

The testing procedure for archaeological hypotheses actually begins in the formulation stage, with the formulation of multiple hypotheses that make mutually exclusive predictions about the data. The use of *multiple working hypotheses* means that as many explanatory alternatives as possible are considered. This minimizes the opportunity for explanatory bias on the part of the investigator and maximizes the chance of finding the best available explanation. In the example cited earlier archaeologists working in the Santa Bárbara area set forth at least two mutually exclusive hypotheses. If Copán and the crossroads were the key to Gualjoquito's prosperity, the predictions outlined above should be met. If, however, other resources underlay its leaders' successes, the data would match predictions from models other than the one described here. Three years of subsequent data collection and analysis supported the first hypothesis.

In this and other situations the goal is to invalidate all but one hypothesis. The surviving hypothesis may then be advanced, not as proven, but as the best possible explanation given the present state of knowledge. All science involves the assumption that contemporary explanations will be modified or replaced as new data become available.

Cultural Processual Interpretation

The models we discuss in this book are not necessarily restricted to either cultural historical or cultural processual interpretation. Although the descriptive models discussed earlier are usually associated with cultural historical reconstruction, they may also be applied in cultural processual interpretations. Cultural historical models often generate hypotheses that are tested, modified, and advanced as explanations for prehistoric cultural processes. But just as some models are used more frequently in cultural historical reconstruction, certain others are primarily associated with cultural processual explanation.

Systems models recognize that an organization represents more than a simple sum of its parts; they emphasize the study of the relations between parts. Two kinds of systems can be defined: open and closed. Closed systems receive no matter, energy, or information from other systems; all sources of change are internal. Open systems exchange matter, energy, and information with other systems; change can come either from within or from outside. Living organisms and sociocultural systems are both examples of open systems. In order to understand how systems operate, we will examine systems models that are often applied to cultural processual interpretation.

We will begin with a simple closed systems model. As an example, consider the components and relationships within a self-regulated temperature control system, such as those found in many modern buildings (Fig. 8.9). The components in the system are the air in the room or building, the thermometer, the thermostat, and the heater or air conditioner. In this case a change in the air

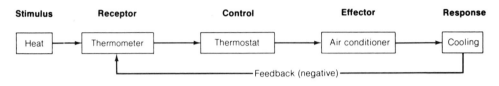

FIGURE 8.9

Diagram of a homeostatic temperature control system, illustrating the operation of a closed system.

temperature is the stimulus that is detected by the thermometer and transmitted to the thermostat. When the temperature rises above a predetermined level, the thermostat triggers the air conditioner. The cooling response acts as *feedback* by stimulating the same interdependent components to shut down the air conditioner once the temperature has gone below the critical level.

This closed system illustrates how certain systems maintain a stable condition or *steady state*. When a specific change in one part of the system threatens the steady state, this stimulates a response from other component parts. When the steady state has been restored, a feedback loop shuts down the response. Feedback of this kind is *negative* in the sense that it dampens or cuts off the system's response and thus maintains a condition of *dynamic equilibrium* in which the system's components are active, but the overall system is stable and unchanging. Although they are useful for illustrating the operation of systems, such models are applicable only to unchanging and stable aspects of human societies.

Since archaeologists are more often concerned with processes of culture change, we must also consider dynamic systems models that can account for cumulative systemic change. The most commonly applied model for this deals with *positive feedback*, which stimulates change within the system. An interesting application of these concepts to an archaeological situation is Kent Flannery's systems model for the development of food production in Mesoamerica. In setting forth the model, Flannery first describes the food procurement system used by peoples of highland Mexico between about 8000 and 5000 B.C. (Fig. 8.10). The components of this system were the people themselves, their technology—including knowledge and equipment—for obtaining food, and the plants and animals actually used for food.

People in the highland valleys lived in small groups, periodically coming together into larger "macrobands" but not settling down in permanent villages. The subsistence technology available to them included knowledge of edible plants and animals that could be procured by gathering and hunting techniques, as well as the implements and facilities of procurement. Among the food items actively used were cactus, avocado, white-tailed deer, rabbits, and so on. Wild grasses related to maize were sometimes eaten but were not a very important part of the diet.

This food procurement system was regulated and maintained by negative

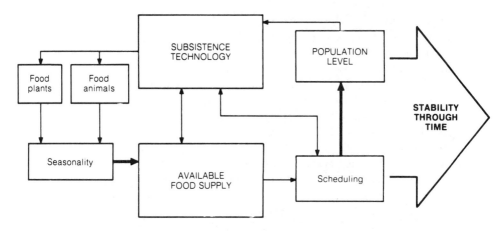

FIGURE 8.10

FIGURE 8.10

Simplified diagram of a system characterized by deviation-counteracting mechanisms (→) that lead to population and cultural stability through time; based on
data from prehistoric Mesoamerica (ca. 8000–5000 B.C.). The larger arrow at the
right indicates the trajectory of the system as a whole.

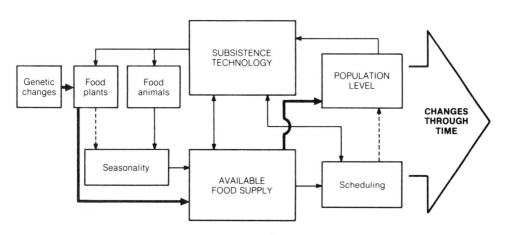

FIGURE 8.11

Simplified diagram of a system characterized by deviation-amplifying mechanisms that both weaken the deviation-counteracting mechanisms in Figure 8.10
and lead to population growth and cultural change, stimulated by genetic changes;
based on data from prehistoric Mesoamerica (after 5000 B.C.).

feedback, acting through seasonality and scheduling. Seasonality refers to characteristics of the food resources themselves; some were available during only one season or another. To gather enough food the people had to go where it was available. Periodic abundance of particular resources allowed people to come together into temporary macrobands, but the seasons of lean resources placed sharply defined limits on both total valley population and effective social group size. Scheduling, the other negative feedback mechanism, refers to the people's organizational response to seasonality. Seasonally scheduled population movement and diet diversity prevented exhaustion of resources by overexploitation, but it also kept population levels low.

This stable system persisted for several thousand years, but, according to Flannery, sometime after 5000 B.C., genetic changes in some of the wild maize stimulated a positive feedback system (Fig. 8.11). Improved traits of the maize, such as larger cob size, induced people to reproduce the "improved" grass by sowing. This behavior gradually altered scheduling patterns. For instance, planting and harvesting requirements increased the time spent in spring and autumn camps, precisely where larger population gatherings had been feasible before. The larger, more stable population groupings then invested more time and labor in improving the quality and quantity of crop yield; and this positive feedback continued to induce change in the subsistence system. For example, irrigation technology was developed to extend agriculture and settlement into more arid zones. As Flannery says, the "positive feedback following these initial genetic changes caused one minor [sub]system to grow out of all proportion to the others, and eventually to change the whole ecosystem of the Southern Mexican Highlands."

Although some cultural systems may maintain a state of dynamic equilibrium for long periods of time, all cultures do change. Not all change involves growth, however. Sometimes positive feedback results in cultural loss or decline, and ultimately in dissolution of the system. The modern case of the Ik of East Africa, described by ethnographer Colin Turnbull, provides an example of such decline. Disruption of traditional behavior patterns by such factors as forced migration from preferred lands has led to apathy, intragroup hostility, a devaluation of human life, and population decline. The result in this case is as dramatically bleak as Flannery's is dramatically positive. Most cases of cultural change are less extreme, as cultural systems are affected simultaneously by both growth and decline of subsystems within them, in a gradual and cumulative course of change.

Cultural ecological models provide a more sophisticated understanding of the interaction between culture and environment than the older, cultural historical model discussed previously. Whereas the cultural historical approach often treated environment as a single entity, cultural ecology considers a given culture as interacting with an environmental system composed of three complex subsystems: (1) the physical landscape, (2) the biological environment, and (3) the cultural environment—other adjacent human groups (Fig. 8.12).

For any given society, the sum of specific interactions contained within an overall cultural ecological system describes the nature of the society's *cultural adaptation*. Each society adjusts itself or adapts to its environment primarily

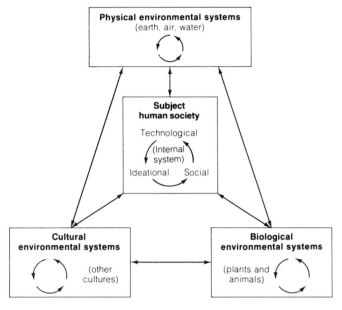

FIGURE 8.12

The cultural ecological system, illustrating the relationships between a given culture (subject human society) and its environment, composed of physical, cultural, and biological subsystems (compare with Fig. 8.8).

through its technological system, but also, secondarily, through the social and ideological systems. The technological system interacts directly with all three components of the environment—physical, biological, and cultural—by providing, for instance, the tools and techniques required for securing shelter, food, and defense. The social system adapts by integrating and organizing society. The relation described earlier between band organization and seasonality and scheduling in preagricultural highland Mexican societies is an example of social system adaptation to the biological environment. And the ideological system is adaptive in that it reinforces the organization and integration of society by providing motivation, explanation, and confidence in the appropriateness of the technological and social adaptations.

Of course the full set of interactions within such a complex system is difficult to study all at once. As a result archaeologists often begin by isolating one or more of the subordinate systems directly involved in cultural adaptation. The technological system is the obvious focus of studies seeking to understand the adaptive process. Fortunately for the prehistoric archaeologist, not only is the technological subsystem a most obvious agent of cultural adaptation, but also the remains of ancient technology are usually the fullest part of the archaeological record. Technological data may be used to reconstruct a particular aspect of the technological system such as subsistence. Archaeologists then integrate their detailed models of different subsystems to create complex models of overall cultural adaptation.

Because of the mass of information involved in such models, computers are often used for information storage. Computers also enable the archaeologist to perform experimental manipulation of the models. After a hypothetical change is introduced in one component of the stable hypothetical system, a *computer simulation* determines what kind of feedback would be induced by the original change. For example, Ezra Zubrow has used computer simulations to examine relationships among human population size and structure, biological resources of the environment, and settlement location in the prehistoric Southwest. He finds that changing the characteristics of any of these system components produces different projected courses of population growth and decline.

In an analogy to biological adaptation some archaeologists measure the effectiveness of cultural adaptation by the rate of population growth and resultant population size. In this sense population growth and size are a measurable response to the overall cultural ecological system (see Fig. 8.12). With regard to population increase some societies are characterized by one or more positive feedback mechanisms. For example, changes in the technological system that provide more efficient food production and storage capabilities may increase population. Changes made in the social or ideational systems to accommodate the population growth may in turn facilitate food distribution or expansion via conquest or colonization to open new areas for food production and further population growth. This may place new stress on the technology, which must respond with new changes to increase the food supply, and so forth. The result is an interrelated change-increase cycle, perhaps best illustrated by the phenomenon of recent world population growth.

However, successful adaptation (biological or cultural) can also be marked by stability of population size. Some societies maintain population stability by negative feedback mechanisms, including culturally acceptable population control methods (birth control, infanticide, warfare), migration, and social fission. Environmental mechanisms, including periodic famine or endemic disease, also contribute to the maintenance of such systems.

Multilinear cultural evolutionary models constitute the final perspective on cultural processual interpretation available today. These models combine the systemic view of culture and the adaptation concept of cultural ecology. They view the evolution of culture as the cumulative changes in a system resulting from the continuous process of cultural adaptation over extensive periods of time. But how does the archaeologist reveal the causes of evolutionary change? Two schools of thought have emerged: The first emphasizes the identification of universal prime movers of cultural change; the second seeks multiple and variable causes.

The search for *prime movers* emphasizes the identification of a few specific, primary factors that underlie the process of culture change and, ultimately, cultural evolution. It is based on the premise that the regularities and patterns in evolutionary change are results of regularities of cause. Accordingly, this approach emphasizes the testing of broad hypotheses that seek the fundamental, far-reaching causes of all cultural change.

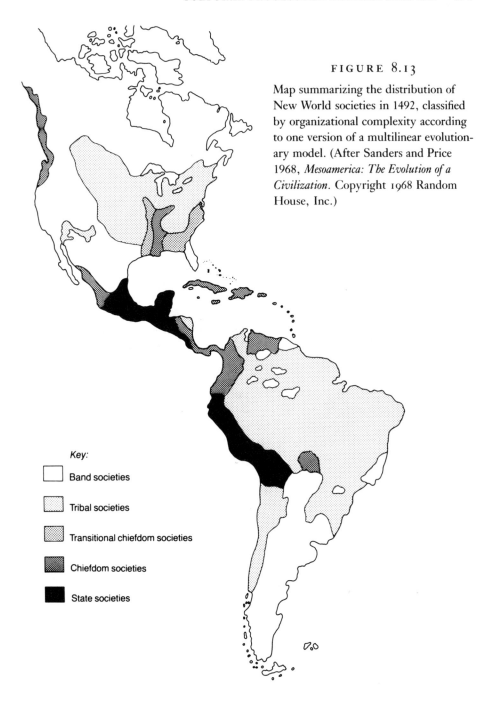

FIGURE 8.13

Map summarizing the distribution of New World societies in 1492, classified by organizational complexity according to one version of a multilinear evolutionary model. (After Sanders and Price 1968, *Mesoamerica: The Evolution of a Civilization*. Copyright 1968 Random House, Inc.)

Key:

☐ Band societies

▨ Tribal societies

▨ Transitional chiefdom societies

▨ Chiefdom societies

■ State societies

Population growth is often proposed as a fundamental cause of cultural change. This prime mover has been applied in various regions to explain the course of cultural evolution. For example, William T. Sanders and Barbara Price based their thesis for the evolution of pre-Columbian Mesoamerican culture on population growth and its effects on two secondary factors, competition and co-operation (Fig. 8.13). Other prime movers, such as warfare, have been proposed to explain specific evolutionary developments, such as the rise of complex state societies.

The *multivariate strategy* attempts to delineate the basic processes of culture change in a different manner, in this case by focusing research on specific sub-systems that are most directly involved in adaptation. To identify the focus of change research of this kind may test hypotheses concerned, for example, with a variety of alternative subsistence modes or with the acquisition and distribution of critical natural resources. Since each instance of change is considered unique, this model holds that no single factor or small group of "prime movers" causes cultural change. Cultural evolution, the overall product of change, is the prod-uct of a multitude of relatively small adaptive adjustments, of the sort that are a constant feature of all cultural systems. This perspective gives the multivariate model of culture change its name. Specific examples, such as Flannery's thesis about the transformation from hunting-and-gathering subsistence to food pro-duction, build on this premise and call for substantial cumulative cultural changes over a sufficient period of time.

The multivariate concept of cultural evolution is based on cultural ecologi-cal and systemic cultural models. This approach requires the archaeologist to identify the components of, and understand the relationships among, the spe-cific subsystems crucial to cultural adaptation. This is not an easy task, espe-cially given the inherent limitations of archaeological data. The archaeologist must formulate and test a series of sophisticated hypotheses, using data that are often difficult to collect. As in the case of the transformation to food production in Mesoamerica, described earlier in this chapter, such research may offer multi-variate explanations of fundamental culture change.

THE PAST AS CULTURE HISTORY AND PROCESS

When the cultural processual approach was being formulated in the 1960s, some of its proponents argued that the cultural historical approach was obsolete. Now that we have discussed both approaches to the reconstruction of the past, we can evaluate the merits of both the cultural historical and cultural processual approaches.

If science relies on a combination of inductive and deductive methods to increase our understanding of the world, archaeology, as a scientific discipline, should be no different. This means that the inductively based cultural historical approach is not invalid but provides a necessary and vital basis for the de-ductively oriented cultural processual approach. Rather than being mutually ex-

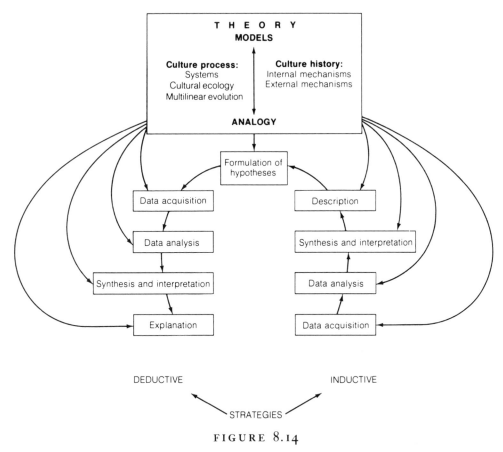

FIGURE 8.14

Diagram of the complementary roles of inductive and deductive research strategies in archaeology.

clusive, these two approaches together form a coherent overall strategy for prehistoric archaeology (Fig. 8.14).

In this strategy data are used inductively to generate temporal and spatial frameworks that define the past. Thus cultural historical interpretations provide the foundation for deductive inquiry designed to identify specific causes of cultural change or stability. Variations within the cultural historical framework may be identified, and "normative" cultural concepts may be used initially to describe these changes. But only rigorously tested propositions can identify the cause of change and begin to explain cultural processes.

In summary, rather than being obsolete or invalid, cultural historical interpretations provide the necessary framework on which cultural processual interpretations are made. The day may come when archaeologists complete the culture historical framework for all world areas and all prehistoric periods. Yet given the tremendous diversity and time depth of human culture and the toll from destruction of archaeological remains, that day still seems far in the future. In the meantime archaeology is also pursuing the second aspect of its strategy by generating and testing an increasing number of research questions designed to reveal the process of prehistoric cultural change.

SUMMARY

The past is reconstructed from its material remains by synthesizing all analyzed data and interpreting them in light of the various research questions. Interpretation attempts both to describe what, when, and where the events of the past happened, and to explain how and why the events of the past happened. Two complementary approaches are used: Cultural historical reconstructions set the foundation by identifying the "what, when, and where," and cultural processual reconstructions follow (often using hypotheses generated from this descriptive reconstruction) to identify the "how and why."

These approaches to archaeological interpretation are guided by one or more cultural frameworks. These are not mutually exclusive, but represent different perspectives in the study of culture. The normative concept of culture is focused on the form of cultural attributes in both time and space as reflections of consensus human behavior (norms). The cultural ecological concept of culture stresses the interrelationships and purposes of cultural components within an overall system and the specific adaptive interactions between culture and its environment. Based on this systemic framework, the multilinear cultural-evolutionary concept emphasizes the trajectory of change that each cultural system follows through time.

Cultural historical reconstruction is concerned with identifying the events of the past, based on a temporal and spatial synthesis of data (time represented by the concept of tradition, space represented by the concept of horizon). Descriptive models based on the normative concept of culture are used to account for the similarities and differences observed in the data. Differences are usually emphasized and are seen as reflections of culture change ascribed to factors originating either inside (invention, selection, drift, and revival) or outside (diffusion, trade, migration, conquest, and environmental change) a particular culture.

Cultural processual reconstruction explains the causes of culture change by testing a series of competing hypotheses. Explanatory models based on functional, ecological, or multilinear evolutionary concepts of culture are most often used in such reconstructions. The functional and ecological perspectives emphasize reconstructions at one or more specific points in time, and seek causality from the interaction process within cultural systems and with their environment. The evolutionary perspective emphasizes reconstructions through time and seeks causality from the identification of single universal (prime movers) or multiple (multivariate) factors.

· 9 ·

Archaeology Today

ARCHAEOLOGY TODAY FACES a challenge to its very existence in the accelerating destruction of the remains of past societies. As we saw at the beginning of this book, the processes of transformation affect all forms of archaeological data, whether by natural forces or the impact of later societies. In recent decades, however, the toll of archaeological destruction has reached immense proportions. Critical information has been lost forever, and many archaeologists fear that unless immediate action is taken, the bulk of the data base will be completely destroyed in the near future (Fig. 9.1).

During the past few years archaeologists have increasingly attempted to stimulate public awareness and concern over the threatened status of archaeological remains throughout the world. This concern is especially apparent in the United States, where public awareness and government protection of archaeological remains have traditionally lagged behind other nations. There are encouraging signs that this situation is changing. An important book by C. R. McGimsey, a leading advocate of public and governmental support for archaeology in the United States, reviewed the situation in the early 1970s and made recommendations for future programs on both state and federal levels. McGimsey summarized the basic issues as follows:

The next fifty years—some would say twenty-five—are going to be the most critical in the history of American archaeology. What is recovered, what is preserved, and how these goals are accomplished during this period will largely determine for all time *the knowledge available to subsequent generations of Americans concerning their heritage from the past. . . . The next generation cannot study or preserve what already has been destroyed.*

(MCGIMSEY 1972:3)

195

FIGURE 9.1

A looted Maya tomb in northern Guatemala, strewn with shattered pottery, is mute testimony to the accelerating destruction of archaeological evidence throughout the world, one of archaeology's most difficult challenges. Tragically, in some areas of the world, most or all archaeological sites have been severely damaged by looting. (Photo by Ian Graham, Peabody Museum.)

The destruction of archaeological evidence has two sources. On the one hand there is the looter who robs the remnants of ancient societies for artifacts or "art" that can be sold to collectors. On the other hand there are the constant destructive effects of expanding societies all over the world. Everyday activities such as farming and construction, though not intended to obliterate archaeological information, nevertheless take their toll.

LOOTING AND ANTIQUITIES COLLECTING

Antiquities collecting is fueled by the looting of archaeological sites—the illicit digging of sites by nonarchaeologists, who seek not information about the past but only objects with prestige, esthetic, or economic value. Even the weekend souvenir hunter causes real damage to the archaeological record, but on a global scale the rapid acceleration of archaeological site destruction by looting has been caused by the demand for ancient artifacts with commercial value. As long as collectors consider certain kinds of archaeological remains to be art, the economics of supply and demand will lead to the plundering of sites to find artifacts with commercial value (Fig. 9.2). In this process, of course, information on the archaeological association and context of these objects is lost, and associated artifacts that lack commercial value are often destroyed.

Most archaeologists recognize that the looting of sites can never be stopped completely. Under most circumstances about all that can be done is to reduce the toll until it reaches less significant proportions, as it has in China due to aroused national concern and government vigilance. New laws are needed to restrict domestic and international traffic in archaeological materials, and present laws should be better enforced. International cooperation and standardization of import-export regulations would help, but customs laws alone cannot solve the problem.

The only effective way to reduce archaeological looting is to discourage the collector. If collectors no longer sought "art" from archaeological contexts, there would be no market for archaeological items and thus no incentive for the plundering of sites. Paintings, sculptures, or other works specifically produced for the art market or art patrons are not included here. But the line must be drawn at any item that derives from an archaeological context, be it a Maya vase from a tomb or a Greek sculpture dragged from the bottom of the sea. The distinction is based on context: Archaeological remains ripped from their archaeological context have already lost their scientific value. Archaeologists must therefore direct their efforts to preventing further destruction of sites (Fig. 9.3).

Collectors include a diverse group of both individuals and institutions. Only a few decades ago, most museums acquired at least some of the objects in their archaeological collections by purchase and thus directly or indirectly encouraged looting. Fortunately that situation has changed: Most museums have promised to abide by international agreements prohibiting commercial dealings

FIGURE 9.2

This aerial photograph shows Oldtown Village in New Mexico, one of the many sites of the prehistoric Mimbres culture that have been transformed by looters into cratered wastelands. Scenes like this are becoming all too common in many areas of the world, as collectors increase their demand for "authentic" archaeological specimens. (Photo after *The Mimbres People: Ancient Pueblo Painters of the American Southwest*, by Steven A. LeBlanc, © 1983 Thames and Hudson, Ltd.)

in archaeological materials. The individual collector remains the greatest problem, for although museum acquisitions often become public knowledge, purchases of archaeological materials by private individuals usually take place privately and remain unknown to others. We do not mean to imply that collectors are evil. Many may not even be aware of the destruction of knowledge that continued collecting spawns. But they should be made aware, for as long as they go on buying, looting will continue.

For example, as northeast Thailand attracted growing archaeological interest in the 1970s, becoming known as a precocious rival to the ancient Near East as a center for the emergence of civilization, the demand for red-painted pottery from Ban Chiang and related sites stepped up dramatically. By the mid-1970s, archaeologists working in the region had trouble locating sites that had not been

(a)

(b)

FIGURE 9.3

Valuable archaeological evidence is often destroyed because it is sought by collectors and commands a high price on the "art" market. (a) Stela 1 from Jimbal, Guatemala, photographed shortly after its discovery in 1965. (b) Less than ten years later, looters had sawed off the top panel to steal the sculpted figures; in the process, they destroyed the head of the Maya ruler and the top of the hieroglyphic inscription. (Photo (a) courtesy of the Tikal Project, the University Museum, University of Pennsylvania; photo (b) courtesy of Joya Hairs.)

damaged or leveled by looting. The seemingly insatiable demand for pottery that caused so much destruction also spawned a thriving business in the local production of high-quality fakes. By the early 1980s, Ban Chiang pots, authentic and fake, were bringing $3000 or more a piece on the illicit "art" market.

The question remains how collectors are to be discouraged from seeking and purchasing looted archaeological materials. Since the root of the problem is economic, clearly the solution must be economic as well. One promising line of legal action, already implemented by some governments, involves changes in the inheritance laws so that individuals cannot bequeath archaeological collections to their heirs. Like legitimate art, most antiquities increase in value over time and thus represent an investment. But under this type of legislation, items defined as archaeological materials pass instead to the state. Collectors may think twice about purchasing "art" that will ultimately be taken by the government.

The antiquities problem is as complex as it is urgent. In formulating antiquities legislation, considerations of politics and patronage often weigh more heavily than the security of archaeological materials. Archaeologists and other interested people must therefore fight to protect the past, or we shall lose it forever.

DESTRUCTION IN THE NAME OF PROGRESS

Vandalism and looting are serious problems, but well-intentioned activities can also be harmful. Although done in the name of progress, activities such as opening new lands to agriculture, constructing new roads and buildings, and creating flood-control projects inevitably destroy countless remains of past human activity. Almost any action that affects the earth's surface is a threat to the archaeological record. Even under the best of circumstances, we can never answer all our questions about past cultural development, but as the physical remains continue to be obliterated, our ability to ask any new questions at all is drastically cut.

Obviously we cannot simply stop population and construction growth, so a considerable number of sites are going to be destroyed. But an increasing number of archaeologists are adopting a conservationist attitude toward cultural remains. This attitude involves a heightened emphasis on planning and a restructuring of the relative roles of excavation and reconnaissance/survey in archaeological research. As we discussed in Chapter 3, archaeologists have a responsibility to the future, when greater resources and more sophisticated techniques may allow a more complete recovery of data. Unthreatened sites should never be completely excavated; a portion should always be left undisturbed for future archaeologists to investigate. But even for sites threatened with imminent destruction, there has been a change of attitude. In such situations the traditional response was to excavate quickly and recover as much data as possible—sometimes literally one step ahead of construction crews. Now, however, with the invaluable assistance of a growing array of supportive legislation, archaeologists are often able to take the time to assess the situation, reconnoiter the area concerned, and then—*if appropriate*—conduct excavations.

CULTURAL RESOURCE MANAGEMENT

Archaeologists have always attempted to respond to the threat of destruction, but until fairly recently, the general public and governmental policy in most nations have shown little concern for this problem. Fortunately, after years of neglect and destruction, many countries have begun to enact firm protective legislation based on the premise that the remains of the historic and prehistoric past are a nonrenewable national resource like such natural resources as petroleum or mineral deposits.

With continuing expansion in preservationist legislation, archaeologists have been needed in growing numbers to conduct the surveys and other work the new laws require. As a consequence, a new specialty has arisen within archaeology: cultural resource management (CRM). As noted in Chapter 1, this specialty has become the fastest-developing area within American archaeology, and private CRM consulting firms now rival colleges and government agencies as employment places for professional archaeologists.

The motives for such conservation efforts are both humanistic and scientific, but they also have a very practical basis. Knowledge of the past fosters self-esteem and national unity. It also fosters economic development. Tourism, founded at least in part on a well-documented and spectacular past, is a multi-million dollar business in some nations. Sites such as Teotihuacán in Mexico, the Great Pyramids in Egypt, Machu Picchu in Peru, and Williamsburg in the United States not only serve as symbols of national heritage but also attract millions of tourists every year (Fig. 9.4). In Egypt the Aswan Dam salvage project, which was conducted in the 1960s, was organized by UNESCO to save the magnificent site of Abu Simbel (Fig. 9.5). This massive effort cost an estimated $40,000,000, of which the government of Egypt supplied more than half. The program also included work in less spectacular aspects of archaeology, such as locating prehistoric occupation sites. Although this work was less heavily funded, its inclusion was important, for it underwrote collection of much valuable archaeological data that would otherwise have been lost.

In the United States a series of federal laws dating back to 1906 have been enacted to conserve archaeological sites (Table 9.1). Until recently, however, other countries, including several in Europe and Latin America, were far ahead of the United States in providing legal protection for their archaeological resources. Fortunately in the last two decades an important series of laws has helped the United States catch up, although additional protective measures are still required in some areas.

FIGURE 9.4

Archaeological remains are recognized national symbols for many countries, as well as providing huge revenues from tourists. One of the most famous examples is Teotihuacán, Mexico.

FIGURE 9.5

The spectacular remains of the temple of Abu Simbel were saved from the rising waters behind the Aswan Dam by being cut apart, moved, and reassembled on higher ground at a cost of over $40 million. (Courtesy of David O'Connor.)

TABLE 9.1

Major U.S. Federal Legislation
for the Protection of Archaeological Resources

Antiquities Act of 1906	Protects sites on federal lands
Historic Sites Act of 1935	Provides authority for designating National Historic Landmarks and for archaeological survey before destruction by development programs
National Historic Preservation Act of 1966 (amended 1976 and 1980)	Strengthens protection of sites via National Register; integrates state and local agencies into national program for site preservation
National Environmental Policy Act of 1969	Requires all federal agencies to specify impact of development programs on cultural resources
Archaeological Resources Protection Act of 1979	Provides criminal and civil penalties for looting or damaging sites on public and Native American lands
Convention on Cultural Property of 1982	Authorizes U.S. participation in 1970 UNESCO convention to prevent illegal international trade in cultural property
Cultural Property Act of 1983	Provides sanctions against U.S. import or export of illicit antiquities

For example, historic shipwrecks have been a recent focus of legislative attention in this country. Traditionally under the jurisdiction of federal maritime salvage laws, shipwrecks of all ages have been available for exploitation by divers and commercial salvage companies. Recent wrecks are often beneficially salvaged, but lack of discrimination between these and older remains has resulted in treasure seekers' destroying many shipwrecks with unique archaeological and historical value, sometimes by innocently removing isolated "souvenirs" and sometimes by dismantling entire sunken ships.

In several recent cases in Florida, for instance, current federal admiralty law has taken precedence over state laws designed to protect underwater archaeological resources. The broader implication of the Florida rulings is that, without new federal legislation, no state can assert confident and effective protective authority over historical shipwrecks. Some specific results of these rulings have been vividly described by Wilburn Cockrell, Underwater Archaeologist for the State of Florida, as in the case of the 1733 wreck of the *San Jose*, originally slated to become the world's first underwater shipwreck park, but which is now completely looted, almost all of its contents destroyed or scattered, so that all that remains is "simply a hole in the ocean floor, with even the ballast stones removed for a fireplace." This tragic case contrasts strongly with the fate of the 1554 wreck of the *San Esteban*, excavated off the coast of Texas in 1973, under the sponsorship of the Texas State Antiquities Committee. The results of this effort include recovery of important new data on little-known 16th-century ship architecture and construction methods, plus conservation of the remains of the ship and its contents, and publication of the results in book, movie, and exhibition formats aimed at diverse audiences. There is certainly no reason why archaeologists, sport divers, and salvage companies cannot work cooperatively to recover shipwrecks, but unless and until such collaboration becomes the norm, adequate legal protection for these archaeologically valuable remains is sorely needed.

The development of CRM has not been without growing pains, which have stemmed chiefly from several related issues. First of all, the sudden increase in both available funds and demand for archaeologists to conduct studies was not generally foreseen. There has been considerable confusion stemming from the unfamiliar kinds of complexities of the federal laws, regulations, and bureaucratic procedures, and a shortage of qualified archaeologists interested in undertaking the flood of new contracts. Second, archaeologists have had to reexamine the ethics and professional standards appropriate for this kind of work—to resolve competing priorities between preservation and excavation, for example.

A more promising effect has been the increasingly positive attitude of archaeologists in general toward such "contract archaeology" and CRM as areas in which creative research can be carried out. As evidence of this, an expanding number of archaeologists are actively trying to coordinate with government officials, such as State Historic Preservation Officers, to formulate broad regional research goals and priorities. Though flexible, such plans would magnify the applicability of data collected under CRM projects to questions of current cultural-historical, processual, and general theoretical interest.

But CRM isn't the full solution either. The laws providing for such work pertain only to sites on public land or those threatened by government-sponsored projects. Many sites, especially in the eastern portion of the United States where far less land is under public control, are situated on private property. To preserve these sites, threatened just as often by looting, construction development, or simple neglect, archaeologists Mark Michel and Steven LeBlanc conceived a private organization modeled on the successful Nature Conservancy. Incorporated in 1979, the Archaeological Conservancy seeks to identify archaeological sites worthy of protection, secure their preservation through purchase or donation, and educate the public about the need to preserve our cultural heritage (Fig. 9.6).

Once a site has been secured, the Archaeological Conservancy ensures its short-term protection and eventually donates or sells it to a public agency able to undertake long-term conservation. For example, the Conservancy has donated the Fort Craig Site in New Mexico to the Bureau of Land Management and has given two sites—Savage Cave in Kentucky and Powers Fort in Missouri—to local universities as centers for both environmental and archaeological research.

FIGURE 9.6

Oak Creek Pueblo, one of two important Sinagua culture ruins acquired for preservation by the Archaeological Conservancy in 1985. This ruin is located on
Oak Creek in the Verde Valley of central Arizona and dates to A.D. 1200–1450.
At one time there were about 40 Sinagua culture ruins in the area, but most
have been destroyed by looters and by development. The Sinagua are thought
to be ancestors of the modern Hopi. (Photo courtesy of the Archaeological
Conservancy.)

As its resources grow, the Archaeological Conservancy promises to be a major
factor for the protection of archaeological sites in the United States.

Archaeologists are not alone in their concern over protection of cultural resources. A growing number of ethnic groups are making efforts to ensure that
their traditions and heritage are preserved. There is a measure of irony in this
situation since in several instances archaeologists and anthropologists have been
the major target of efforts to defend ethnic cultural resources. Some Native
American groups, for example, resent what they perceive as often callous dis-
regard in archaeological removal of burials and artifacts. In California and elsewhere in the United States, laws now restrict excavation of Native American
sites, and some groups seek return or reburial of materials already excavated. A
similar situation exists in Australia, where new legislation requires that Aborigine skeletal collections in universities and museums be returned to native control.

These and similar situations are examples of a new challenge facing archaeologists: a growing antiarchaeological trend, motivated by the desire to compen-

sate various ethnic groups for very real offenses committed in the past, as well as to protect cultural traditions. While archaeologists were not actively involved in the worst of these past offenses—such as the genocidal treatment suffered by Aborigine groups in Australia and some Native American tribes in the United States—at the very least some archaeologists have excavated sites without considering the feelings or belief systems of the living descendants of those who once occupied these sites.

Both archaeologists and ethnic groups should recognize, however, that the greatest agent of destruction of cultural resources comes from the looter, motivated by monetary greed rather than knowledge or respect for the past. It can only be in the best interests of both parties to join forces to protect cultural resources from looting and, at the same time, cooperate in research designed to increase our knowledge about the past.

We cannot preserve or excavate all sites, and some sites have more to tell us than others. Clearly, then, increased attention should be paid to improving the means by which decisions are made between protection, immediate investigation, and sometimes necessary sacrifice. The question is not whether the past should be protected, but how best to protect it in the context of a rapidly growing and changing world.

THE RESPONSIBILITIES OF ARCHAEOLOGY

The archaeological profession has assumed responsibility for the cultural resources we have inherited from the past. This responsibility includes a variety of obligations, as summarized in a statement of archaeological ethics adopted more than a quarter of a century ago by the Society for American Archaeology:

Collections made by competent archaeologists must be available for examination by qualified scholars; relevant supporting data must also be accessible for study whether the collection is in a museum or other institution or in private hands.

It is the scholarly obligation of the archaeologist to report his findings in a recognized scientific medium. In the event that significance of the collection does not warrant publication, a manuscript report should be prepared and available.

Inasmuch as the buying and selling of artifacts usually results in the loss of context and cultural associations, the practice is censured.

An archaeological site presents problems which must be handled by the excavator according to a plan. Therefore, members of the Society for American Archaeology do not undertake excavations on any site being studied by someone without the prior knowledge and consent of that person.

Willful destruction, distortion, or concealment of the data of archaeology is censured, and provides grounds for expulsion from the Society for American Archaeology, at the discretion of the Executive Committee.

(CHAMPE ET AL. 1961)

This ethical statement expresses values that are as important today as when it was first written. It highlights some of the archaeologist's prime obligations: to protect the archaeological record and to share as widely as possible the information gained from it. Today, most archaeologists would add the obligation to respect the concern of ethnic groups directly affected by their research. Conservation, investigation, and communication—including consideration of concerned groups and education of new generations of archaeologists—are lasting goals for those who seek to know the past.

SUMMARY

Archaeology today faces an unprecedented crisis from the rapidly increasing destruction of archaeological sites—loss of the nonrenewable cultural resources of humankind. While some of this destruction will always be caused by the inescapable disturbances of modern activity, the greatest and most disturbing toll is taken by looting. Most of this intentional destruction is generated to supply an illicit worldwide market in antiquities. Although there is no easy solution to this problem, success has been achieved by protective governmental legislation (in the United States and in many other countries), nongovernmental preservation initiatives such as the Archaeological Conservancy, and the efforts of ethnic groups to protect their cultural heritage. These measures have fostered new attitudes about the past, giving rise to cultural resource management—the mobilization of concerned individuals and organizations to protect and preserve the heritage of all peoples. Archaeologists are central to this effort, for they have a professional responsibility both to protect the record of the past and, through training and publication, to ensure that the knowledge acquired from their research is preserved and passed on to future generations.

· *Glossary* ·

Terms in italics are defined elsewhere in the glossary.

A B S O L U T E   D A T I N G   Determination of age on a specific time scale, as in years before present (*B.P.*) or according to a fixed calendrical system (compare with *relative dating*). (Chapter 6)

A C Q U I S I T I O N   The first stage of *behavioral processes*, in which raw materials are procured (see *manufacture*, *use*, and *deposition*). (Chapter 3)

A C T U A L I S T I C   S T U D I E S   Detailed observations of actual use of materials like those found in the *archaeological record* (*artifacts*, *ecofacts*, and *features*) to produce reliable *general analogies* for *interpretation*. (Chapter 7)

A E R I A L   R E C O N N A I S S A N C E   *Remote sensing* techniques carried out from an aerial platform (balloon, airplane, satellite, etc.); includes direct observation and recording by photographic, radar, or other images. (Chapter 4)

A L L O Y   A mixture of two or more metals, such as bronze (copper and tin), used to make *metal artifacts*. (Chapter 5)

A N A L O G Y   A process of reasoning by which similarity between two entities in some characteristics is taken to imply similarity of other characteristics as well; the basis of most archaeological *interpretation* (see *general* and *specific analogy*). (Chapter 7)

A N A L Y S I S   A stage in archaeological *research design* in which data are isolated, described, and structured, usually via typological *classification*, along with chronological, functional, technological, and constituent determinations (Chapters 3, 5)

A N N E A L I N G   Application of heat in the *manufacture* of *metal artifacts*. (Chapter 5)

A N T H R O P O L O G Y   The comprehensive study of the human species from biological, social, and cultural perspectives using both *synchronic* and *diachronic* views; in North

America it includes the subdisciplines of physical anthropology and cultural anthropology, the latter including *prehistoric archaeology*. (Chapter 1)

ANTIQUARIAN A person with nonprofessional interests in the past, usually someone who studies the past for its artistic or cultural value (compare with *archaeologist* and *looter*). (Chapter 2)

ARBITRARY SAMPLE UNIT A subdivision of the *data universe* with no cultural relevance, such as a *sample unit* defined by a site grid (compare with *nonarbitrary sample unit*). (Chapter 3)

ARCHAEOASTRONOMY Inference of ancient astronomical knowledge through study of alignments and other aspects of the *archaeological record;* combines perspectives of *archaeology* and astronomy. (Chapters 5 and 7)

ARCHAEOLOGICAL CULTURE The maximum grouping of all *assemblages* presumed to represent the sum of human activities carried out within an ancient *culture*. (Chapter 4)

ARCHAEOLOGICAL RECORD The physical remains produced by past human activities, that are sought, recovered, studied, and interpreted by *archaeologists* to reconstruct the past. (Chapter 1)

ARCHAEOLOGIST A professional scholar who studies the human past through its physical remains (compare with *antiquarian* and *looter*). (Chapter 1, 2, and 9)

ARCHAEOLOGY The study of the social and cultural past through material remains, with the aim of ordering, describing, and explaining the meaning of the events of the past. (Chapters 1, 2, and 9)

ARCHAEOMAGNETIC AGE DETERMINATION Measurement of magnetic alignments within undisturbed *features*, such as hearths and kilns, for comparison to known schedules of past magnetic alignments within a region to yield an absolute age. (Chapter 6)

ARTIFACT A discrete, portable object with characteristics resulting wholly or in part from human activity; artifacts are individually assignable to *ceramic*, *lithic*, *metal*, *organic*, or other categories (see also *industry*). (Chapters 3 and 5)

ASSEMBLAGE A gross grouping of all *subassemblages* assumed to represent the sum of human activities carried out within an ancient community (see *archaeological culture*). (Chapter 4)

ASSOCIATION Occurrence of one item of archaeological data adjacent to another and in or on the same *matrix*. (Chapter 3)

ATTRIBUTE The minimal characteristic used as a criterion for grouping artifacts into classes; includes *stylistic*, *form*, and *technological attributes* (also see *classification*). (Chapters 4 and 5)

AUGURING A *subsurface detection* technique using a drill run by either human or machine power to determine the depth and characteristics of archaeological or natural deposits. (Chapter 4)

BATTLESHIP-SHAPED CURVE A lens-shaped graph representing changes in artifact type frequencies through time, from origin to expanding popularity, decline, and finally disappearance. (Chapter 6)

BEHAVIORAL PROCESSES Human activities, including *acquisition, manufacture, use,* and *deposition* behavior, that produce tangible archaeological remains (compare with *transformational processes*). (Chapter 3)

BLADE A long, thin, parallel-sided *flake* usually made from a cylindrical *core* (see *lithic artifacts*). (Chapter 5)

BONE AGE DETERMINATION Use of any of a variety of *relative dating* techniques applicable to bone material, including measurements of the depletion of nitrogen and the accumulation of fluorine and uranium. (Chapter 6)

B.P. Before present; used in age determinations; in calculating radiocarbon dates, "present" means 1950 (a fixed reference date). (Chapter 6)

CENTRAL PLACE THEORY The theory that human settlements space themselves evenly across a landscape, depending on the availability of resources and communication routes, and that these settlements become differentiated, forming a hierarchy of controlling centers called "central places" (see *locational analysis*). (Chapter 7)

CERAMIC ARTIFACTS *Artifacts* of fired clay, belonging to *pottery,* figurine, or other ceramic *industries.* (Chapter 5)

CLASSIFICATION The ordering of phenomena into groups (classes) based on the sharing of *attributes.* (Chapters 2, 4, 5, and 6)

CLEARING EXCAVATIONS Excavations designed primarily to reveal the horizontal and, by inference, functional dimensions of archaeological *sites*—the extent, distribution, and patterning of buried archaeological data (compare with *penetrating excavations*). (Chapter 4)

COLD HAMMERING A technique for making *metal artifacts,* in which the metal is shaped by percussion without heating. (Chapter 5)

COMPUTER SIMULATION STUDIES Reconstructions of the past using computerized *models* of ancient conditions and variables to generate a sequence of events, which can be compared to the known *archaeological record,* thus refining and testing *hypotheses* about the past. (Chapter 8)

CONJOINING STUDIES The refitting of *artifact* and *ecofact* fragments to evaluate the integrity of an archaeological deposit; such studies allow definition of *cumulative features,* such as lithic debris scatters; they sometimes allow reconstruction of ancient *manufacture* and *use* behavior. (Chapters 4 and 5)

CONQUEST Aggressive movement of human groups from one area to another, resulting in the subjugation of the native society. (Chapter 8)

CONSTRUCTED FEATURE A *feature,* such as a house, storeroom, or burial chamber, deliberately built to provide a setting for one or more activities (compare with *cumulative feature*). (Chapter 5)

CONTEXT Characteristics of archaeological data, resulting from combined *behavioral* and *transformational processes,* which are evaluated by means of recorded *association, matrix,* and *provenience* (see *primary context* and *secondary context*). (Chapter 3)

COPROLITES Preserved ancient feces that contain food residues used to reconstruct ancient diet and subsistence activities. (Chapter 5)

CORE A *lithic artifact* from which *flakes* are removed; it is used as a tool or a blank from which other tools are made. (Chapter 5)

CORING A *subsurface detection* technique using a hollow metal tube driven into the ground to lift a column of earth for stratigraphic study. (Chapter 4)

CULTURAL ADAPTATION The sum of the adjustments of a human society to its environment (see *cultural ecology*). (Chapter 8)

CULTURAL DRIFT Gradual cultural change caused by imperfect transmission of information between generations; it is analogous to genetic drift in biology. (Chapter 8)

CULTURAL ECOLOGY The study of the dynamic interaction between human society and its environment, viewing *culture* as the primary adaptive mechanism in the relationship. (Chapters 2, 7, and 8)

CULTURAL EVOLUTION The theory that human societies change via a process analogous to the evolution of biological species (see *unilinear cultural evolution* and *multilinear cultural evolution*). (Chapters 2 and 8)

CULTURAL HISTORICAL INTERPRETATION A largely *inductive* approach to archaeological *interpretation* based on temporal and spatial syntheses of data and the application of general descriptive *models* usually derived from a normative view of *culture*. (Chapter 8)

CULTURAL INVENTION The origin of new cultural forms within a society, by either accident or design. (Chapter 8)

CULTURAL PROCESSUAL INTERPRETATION A largely *deductive* approach to archaeological *interpretation* aimed at delineating the interactions and changes in cultural *systems* by applying both descriptive and explanatory *models* based on ecological and evolutionary views of *culture*. (Chapter 8)

CULTURAL RESOURCE MANAGEMENT (CRM) The conservation and selective investigation of prehistoric and historic remains; specifically, the development of ways and means, including legislation, to safeguard the past. (Chapters 1 and 9)

CULTURAL SELECTION The process that leads to differential retention of cultural traits that increase a society's potential for successful *cultural adaptation*, while eliminating maladaptive traits. (Chapter 8)

CULTURE The concept that underlies and unites the discipline of *anthropology* and, in its various definitions, acts as a central *model* by which archaeological data are interpreted; a definition suited to *archaeology* sees culture as the cumulative resource of human society that provides the means for nongenetic adaptation to the environment by regulating behavior in three areas—*technology*, *social systems*, and *ideological systems*. (Chapters 1 and 2)

CULTURE AREA A spatial unit defined by *ethnographically* observed cultural similarities within a given geographical area; used archaeologically to define spatial limits to *archaeological cultures* (see also *time–space grids*). (Chapter 8)

CUMULATIVE FEATURE A *feature* without evidence of deliberate construction, resulting instead from accretion, such as in a *midden*, or subtraction, such as in a quarry (compare with *constructed feature*). (Chapter 5)

DATA ACQUISITION A stage in archaeological *research design* in which data are gathered, normally by three basic procedures—*reconnaissance*, *surface survey*, and *excavation*. (Chapters 3 and 4)

DATA PROCESSING A stage in archaeological *research design* usually involving, in the case of *artifacts*, cleaning, conserving, labeling, inventorying, and cataloging. (Chapters 3 and 4)

DATA UNIVERSE A defined area of archaeological investigation, often a *region* or *site*, bounded in time and geographical space. (Chapter 3)

DEDUCTION A process of reasoning by which an investigator tests the validity of a generalization or law by deriving one or more *hypotheses* and applying these to specific observations (compare with *induction*). (Chapters 1 and 8)

DENDROCHRONOLOGY The study of tree ring growth patterns, which are linked to develop a continuous chronological sequence. (Chapter 6)

DEPOSITION The last stage of *behavioral processes*, in which *artifacts* are discarded (see *acquisition, manufacture,* and *use*). (Chapter 3)

DIACHRONIC Pertaining to phenomena as they occur or change over a period of time; a chronological perspective (compare with *synchronic*). (Chapter 1)

DIFFUSION Transmission of ideas from one *culture* to another. (Chapter 8)

DIRECT DATING Determining the age of archaeological data by analysis of the *artifact, ecofact,* or *feature* itself (compare with *indirect dating*). (Chapter 6)

DIRECT PERCUSSION A technique used for the manufacture of chipped stone *artifacts* in which *flakes* are produced by striking a *core* with a hammerstone or by striking the core against a fixed stone or anvil (compare with *indirect percussion* and *pressure flaking*). (Chapter 5)

DISPOSAL See *deposition*.

ECOFACT Nonartifactual evidence from the past that has cultural relevance; the category includes both *inorganic* and *organic ecofacts*. (Chapters 3 and 5)

ETHNOARCHAEOLOGY *Ethnographic* studies designed to aid archaeological *interpretation*, such as descriptions of *behavioral processes*; especially the ways material items enter the *archaeological record* (see *analogy*). (Chapter 7)

ETHNOCENTRISM Observational bias in which other societies are evaluated by standards relevant to the observer's *culture*. (Chapters 2 and 9)

ETHNOGRAPHY The comparative study of contemporary *cultures*; part of the subdiscipline of cultural *anthropology*. (Chapter 1)

ETHNOLOGY The comparative study of contemporary *cultures*; part of the subdiscipline of cultural *anthropology*. (Chapter 1)

EXCAVATION A method of *data acquisition* in which *matrix* is removed to discover and retrieve archaeological data from beneath the ground, revealing the three-dimensional structure of the data and *matrix*, both vertically (see *penetrating excavations*) and horizontally (see *clearing excavations*). (Chapters 3 and 4)

EXCHANGE SYSTEMS *Systems* for trade or transfer of goods, services, and ideas between individuals and societies. (Chapter 7)

EXPERIMENTAL ARCHAEOLOGY Studies designed to aid archaeological *interpretation* by attempting to duplicate aspects of *behavioral processes* experimentally under carefully controlled conditions (see *analogy*). (Chapter 7)

EXPLANATION The end product of scientific research; in *archaeology* this refers to determining what happened in the past and when, where, how, and why it happened (see *interpretation*). (Chapters 1, 7, and 8)

FEATURE   A nonportable *artifact*, not recoverable from its *matrix* without destroying its integrity (see *constructed feature* and *cumulative feature*). (Chapters 3 and 5)

FEEDBACK   A response to a stimulus that acts within a *system* (see *negative feedback* and *positive feedback*). (Chapter 8)

FLAKE   A *lithic artifact* detached from a *core*, either as waste or as a tool. (Chapter 5)

FORM   The physical characteristics—arrangement, composition, size, and shape—of any component of a *culture* or cultural *system;* in archaeological research, the first objective is to describe and analyze the physical *attributes* (form) of data to determine distributions in time and space (see *function*). (Chapters 1 and 2)

FORM ATTRIBUTES   *Attributes* based on the physical characteristics of an *artifact*, including overall shape, shape of parts, and measurable dimensions; leads to form *classification*. (Chapters 4 and 5)

FORM TYPES   *Artifact* classes based on *form attributes*. (Chapters 4 and 5)

FORMULATION   The first stage in archaeological *research design*, involving definition of the research problem and goals, background investigations, and feasibility studies. (Chapter 3)

FREQUENCY SERIATION   A *relative dating* technique in which artifacts or other archaeological data are chronologically ordered by ranking their relative frequencies to conform with *battleship-shaped curves* (see *seriation*). (Chapter 6)

FUNCTION   The purpose or use of a component of a *culture* or of a cultural *system;* the second goal of archaeological research is analysis of data and their relationships to determine function, thus reconstructing ancient behavior (see *form*). (Chapters 1 and 2)

GENERAL ANALOGY   An *analogy* used in archaeological *interpretation* based on broad and generalized comparisons that are documented across many cultural *traditions* (see *actualistic studies*). (Chapter 7)

GEOCHRONOLOGY   Age determination by *association* with geological formations. (Chapter 6)

GLAZE   A specialized *slip* applied to *pottery*, which produces an impermeable and glassy surface when fired at high temperatures (see *vitrification*). (Chapter 5)

GROUND RECONNAISSANCE   The traditional method for the discovery of archaeological *sites* by visual inspection from ground level. (Chapter 4)

GROUND SURVEY   A *surface survey* technique using direct observation to gather archaeological data present on the ground surface; specifically, mapping and surface collection. (Chapter 4)

GROUND TRUTH   Determination of the causes of patterns revealed by *remote sensing*, such as by examining ground surface features identified by aerial photography. (Chapter 4)

HALF-LIFE   The period required for one-half of a radioactive isotope to decay and form a stable element; this decay rate, expressed as a statistical constant, provides the measurement scale for *radiometric age determination*. (Chapter 6)

HISTORICAL ARCHAEOLOGY   The area of *archaeology* concerned with literate societies, in contrast to *prehistoric archaeology* (although the distinction is not always clear-cut). For obvious reasons historical archaeology is often allied to the discipline of *history*. (Chapter 1)

HISTORY   The study of the past through written records, which are compared, judged for accuracy, placed in chronological sequence, and interpreted in light of preceding, contemporary, and subsequent events. (Chapters 1 and 7)

HORIZON   Cross-cultural regularities at one point in time; the spatial baseline of the New World *cultural historical interpretation* synthesis proposed in 1958 by Willey and Phillips (compare with *tradition*). (Chapter 8)

HORIZONTAL STRATIGRAPHY   Chronological sequences based on successive horizontal displacements, such as sequential beach terraces, analogous to *stratigraphy*. (Chapter 6)

HYPOTHESIS   A proposition, often derived from a broader generalization or law, that postulates relationships between two or more variables based on specified assumptions. (Chapter 1)

IDEOLOGICAL SYSTEMS   One of three components of *culture*; the knowledge or beliefs used by human societies to understand and cope with their existence (see also *technology* and *social systems*). (Chapters 2 and 7)

IMPLEMENTATION   The second stage in archaeological *research design*; it involves obtaining permits, raising funds, and making logistical arrangements. (Chapter 3)

INDIRECT DATING   Determination of the age of archaeological data by *association* with a *matrix* or object of known age (compare *direct dating*). (Chapter 6)

INDIRECT PERCUSSION   A technique used to manufacture chipped stone *artifacts*, in which *flakes* are produced by striking a punch, usually made of wood or bone, placed against a *core* (compare with *direct percussion* and *pressure flaking*). (Chapter 5)

INDUCTION   A process of reasoning by which one proceeds from a series of specific observations to derive a general conclusion (compare with *deduction*). (Chapters 1 and 8)

INDUSTRY   A gross *artifact* category defined by shared material and *technology*, such as a chipped stone industry or a *pottery* industry. (Chapter 5)

INEVITABLE VARIATION   The premise that all cultures vary and change through time without specific cause; a general and unsatisfactory descriptive *model* sometimes implied in *cultural historical interpretation*. (Chapter 8)

INORGANIC ECOFACTS   *Ecofacts* derived from nonbiological remains, including soils, minerals, and the like (compare with *organic ecofacts*). (Chapter 5)

INTERPRETATION   A stage in archaeological *research design* involving the *synthesis* of results of data *analysis* and the *explanation* of their meaning, allowing a reconstruction of the past. (Chapters 3, 7, and 8)

LAW OF SUPERPOSITION   The principle that the sequence of observable *strata*, from bottom to top, reflects the order of deposition, from earliest to latest (see *stratigraphy*). (Chapter 4)

LITHIC ARTIFACTS   *Artifacts* made from stone, including chipped stone and ground stone *industries*. (Chapter 5)

LOCATIONAL ANALYSIS   Techniques from geography used to study locations of human settlement and to infer the determinants of these locations (see *central place theory*). (Chapter 7)

LOOTER An individual who plunders archaeological *sites* to find *artifacts* of commercial value, at the same time destroying the evidence that *archaeologists* rely on to understand the past (compare with *antiquarian* and *archaeologist*). (Chapters 1, 2, and 9)

MAGNETOMETER A device used in *subsurface detection* that measures minor variations in the earth's magnetic field, often revealing archaeological *features* as magnetic anomalies. (Chapter 4)

MANUFACTURE The second stage of *behavioral processes* in which raw materials are modified to produce *artifacts* (see *acquisition*, *use*, and *deposition*). (Chapter 3)

MATRIX The physical medium that surrounds, holds, or supports archaeological data. (Chapter 3)

METAL ARTIFACTS *Artifacts* made from metal, including copper, bronze, and iron *industries*. (Chapter 5)

METATE A common New World term for ground stone basins used to process grains. (Chapter 5)

MIDDEN An accumulation of debris, resulting from human *disposal* behavior, removed from areas of *manufacture* and *use*; it may be the result of one-time refuse disposal or long-term disposal, resulting in *stratification*. (Chapters 3 and 5)

MIGRATION Movement of human populations from one area to another, usually resulting in cultural contact. (Chapter 8)

MODEL A theoretical scheme constructed to understand a specific set of data or phenomena; descriptive models deal with the form and structure of phenomena, and explanatory models seek underlying causes for phenomena; models may also be *diachronic* or *synchronic*. (Chapters 1, 2, and 8)

MULTILINEAR CULTURAL EVOLUTION A theory of *cultural evolution* proposing that each society pursues an individual evolutionary career shaped by accumulated specific *cultural adaptations* (compare with *unilinear cultural evolution*). (Chapters 2 and 8)

MULTIPLE WORKING HYPOTHESES The simultaneous testing of alternative *hypotheses* to minimize bias and maximize the chances of finding the best available choice. (Chapter 8)

MULTIVARIATE STRATEGY A class of *models* of *multilinear cultural evolution* that views major cultural changes as the result of multiple, relatively small, adaptive adjustments (compare with *prime movers*). (Chapter 8)

NATURAL SECONDARY CONTEXT A *secondary context* resulting from natural *transformational processes* such as erosion or animal and plant activity (compare with *use-related secondary context*). (Chapter 3)

NEGATIVE FEEDBACK A response to changing conditions that acts to dampen or stop a *system's* reaction. (Chapter 8)

NONARBITRARY SAMPLE UNIT A subdivision of the *data universe* with cultural relevance, such as *sample units* defined by rooms or houses (compare with *arbitrary sample unit*). (Chapter 3)

NORMS Rules that govern behavior in a particular society. (Chapter 8)

OBSIDIAN HYDRATION Adsorption of water on exposed surfaces of obsidian; if the local hydration rate is known and constant, this phenomenon can be used as an *absolute dating* technique through measurement of the thickness of the hydration layer. (Chapter 6)

ORGANIC ARTIFACTS *Artifacts* made of organic materials, including wood, bone, horn, fiber, ivory, or hide *industries*. (Chapter 5)

ORGANIC ECOFACTS *Ecofacts* derived from plant, animal, and human remains (compare with *inorganic ecofacts*). (Chapter 5)

PENETRATING EXCAVATIONS *Excavations* designed primarily to reveal the vertical and temporal dimensions within archaeological deposits—the depth, sequence, and composition of buried data (compare with *clearing excavations*). (Chapter 4)

PERIOD A broad and general chronological unit defined for a *site* or *region*, based on combined data such as sets of contemporary *artifact* types (see also *time–space grid*). (Chapter 8)

PHYTOLITHS Microscopic silica bodies that form in living plants, providing a durable floral *ecofact* that allows the identification of plant remains in archaeological deposits. (Chapter 5)

POPULATION The aggregate of all *sample units* within a *data universe*. (Chapter 3)

POSITIVE FEEDBACK A response to changing conditions that acts to stimulate further reactions within a *system*. (Chapter 8)

POTASSIUM-ARGON AGE DETERMINATION A *radiometric* dating technique based on the *half-life* of the radioactive isotope of potassium (^{40}K) that decays to form argon (^{40}Ar). (Chapter 6)

POTTERY A class of *ceramic artifacts* in which clay is formed into containers (by hand, in molds, or using a potter's wheel), often decorated, and fired. (Chapter 5)

PREHISTORIC ARCHAEOLOGY In contrast to *historical archaeology*, the area of *archaeology* concerned with preliterate or nonliterate societies; prehistoric archaeology in North America is considered a part of the discipline of *anthropology*. (Chapter 1)

PRESSURE FLAKING A technique for manufacturing chipped stone *artifacts*, in which *flakes* or *blades* are produced by applying pressure against a *core* with a punch usually made of wood or bone (compare with *direct percussion* and *indirect percussion*). (Chapter 5)

PRIMARY CONTEXT The condition in which *provenience*, *association*, and *matrix* have not been disturbed since the original *deposition* of archaeological data (compare with *secondary context*). (Chapter 3)

PRIME MOVERS Factors crucial to stimulating major cultural change; they are emphasized in some *models* of *multilinear cultural evolution* (compare with *multivariate strategy*). (Chapter 8)

PROVENIENCE The three-dimensional location of archaeological data within or on the *matrix* at the time of discovery. (Chapter 3)

PSEUDOARCHAEOLOGY Use of real or imagined archaeological evidence to justify nonscientific accounts about the past. (Chapter 1)

PUBLICATION   The final stage of archaeological *research design*, providing reports of the data and *interpretations* resulting from archaeological research. (Chapters 3 and 9)

QUERN   A common Old World term for ground stone basins used to process grains. (Chapter 5)

RADAR   An instrument used in *subsurface detection* that records differential reflection of radar pulses from buried *strata* and *features*. (Chapter 4)

RADIOCARBON AGE DETERMINATION   A *radiometric age determination* technique based on measuring the decay of the radioactive isotope of carbon (^{14}C) to stable nitrogen (^{14}N). (Chapter 6)

RADIOMETRIC AGE DETERMINATION   A variety of *absolute dating* techniques based on the transformation of unstable radioactive isotopes into stable elements (see *potassium-argon age determination* and *radiocarbon age determination*). (Chapter 6)

RECONNAISSANCE   A method of *data acquisition* in which archaeological remains are systematically identified, including both discovery and plotting of their location; it is often conducted along with *surface survey*. (Chapter 4)

REGION   A geographically defined area containing a series of interrelated human communities that share a single cultural-ecological *system*. (Chapter 3)

RELATIVE DATING   Determining chronological sequence without reference to a fixed time scale (compare with *absolute dating*). (Chapter 6)

REMOTE SENSING   *Reconnaissance* and *surface survey* methods involving aerial or subsurface detection of archaeological data. (Chapter 4)

RESEARCH DESIGN   A systematic plan to coordinate archaeological research to ensure the efficient use of resources and to guide the research according to the *scientific method* (see *formulation, implementation, data acquisition, data processing, analysis, interpretation,* and *publication*). (Chapter 3)

RESISTIVITY DETECTOR   An instrument used in *subsurface detection* that measures differences in the conductivity of electrical current and thus may identify archaeological *features*. (Chapter 4)

RETOUCH   A technique of chipped stone *artifact manufacture* in which *pressure flaking* is used to remove small steep *flakes* to modify the edges of flake tools. (Chapter 5)

SAMPLE DATA ACQUISITION   Investigation of only a portion of the *sample units* in a *population* by probabilistic or nonprobabilistic sampling (compare with *total data acquisition*). (Chapters 3, 4, 5, and 9)

SAMPLE UNIT   The basic unit of archaeological investigation; a subdivision of the *data universe*, defined by either arbitrary or nonarbitrary criteria (see *arbitrary sample units* and *nonarbitrary sample units*). (Chapter 3)

SCIENCE   The systematic pursuit of knowledge about natural phenomena (in contrast to the nonnatural or supernatural) by a continually self-correcting method of testing and refining the conclusions that result from observation (see *scientific method*). (Chapters 1 and 8)

SCIENTIFIC METHOD   The operational means of *science*, by which natural phenomena are observed and conclusions are drawn and tested, using both *induction* and *deduction*. (Chapters 1 and 8)

SECONDARY CONTEXT The condition in which *provenience, association,* and *matrix* have been wholly or partially altered by *transformational processes* after original *deposition* of archaeological data (compare with *primary context*). (Chapter 3)

SERIATION Techniques used to order materials in a *relative dating* sequence in such a way that adjacent items in the series are more similar to each other than to items farther apart in the series (see *frequency seriation* and *stylistic seriation*). (Chapter 6)

SETTLEMENT ARCHAEOLOGY The study of the spatial distribution of ancient activities from the remains of single activity areas to entire *regions*. (Chapter 7)

SHOVEL TESTING A *subsurface detection* technique using either post hole diggers or shovels to determine rapidly the density and distribution of archaeological remains. (Chapter 4)

SITE A spatial clustering of archaeological data, comprising *artifacts, ecofacts,* and *features* in any combination. (Chapter 3)

SLIP A solution of clay and water applied to *pottery* to provide color and a smooth, uniform surface (see also *glaze*). (Chapter 5)

SMELTING Application of heat to ores to extract metals prior to the *manufacture* of *metal artifacts*. (Chapter 5)

SOCIAL SYSTEMS One of the three basic components of *culture;* the means by which human societies organize themselves and their interactions with other societies (see also *technology* and *ideological systems*). (Chapters 2 and 7)

SPECIFIC ANALOGY An *analogy* used in archaeological *interpretation* based on specific comparisons that are documented within a single cultural *tradition*. (Chapter 7)

STRATA The definable layers of archaeological *matrix* or *features* revealed by *excavation* (see *stratification*). (Chapter 4)

STRATIFICATION Multiple *strata* whose order of deposition reflects the *law of superposition* (see *stratigraphy*). (Chapter 4)

STRATIGRAPHY The archaeological evaluation of the significance of *stratification* to determine the temporal sequence of data within stratified deposits by using the *law of superposition* and *context* evaluations; also a *relative dating* technique. (Chapters 4 and 6)

STYLISTIC ATTRIBUTES *Attributes* defined by the surface characteristics of *artifacts*—color, texture, decoration, and so forth—leading to stylistic *classifications*. (Chapters 4 and 5)

STYLISTIC SERIATION A *relative dating* technique in which *artifacts* or other data are ordered chronologically according to stylistic similarities (see *seriation*). (Chapter 6)

STYLISTIC TYPES *Artifact* classes based on *stylistic attributes*. (Chapters 4 and 5)

SUBASSEMBLAGE A grouping of *artifact* classes, based on *form* and *functional* criteria, that is assumed to represent a single occupational group within an ancient community (see *assemblage* and *archaeological culture*). (Chapter 4)

SUBSURFACE DETECTION *Remote sensing* techniques carried out from ground level, including *auguring, coring, shovel testing,* and use of a *magnetometer, resistivity detector, radar,* and similar means. (Chapter 4)

SURFACE SURVEY A method of *data acquisition* in which data are gathered and evaluated from the surface of archaeological *sites,* usually by mapping of *features* and surface collection of *artifacts* and *ecofacts*. (Chapter 4)

SYNCHRONIC Pertaining to phenomena at one point in time; a concurrent perspective (compare with *diachronic*). (Chapter 1)

SYSTEM An organization that functions through the interdependence of its parts. (Chapter 8)

TAPHONOMY The study of the *transformational processes* affecting *organic ecofacts* after the death of the original organisms. (Chapter 5)

TECHNOLOGICAL ATTRIBUTES *Attributes* comprising raw material characteristics (constituents) and characteristics resulting from *manufacturing* methods; leads to technological *classifications*. (Chapters 4 and 5)

TECHNOLOGICAL TYPES *Artifact* classes based on *technological attributes*. (Chapters 4 and 5)

TECHNOLOGY One of the three basic components of *culture;* the means used by human societies to interact directly with, and adapt to, the environment (see *ideological* and *social systems*). (Chapters 2 and 7)

TEMPER A nonplastic substance (such as sand) added to clay prior to *pottery manufacture* to reduce shrinkage and breakage during drying and firing. (Chapter 5)

THREE-AGE SYSTEM A traditional *diachronic model* describing the sequence of technological *periods* in the Old World, each period characterized by predominant use of stone, bronze, or iron tools. (Chapter 2)

TIME–SPACE GRIDS A synthesis of temporal and spatial distributions of data used in *cultural historical interpretation*, based on *period* sequences within *culture areas*. (Chapter 8)

TOTAL DATA ACQUISITION Investigation of all *sample units* in a *population* (compare with *sample data acquisition*). (Chapters 3, 4, 5, and 9)

TRADE Transmission of material objects from one society to another; a descriptive cultural *model* used in *cultural historical interpretation* (see *exchange systems*). (Chapters 7 and 8)

TRADITION Cultural continuity through time; the temporal basis of the New World *cultural historical interpretation* synthesis proposed in 1958 by Willey and Phillips (compare with *horizon*). (Chapter 8)

TRANSFORMATIONAL PROCESSES Conditions and events that affect archaeological data from the time of *deposition* to the time of recovery (compare with *behavioral processes;* see also *taphonomy*). (Chapter 3)

TRANSPOSED PRIMARY CONTEXT *Primary context* that results from discard activities, leading to *midden* formation (compare with *use-related primary context*). (Chapter 3)

TYPE A class of data defined by a consistent clustering of *attributes* (see *classification*). (Chapter 8)

UNILINEAR CULTURAL EVOLUTION A 19th-century version of *cultural evolution* holding that all human societies change according to a single, fixed evolutionary course, passing through the same stages (described as "savagery," "barbarism," and "civilization" by Lewis Henry Morgan). (Chapters 2 and 8)

USE The third stage of *behavioral processes*, in which *artifacts* are utilized (see *acquisition, manufacture,* and *deposition*). (Chapter 3)

USE-RELATED PRIMARY CONTEXT *Primary context* that results from abandonment of materials during either *manufacture* or *use* (compare with *transposed primary context*). (Chapter 3)

USE-RELATED SECONDARY CONTEXT A *secondary context* resulting from disturbance by human activity after original *deposition* of materials (compare with *natural secondary context*). (Chapter 3)

VITRIFICATION Melting and fusion of glassy minerals within clay during high-temperature firing of *pottery* (above 1000° C), resulting in loss of porosity. (Chapter 5)

· *Bibliography* ·

NOTE: This brief bibliography is an introduction to the vast literature on archaeology and the human past. The works listed include books and articles, both recent and "classic" pieces. Numbers in parentheses at the end of each listing indicate the chapter or chapters to which each is most relevant. A fuller bibliography can be found in *Archaeology: Discovering Our Past* (Sharer and Ashmore 1987). Of course, we also recommend that the interested reader explore the local library for other works, including new books and issues of magazines and journals. In general, periodicals such as *Archaeology, National Geographic, Natural History, Scientific American,* and *Smithsonian* publish articles for the broadest audience. Journals such as *American Antiquity, American Scientist, Journal of Field Archaeology, Nature,* and *Science* are more technical in content and language.

Agurcia Fasquelle, R. 1986. Snakes, jaguars, and outlaws: Some comments on Central American archaeology. In *Research and Reflections in Archaeology and History. Essays in Honor of Doris Stone,* ed. E. W. Andrews V, pp. 1–9. New Orleans: Middle American Research Institute, Tulane University. (3)

Ammerman, A. J. 1981. Surveys and archaeological research. *Annual Review of Anthropology* 10: 63–88. (3,4)

Andresen, J. M., B. F. Byrd, M. D. Elson, R. H. McGuire, R. G. Mendoza, E. Staski, and J. P. White. 1981. The deer hunters: Star Carr reconsidered. *World Archaeology* 13: 31–46. (5,7)

Arnold, D. 1985. *Ceramic Theory and Cultural Process.* Cambridge: Cambridge University Press. (5,7,8)

Aveni, A. F. 1980. *Skywatchers of Ancient Mexico.* Austin: University of Texas Press. (7)

Aveni, A. F., ed. 1982. *Archaeoastronomy in the New World.* Cambridge: Cambridge University Press. (7)

Baillie, M. G. L. 1982. *Tree-Ring Dating and Archaeology*. Chicago: University of Chicago Press. (6)

Bannister, B. 1970. Dendrochronology. In *Science in Archaeology*, 2nd ed., ed. D. Brothwell and E. S. Higgs, pp. 191–205. New York: Praeger. (6)

Bartlett, M. H., T. M. Kolaz, and D. A. Gregory. *Archaeology in the City: A Hohokam Village in Phoenix, Arizona*. Tucson: University of Arizona Press. (1,3)

Bass, G. F. 1966. *Archaeology Under Water*. London: Thames & Hudson. (1,3,4)

Bass, W. M. 1986. *Human Osteology: A Laboratory and Field Manual of the Human Skeleton*. Columbia, Mo.: Missouri Archaeological Society. (5)

Bassett, C. A. 1986. The culture thieves. *Science 86* 7 (6): 22–29. (9)

Behrensmeyer, A. K., and A. P. Hill, eds. 1980. *Fossils in the Making: Vertebrate Taphonomy and Paleoecology*. Chicago: University of Chicago Press. (3)

Benson, E. P., ed. 1979. *Pre-Columbian Metallurgy of South America*. Washington, D.C.: Dumbarton Oaks. (5,7)

Binford, L. R. 1962. Archaeology as anthropology. *American Antiquity* 28: 217–225. (1,7,8)

———. 1967. Smudge pits and hide smoking: The use of analogy in archaeological reasoning. *American Antiquity* 32: 1–12. (7)

———. 1972. *An Archeological Perspective*. New York: Seminar Press. (1,3,7,8)

———. 1978. *Nunamiut Ethnoarchaeology*. New York: Academic Press. (3,5,7)

———. 1981. *Bones: Ancient Men and Modern Myths*. New York: Academic Press. (3,5,7)

———. 1983a. *In Pursuit of the Past: Decoding the Archaeological Record*. New York: Thames & Hudson. (1,3,7,8)

———. 1983b. *Working at Archaeology*. New York: Academic Press. (1,3,7,8)

Binford, L. R., and S. R. Binford. 1969. Stone tools and human behavior. *Scientific American* 220 (4): 70–84. (5,7)

Blumenschine, R. J. 1987. Letting lions speak for fossil bones. In *Archaeology: Discovering Our Past*, by R. J. Sharer and W. Ashmore, pp. 330–331. Palo Alto: Mayfield. (5,7)

Bordaz, J. 1970. *Tools of the Old and New Stone Age*. Garden City, N.Y.: Natural History Press. (5)

Bordes, F., and D. de Sonneville-Bordes. 1970. The significance of variability in Paleolithic assemblages. *World Archaeology* 2: 61–73. (7)

Brain, C. K. 1981. *The Hunters or the Hunted? An Introduction to African Cave Taphonomy*. Chicago: University of Chicago Press. (3,5,7)

Bray, W. and D. Trump. 1982. *The Penguin Dictionary of Archaeology*. 2nd ed. Harmondsworth: Penguin Books, Ltd. (1,3,4,5)

Brothwell, D. R. 1981. *Digging Up Bones*. 3rd ed. Ithaca, N.Y.: Cornell University Press. (5)

Bunn, H. T. 1981. Archaeological evidence for meat-eating by Plio-Pleistocene hominids from Koobi Fora and Olduvai Gorge. *Nature* 291: 574–577. (3,5,7)

Bunn, H. T., J. W. K. Harris, G. Isaac, Z. Kaufulu, E. Kroll, K. Schick, N. Toth, and A. K. Behrensmeyer. 1980. FxJj50: An early Pleistocene site in northern Kenya. *World Archaeology* 12: 109–136. (3,5,7)

Butzer, K. W. 1982. *Archaeology as Human Ecology: Method and Theory for a Contextual Approach*. New York: Cambridge University Press. (1,3,4,7)

Champe, J. L., D. S. Byers, C. Evans, A. K. Guthe, H. W. Hamilton, E. B. Jelks, C. W. Meighan, S. Olafson, G. I. Quimby, W. Smith, and F. Wendorf. 1961. Four statements for archaeology. *American Antiquity* 27: 137–138. (1,9)

Champion, S. 1980. *A Dictionary of Terms and Techniques in Archaeology*. Oxford: Phaidon Press. (1,3,4,5)

Chang, K. C. 1972. *Settlement Patterns in Archaeology*. Modules in Anthropology, no. 24. Reading, Mass.: Addison-Wesley. (3,7)

Chapman, R., I. Kinnes, and K. Randsborg, eds. 1981. *The Archaeology of Death*. Cambridge: Cambridge University Press. (5,7)

Chapman, R. C. 1987. Encounters with the historic dead. In *Archaeology: Discovering Our Past*, by R. J. Sharer and W. Ashmore, pp. 484–485. Palo Alto: Mayfield. (9)

Charleton, T. H. 1981. Archaeology, ethnohistory, and ethnology: Interpretive interfaces. In *Advances in Archaeological Method and Theory*, vol. 4, ed. M. B. Schiffer, pp. 129–176. New York: Academic Press. (1,7)

Chippindale, C. 1986. Stonehenge astronomy: Anatomy of a modern myth. *Archaeology* 39 (1): 48–52. (1,7)

Clark, J. G. D. [1954] 1971. *Excavations at Star Carr*. Reprint. Cambridge: Cambridge University Press. (5,7)

Clarke, D. L. 1972. A provisional model of an Iron Age society. In *Models in Archaeology*, ed. D. L. Clarke, pp. 801–869. London: Methuen. (7)

Cleere, H., ed. 1984. *Approaches to the Archaeological Heritage: A Comparative Study of World Cultural Resource Management Systems*. Cambridge: Cambridge University Press. (1,9)

Coggins, C. C. 1972. Archaeology and the art market. *Science* 175: 263–266. (1,9)

Coles, J. 1973. *Archaeology by Experiment*. New York: Scribner's. (7)

———. 1984. *The Archaeology of Wetlands*. Edinburgh: Edinburgh University Press. (3,4)

Conrad, G. W., and A. A. Demarest. 1984. *Religion and Empire: The Dynamics of Aztec and Inca Expansionism*. Cambridge: Cambridge University Press. (7,8)

Cowgill, G. L. 1974. Quantitative studies of urbanism at Teotihuacan. In *Mesoamerican Archaeology: New Approaches*, ed. N. Hammond, pp. 363–397. Austin: University of Texas Press. (4,7)

Daniel, G. 1981. *A Short History of Archaeology*. London: Thames & Hudson. (2)

Davis, H. A. 1982. Professionalism in archaeology. *American Antiquity* 47: 158–162. (1,9)

Deetz, J. F. 1977. *In Small Things Forgotten: The Archaeology of Early American Life*. Garden City, N.Y.: Doubleday/Anchor. (1,7,8)

DeNiro, M. J. 1987. Stable isotopy and archaeology. *American Scientist* 75: 182–191. (5,7)

Dimbleby, G. W. 1985. *The Palynology of Archaeological Sites*. Orlando: Academic Press. (5,7)

Ebert, J. I. 1984. Remote sensing applications in archaeology. In *Advances in Archaeologi-*

cal Method and Theory, vol. 7, ed. M. B. Schiffer, pp. 293–362. Orlando: Academic Press. (4)

Elachi, C. 1982. Radar images of the earth from space. *Scientific American* 247 (6): 54–61. (4)

Ericson, J. E., and T. K. Earle, eds. 1982. *Contexts for Prehistoric Exchange*. New York: Academic Press. (7)

Estes, J. E., J. R. Jensen, and L. R. Tinney. 1977. The use of historical photography for mapping archaeological sites. *Journal of Field Archaeology* 4: 441–447. (4)

Fagan, B. M. 1975. *The Rape of the Nile*. New York: Scribner's. (2,9)

———. 1978. *Quest for the Past: Great Discoveries in Archaeology*. New York: Scribner's. (2)

———. 1985. *The Adventure of Archaeology*. Washington, D.C.: National Geographic Society. (1,2,3)

Finney, B. R. 1977. Voyaging canoes and the settlement of Polynesia. *Science* 196: 1277–1285. (7)

Flannery, K. V. 1967. Culture history vs. cultural process: A debate in American archaeology. *Scientific American* 217 (2): 119–122. (2,8)

———. 1968. Archeological systems theory and early Mesoamerica. In *Anthropological Archeology in the Americas*, ed. B. J. Meggers, pp. 67–87. Washington, D.C.: Anthropological Society of Washington. (8)

———. 1972. The cultural evolution of civilizations. *Annual Review of Ecology and Systematics* 2: 399–426. (8)

———, ed. 1976. *The Early Mesoamerican Village*. New York: Academic Press. (1,3,4,7,8)

———. 1987. Coping with explanation in archaeology: Advice from The Master. In *Archaeology: Discovering Our Past*, by R. J. Sharer and W. Ashmore, pp. 581–583. Palo Alto: Mayfield. (8)

Ford, J. A. 1954. The type concept revisited. *American Anthropologist* 56: 42–53. (4)

Ford, R. I. 1983. The Archaeological Conservancy, Inc.: The goal is site preservation. *American Archaeology* 3: 221–224. (9)

Friedman, I., and F. W. Trembour. 1978. Obsidian: The dating stone. *American Scientist* 66: 44–51. (6)

Frink, D. S. 1984. Artifact behavior within the plow zone. *Journal of Field Archaeology* 11: 356–363. (3)

Geismar, J. H. 1987. Digging into a seaport's past [Manhattan]. *Archaeology* 40 (1): 30–35. (1,4,7)

Giesecke, A. G. 1987. The Abandoned Shipwreck Bill: Protecting our threatened cultural heritage. *Archaeology* 40 (4): 50–53. (9)

Gilbert, R. I., Jr., and J. H. Mielke, eds. 1985. *The Analysis of Prehistoric Diets*. Orlando: Academic Press. (5,7)

Gladfelter, B. G. 1981. Developments and directions in geoarchaeology. In *Advances in Archaeological Method and Theory*, vol. 4, ed. M. B. Schiffer, pp. 343–364. New York: Academic Press. (3,5,7)

Gould, R. A. 1980. *Living Archaeology*. Cambridge: Cambridge University Press. (7,8)

Gould, S. J. 1985. *The Flamingo's Smile*. New York: Norton. (1,8)

———. 1986. Evolution and the triumph of homology, or why history matters. *American Scientist* 74: 60–69. (1,8)

Green, E. L., ed. 1984. *Ethics and Values in Archaeology*. New York: Free Press. (1,9)

Hadingham, E. 1984. *Early Man and the Cosmos*. New York: Walker. (7)

Hamilton, S. L., and R. Woodward. 1984. A sunken 17th-century city: Port Royal, Jamaica. *Archaeology* 37 (1): 38–45. (1,3,4)

Harris, E. C. 1979. *Principles of Archaeological Stratigraphy*. London: Academic Press. (4,6)

Hart, D., ed. 1983. *Disease in Ancient Man*. Agincourt, Ontario: Irwin. (5,7)

Hassan, F. A. 1981. *Demographic Archaeology*. New York: Academic Press. (5,7)

Haviland, W. A. 1985. *Anthropology*, 4th ed. New York: Holt, Rinehart and Winston. (1,7,8)

Hedges, R. E. M., and J. A. J. Gowlett. 1986. Radiocarbon dating by accelerator mass spectrometry. *Scientific American* 254 (1): 101–107. (6)

Heggie, D. C., ed. 1982. *Archaeoastronomy in the Old World*. Cambridge: Cambridge University Press. (7)

Hester, T. A., R. F. Heizer, and J. A. Graham, eds. 1975. *Field Methods in Archaeology*. 6th ed. Palo Alto: Mayfield. (1,3,4,5)

Heyerdahl, T. 1950. *The Kon-Tiki Expedition: By Raft Across the South Seas*. London: Allen & Unwin. (7)

Higgenbotham, C. D. 1983. Native Americans versus archaeologists: The legal issues. *American Indian Law Review* 10: 91–115. (9)

Hill, J. N., and R. K. Evans. 1972. A model for classification and typology. In *Models in Archaeology*, ed. D. L. Clarke, pp. 231–273. London: Methuen. (3,4)

Hodder, I., ed. 1982. *Symbolic and Structural Archaeology*. Cambridge: Cambridge University Press. (7,8)

Hodder, I., and M. Hassall. 1971. The non-random spacing of Romano-British walled towns. *Man* 6: 391–407. (7)

Hyslop, J. 1984. *The Inka Road System*. Orlando: Academic Press. (5,7)

Isbell, W. H. 1978. The prehistoric ground drawings of Peru. *Scientific American* 239 (4): 140–153. (1,7)

Johnstone, P. 1980. *The Sea-Craft of Prehistory*. Cambridge: Harvard University Press. (1,5)

Joukowsky, M. 1980. *A Complete Manual of Field Archaeology*. Englewood Cliffs, N.J.: Prentice-Hall. (1,3,4,5,6)

Jovanovič, B. 1980. The origins of copper mining in Europe. *Scientific American* 242 (5): 152–167. (5,7)

Keeley, L. H. 1977. The functions of Paleolithic stone tools. *Scientific American* 237 (5): 105–126. (5,7)

———. 1980. *Experimental Determination of Stone Tool Uses: A Microwear Analysis*. Chicago: University of Chicago Press. (5,7)

Kenworthy, M. A., E. M. King, M. E. Ruwell, and T. Van Houten. 1985. *Preserving Field Records: Archival Techniques for Archaeologists and Anthropologists*. Philadelphia: University Museum, University of Pennsylvania. (4)

King, M. E. 1978. Analytical methods and prehistoric textiles. *American Antiquity* 43: 89–96. (5,7)

King, T. F. 1978. *The Archaeological Survey: Methods and Uses*. Washington, D.C.: U.S. Department of the Interior, Heritage Conservation and Recreation Service. (4)

———. 1983. Professional responsibility in public archaeology. *Annual Review of Anthropology* 12: 143–164. (1,9)

Klein, R. G., and K. Cruz-Uribe. 1984. *The Analysis of Animal Bones from Archaeological Sites*. Chicago: University of Chicago Press. (5,7)

Kolata, A. 1987. Tiwanaku and its hinterland. *Archaeology* 40 (1): 36–41. (5,7,8)

Lange, F., N. Mahaney, J. B. Wheat, and M. L. Chenault. 1986. *Yellow Jacket: A Four Corners Anasazi Ceremonial Center*. Boulder, Colo.: Johnson Books. (1,3)

LeBlanc, S. A. 1983. *The Mimbres People: Ancient Pueblo Painters of the American Southwest*. New York: Thames & Hudson. (1,3,4,9)

———. 1987. Of pots and pillage. In *Archaeology: Discovering Our Past*, by R. J. Sharer and W. Ashmore, pp. 546–547. Palo Alto: Mayfield. (1,9)

Lechtman, H. 1984. Pre-Columbian surface metallurgy. *Scientific American* 250 (6): 56–63. (5,7)

Lee, R. B., and I. DeVore, eds. 1968. *Man the Hunter*. Chicago: Aldine. (7)

Leone, M. P. 1982. Some opinions about recovering mind. *American Antiquity* 47: 742–760. (7)

Levin, A. M. 1986. Excavation photography: A day on a dig. *Archaeology* 39 (1): 34–39. (4)

Lewis-Williams, J. D. 1986. Cognitive and optical illusions in San rock art research. *Current Anthropology* 27: 171–178. (7)

Limp, W. F. 1974. Water separation and flotation processes. *Journal of Field Archaeology* 1: 337–342. (4)

Lipe, W. D. 1974. A conservation model for American archaeology. *The Kiva* 39: 213–245. (1,3,9)

———. 1984. Value and meaning in cultural resources. In *Approaches to the Archaeological Heritage: A Comparative Study of World Cultural Resource Management Systems*, ed. H. Cleere, pp. 1–11. Cambridge: Cambridge University Press. (1,3,9)

Loy, T. H. 1983. Prehistoric blood residues: Detection on tool surfaces and identification of species of origin. *Science* 220: 1269–1271. (5,7)

McGimsey, C. R., III. 1972. *Public Archeology*. New York: Seminar Press. (1,9)

McKusick, M. 1984. Psychic archaeology from Atlantis to Oz. *Archaeology* 37 (6): 48–52. (1)

MacNeish, R. S. 1964. The origins of New World civilization. *Scientific American* 211 (5): 29–37. (3,4,7)

MacNeish, R. S., M. L. Fowler, A. G. Cook, F. A. Peterson, A. Nelken-Terner, and J. A. Neely. 1972. *Excavations and Reconnaissance: The Prehistory of the Tehuacán Valley*, vol. 5. Austin: University of Texas Press. (3,4,7)

MacNeish, R. S., T. C. Patterson, and D. L. Browman. 1975. *The Central Peruvian Interaction Sphere*. Andover, Mass.: Phillips Academy. (7)

Maddin, R., J. D. Muhly, and T. S. Wheeler. 1977. How the Iron Age began. *Scientific American* 237 (4): 122–131. (5,7)

Marshack, A. 1972. Upper Paleolithic notation and symbol. *Science* 178: 817–827. (7)

Meltzer, D. J., D. D. Fowler, and J. A. Sabloff, eds. 1986. *American Archaeology Past and Future: A Celebration of the Society for American Archaeology 1935–1985*. Washington, D.C.: Smithsonian Institution Press. (1,2,7,8)

Michael, H. N. 1985. Correcting radiocarbon dates with tree ring dates at MASCA. *University Museum Newsletter* (University of Pennsylvania) 23 (3): 1–2. (6)

Michel, M. 1981. Preserving America's prehistoric heritage. *Archaeology* 34 (2): 61–63. (9)

Michels, J. W. 1973. *Dating Methods in Archaeology*. New York: Academic Press. (6)

Miller, D. 1980. Archaeology and development. *Current Anthropology* 21: 709–726. (1,9)

Moseley, M. E., and C. J. Mackey. 1974. *Twenty-four Architectural Plans of Chan Chan, Peru: Structure and Form at the Capital of Chimor*. Cambridge: Harvard University, Peabody Museum Press. (7)

Netting, R. M. 1977. *Cultural Ecology*. Menlo Park, Calif.: Cummings. (7,8)

Noël Hume, I. 1969. *Historical Archaeology*. New York: Knopf. (1,5,7)

———. 1979. *Martin's Hundred: The Discovery of a Lost Colonial Virginia Settlement*. New York: Knopf. (1,5,7)

Numbers, R. L. 1982. Creationism in 20th-century America. *Science* 218: 538–544. (1)

Oakley, K. P. 1956. *Man the Tool-Maker*. 3rd ed. London: British Museum. (5)

———. 1970. Analytical methods of dating bones. In *Science in Archaeology*, 2nd ed., ed. D. Brothwell and E. S. Higgs, pp. 35–45. New York: Praeger. (6)

Orme, B., ed. 1982. *Problems in Case Studies in Archaeological Dating*. Atlantic Highlands, N.J.: Humanities Press. (6)

Parrington, M. 1983. Remote sensing. *Annual Review of Anthropology* 12: 105–124. (3,4)

Petrie, W. M. F. 1901. *Diospolis Parva*. Memoir no. 20. London: Egyptian Exploration Fund. (4)

Plog, S., F. Plog, and W. Wait. 1978. Decision making in modern surveys. In *Advances in Archaeological Method and Theory*, vol. 1, ed. M. B. Schiffer, pp. 383–421. New York: Academic Press. (3,4)

Potts, R., and P. Shipman. 1981. Cutmarks made by stone tools on bones from Olduvai Gorge, Tanzania. *Nature* 291: 577–580. (5,7)

Price, T. D., and J. A. Brown, eds. 1985. *Prehistoric Hunter-Gatherers: The Emergence of Cultural Complexity*. Orlando: Academic Press. (7,8)

Pulak, C., and D. A. Frey. 1985. The search for a Bronze Age shipwreck. *Archaeology* 38 (4): 18–24. (1,3,4)

Rapp, G., Jr., and J. A. Gifford, eds. 1985. *Archaeological Geology.* New Haven: Yale University Press. (3,4,5,6,7)

Rathje, W. L. 1978. The ancient astronaut myth. *Archaeology* 31 (1): 4–7. (1)

Renfrew, C. 1971. Carbon 14 and the prehistory of Europe. *Scientific American* 225 (4): 63–72. (6,7,8)

———. 1973. *Before Civilization: The Radiocarbon Revolution and Prehistoric Europe.* New York: Knopf. (6,7,8)

———. 1983. The social archaeology of megalithic monuments. *Scientific American* 249 (5): 152–163. (7,8)

Renfrew, C., and J. F. Cherry, eds. 1986. *Peer Polity Interaction and Socio-Political Change.* Cambridge: Cambridge University Press. (7,8)

Rice, P. M. 1987. *Pottery Analysis: A Sourcebook.* Chicago: University of Chicago Press. (5,7)

Rouse, I. 1962. Introduction to revised edition. In *An Introduction to Southwestern Archaeology* [orig. 1924], by A. V. Kidder. New Haven: Yale University Press. (8)

Rovner, I. 1983. Plant opal phytolith analysis: Major advances in archaeobotanical research. In *Advances in Archaeological Method and Theory,* vol. 6, ed. M. B. Schiffer, pp. 225–266. New York: Academic Press. (5,7)

Sabloff, J. A. 1975. *Ceramics: Excavations at Seibal.* Memoirs of the Peabody Museum of Archaeology and Ethnology, vol. 13, no. 2. Cambridge: Harvard University, Peabody Museum. (4)

———. 1982. Introduction. In *Archaeology: Myth and Reality: Readings from Scientific American,* ed. J. A. Sabloff, pp. 1–26. San Francisco: Freeman. (1)

Schliemann, H. [1881] 1968. *Ilios, the City and Country of the Trojans.* Reissue. New York: Benjamin Blom. (1,2,7)

Schortman, E., P. Urban, W. Ashmore, and J. Benyo. 1986. Interregional interaction in the southeast Maya periphery: The Santa Bárbara Archaeological Project 1983–1984 seasons. *Journal of Field Archaeology* 13: 259–272. (8)

Schrire, C., ed. 1984. *Past and Present in Hunter-Gatherer Studies.* Orlando: Academic Press. (7,8)

Sedat, D. W. 1987. A day in the life of a field archaeologist. In *Archaeology: Discovering Our Past,* by R. J. Sharer and W. Ashmore, pp. 134–135. Palo Alto: Mayfield. (1,9)

Sharer, R. J., and W. Ashmore. 1987. *Archaeology: Discovering Our Past.* Palo Alto: Mayfield.

Sheets, P. D. 1987. Dawn of a new Stone Age in eye surgery. In *Archaeology: Discovering Our Past,* by R. J. Sharer and W. Ashmore, pp. 230–231. Palo Alto: Mayfield. (1,5,9)

Society for American Archaeology. 1986. Statement concerning the treatment of human remains. *Bulletin of the Society for American Archaeology* 4 (3): 7–8. (9)

Spaulding, A. C. 1953. Statistical techniques for the discovery of artifact types. *American Antiquity* 18: 305–313. (4)

Stark, B. L. 1986. Origins of food production in the New World. In *American Archaeology Past and Future: A Celebration of the Society for American Archaeology 1935–1985*, ed. D. J. Meltzer, D. D. Fowler, and J. A. Sabloff, pp. 277–321. Washington, D.C.: Smithsonian Institution Press. (7,8)

Stein, J. K., and W. R. Farrand, eds. 1985. *Archaeological Sediments in Context*. Orono, Maine: Center for the Study of Early Man. (3,4,5,7)

Stuart, G. E. 1976. *Your Career in Archaeology*. Washington, D.C.: Society for American Archaeology. (1,3,9)

Talmadge, V. A. 1982. The violation of sepulture: Is it legal to excavate human burials? *Archaeology* 35 (6): 44–49. (9)

Toth, N. 1987. The first technology. *Scientific American* 256 (4): 112–121. (5,7)

Toth, N., and K. D. Schick. 1986. The first million years: The archaeology of proto-human culture. In *Advances in Archaeological Method and Theory*, vol. 9, ed. M. B. Schiffer, pp. 1–96. Orlando: Academic Press. (5,7,8)

Trigger, B. G. 1968. The determinants of settlement patterns. In *Settlement Archaeology*, ed. K. C. Chang, pp. 53–78. Palo Alto: National Press. (7)

———. 1984. Archaeology at the crossroads: What's new? *Annual Review of Anthropology* 13: 275–300. (2,7,8)

Trinkaus, K. M., ed. 1987. *Polities and Partitions: Human Boundaries and the Growth of Complex Societies*. Tempe, Ariz.: Anthropological Research Papers. (7,8)

Tuan, Y. 1977. *Space and Place: The Perspective of Experience*. Minneapolis: University of Minnesota Press. (7)

Ubelaker, D. H. 1984. *Human Skeletal Remains: Excavation, Analysis, Interpretation*. Manuals on Archaeology. Washington, D.C.: Taraxacum. (5,7)

Ucko, P. J. 1969. Ethnography and archaeological interpretation of funerary remains. *World Archaeology* 1: 262–280. (7)

van der Merwe, N. J. 1982. Carbon isotopes, photosynthesis, and archaeology. *American Scientist* 70: 596–606. (5,7)

van der Merwe, N. J., and P. Avery. 1982. Pathways to steel. *American Scientist* 70: 146–155. (5,7)

Van Noten, F., D. Cahan, and L. Keeley. 1980. A Paleolithic campsite in Belgium. *Scientific American* 242 (4): 48–55. (3,5,7)

Villa, P. 1982. Conjoinable pieces and site formation processes. *American Antiquity* 47: 276–290. (3,4,5,7)

Watson, P. J., S. A. LeBlanc, and C. L. Redman. 1984. *Archaeological Explanation: The Scientific Method in Archaeology*. New York: Columbia University Press. (1,3,7,8)

Wauchope, R. 1962. *Lost Tribes and Sunken Continents*. Chicago: University of Chicago Press. (1,9)

Wertime, T., and S. Wertime, eds. 1982. *Early Pyrotechnology*. Washington, D.C.: Smithsonian Institution Press. (5,7)

Whallon, R., and J. A. Brown, eds. 1982. *Essays on Archaeological Typology*. Evanston, Ill.: Center for American Archeology Press. (3,4)

Wheat, J. B. 1967. A Paleo-Indian bison kill. *Scientific American* 216 (1): 44–52. (5,7)

White, P. 1974. *The Past Is Human*. New York: Taplinger. (1)

Wilk, R. R., and W. L. Rathje, eds. 1982. Archaeology of the household: Building a prehistory of domestic life. *American Behavioral Scientist* 25 (whole no. 6). (7)

Willey, G. R. 1953. *Prehistoric Settlement Patterns in the Virú Valley, Peru*. Bureau of American Ethnology, Bulletin 155. Washington, D.C.: Smithsonian Institution Press. (3,4,7)

————, ed. 1974. *Archaeological Researches in Retrospect*. Cambridge, Mass.: Winthrop. (2,3)

Willey, G. R., and P. Phillips. 1958. *Method and Theory in American Archaeology*. Chicago: University of Chicago Press. (8)

Willey, G. R., and J. A. Sabloff. 1980. *A History' of American Archaeology*. 2nd ed. San Francisco: Freeman. (2,8)

Wilson, J. 1982. *The Passionate Amateur's Guide to Archaeology in the United States*. New York: Collier. (1,3,9)

Wing, E. S., and A. R. Brown. 1980. *Paleonutrition: Method and Theory in Prehistoric Foodways*. New York: Academic Press. (5,7)

Wiseman, J. R. 1984. Scholarship and provenience in the study of artifacts. *Journal of Field Archaeology* 11: 67–77. (1,9)

————. 1985. Odds and ends: Multimedia documentation in archaeology. *Journal of Field Archaeology* 12: 389. (9)

Wolfman, D. 1984. Geomagnetic dating methods in archaeology. In *Advances in Archaeological Method and Theory*, vol. 7, ed. M. B. Schiffer, pp. 363–458. Orlando: Academic Press. (6)

Wood, M. 1985. *In Search of the Trojan War*. New York: Facts on File Publications. (1,2)

Woolley, C. L. 1934. *Ur Excavations*. Vol. 2, *The Royal Cemetery*. Oxford and Philadelphia: British Museum, and University Museum, University of Pennsylvania. (3,4)

Wright, H. T. 1986. The evolution of civilizations. In *American Archaeology Past and Future: A Celebration of the Society for American Archaeology 1935–1985*, ed. D. J. Meltzer, D. D. Fowler, and J. A. Sabloff, pp. 323–365. Washington, D.C.: Smithsonian Institution Press. (7,8)

· *Index* ·